GW01157877

Cooking with Kadai

THE WORLD OF KADAI

Well, where did it all begin? The journey for me began back in 2002, one chilly January night on a roof in Rajasthan, India. Imagine sitting around an old Indian cooking bowl (known as a kadai) that we had bought from a local market and converted into a firebowl. It was one of those memorable nights made even more special by being mesmerised by the flames as we kept ourselves warm.

This fantastic night led me to bring an original kadai back to my home in Shropshire, to continue its use as a firebowl. In no time, as friends enjoyed this concept in my garden, they put in orders for themselves and the exciting new business of Kadai Firebowls was born. It took another few years of using dreadful barbecues, standing on my own to cook as the party ensued behind me, that a new thought emerged. Why not drop a grill into the kadai bowl, where everyone can cook together and I can sit with my friends and actually join in with the fun and laughter. So, this is what I did, and once the cooking was done, we lifted out the grill, threw some more wood on the fire and carried on enjoying the firebowl long into the night.

As sales grew, so did the concept of the first ever barbecue firebowl combination: a set-up where everyone can cook together around a circular bowl, then using the lit fire, easily turn it into a heat source for a social gathering. Since the Palaeolithic period, possibly some 400,000 years ago, humans have used fire to cook and keep warm - it's just that evolution can take a long time to perfect sometimes.

Barbecue cooking is not just about bringing people together or the uniquely flavoured food, but the whole primeval essence of loving being outside around a fire. I hope this book will lead you on a special Kadai journey of your own, full of discovery and lasting memories.

Christo

Christo, Founder of Kadai

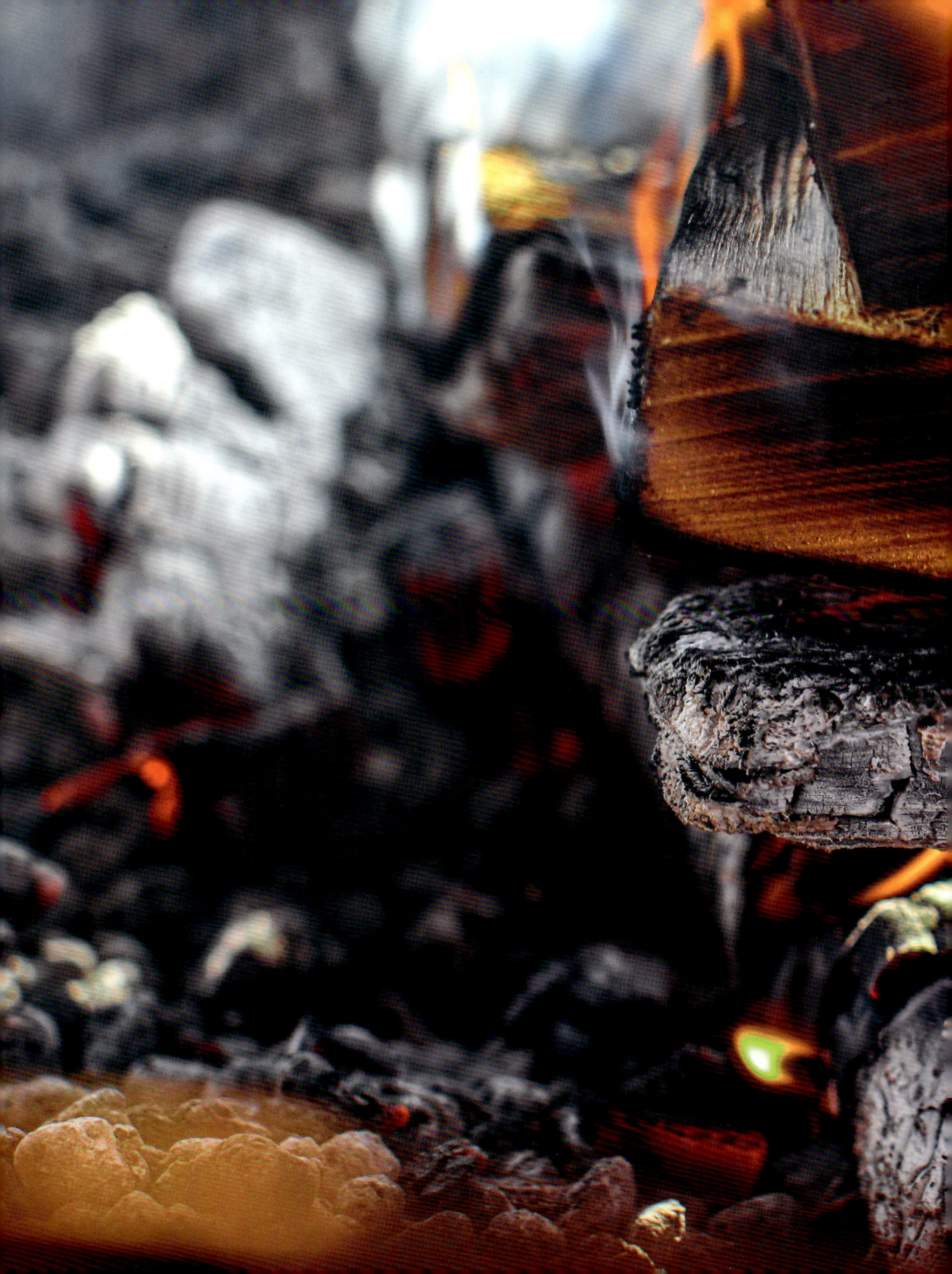

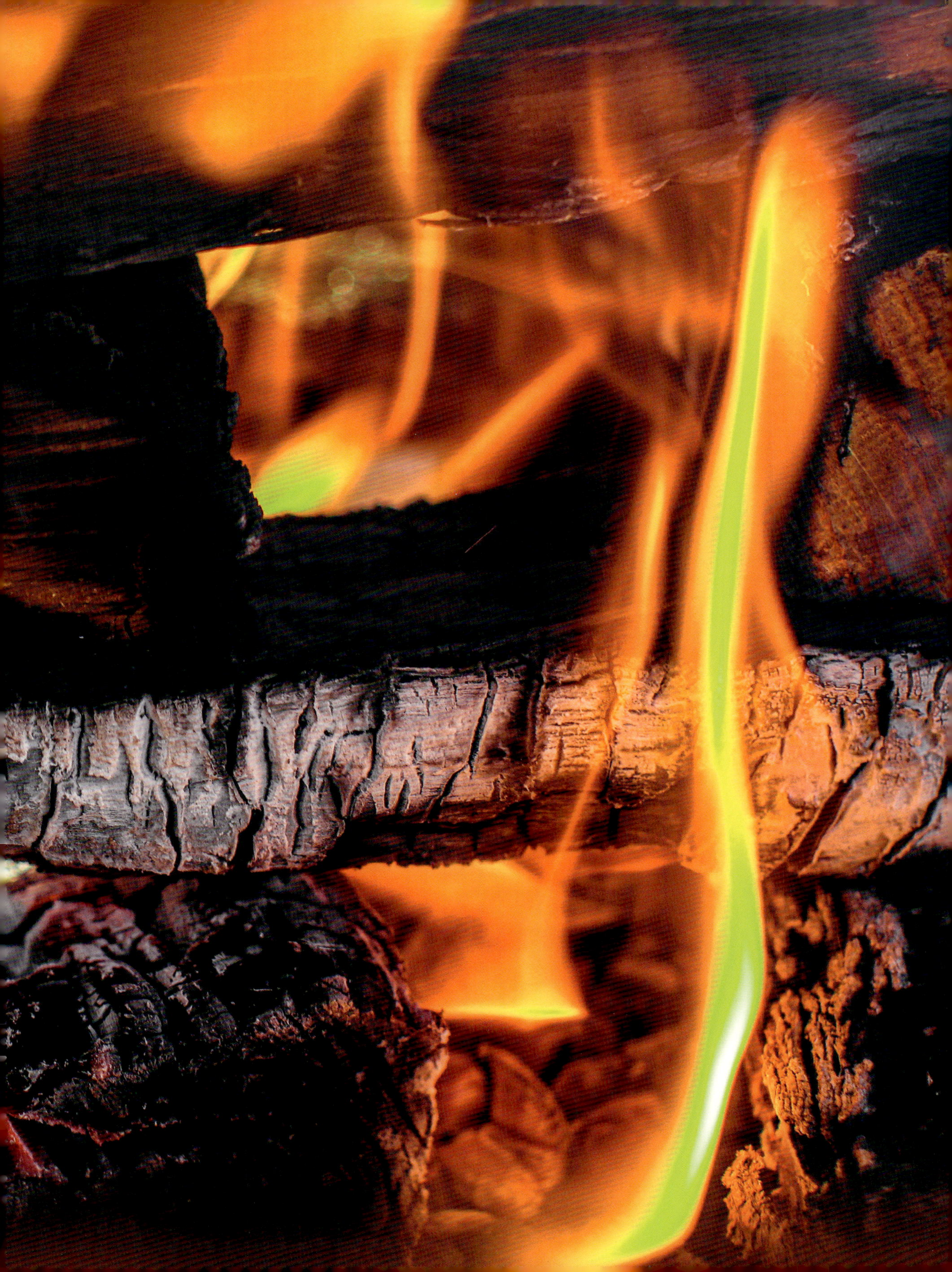

CONTENTS

Introduction — 9

Getting started — 10

Charcoal or wood? — 12

Cooking temperatures — 23

Ways to cook — 26

Kadai care — 40

How to spice things up — 43
Rubs, Marinades & Sauces

Lazy mornings	61
Nibbles & sides	75
Simple & quick	101
If you have time...	127
Feeding family & friends	151
Pizza night	187
Something sweet	207
Drinks from the grill	223
Index	232
Acknowledgements	236

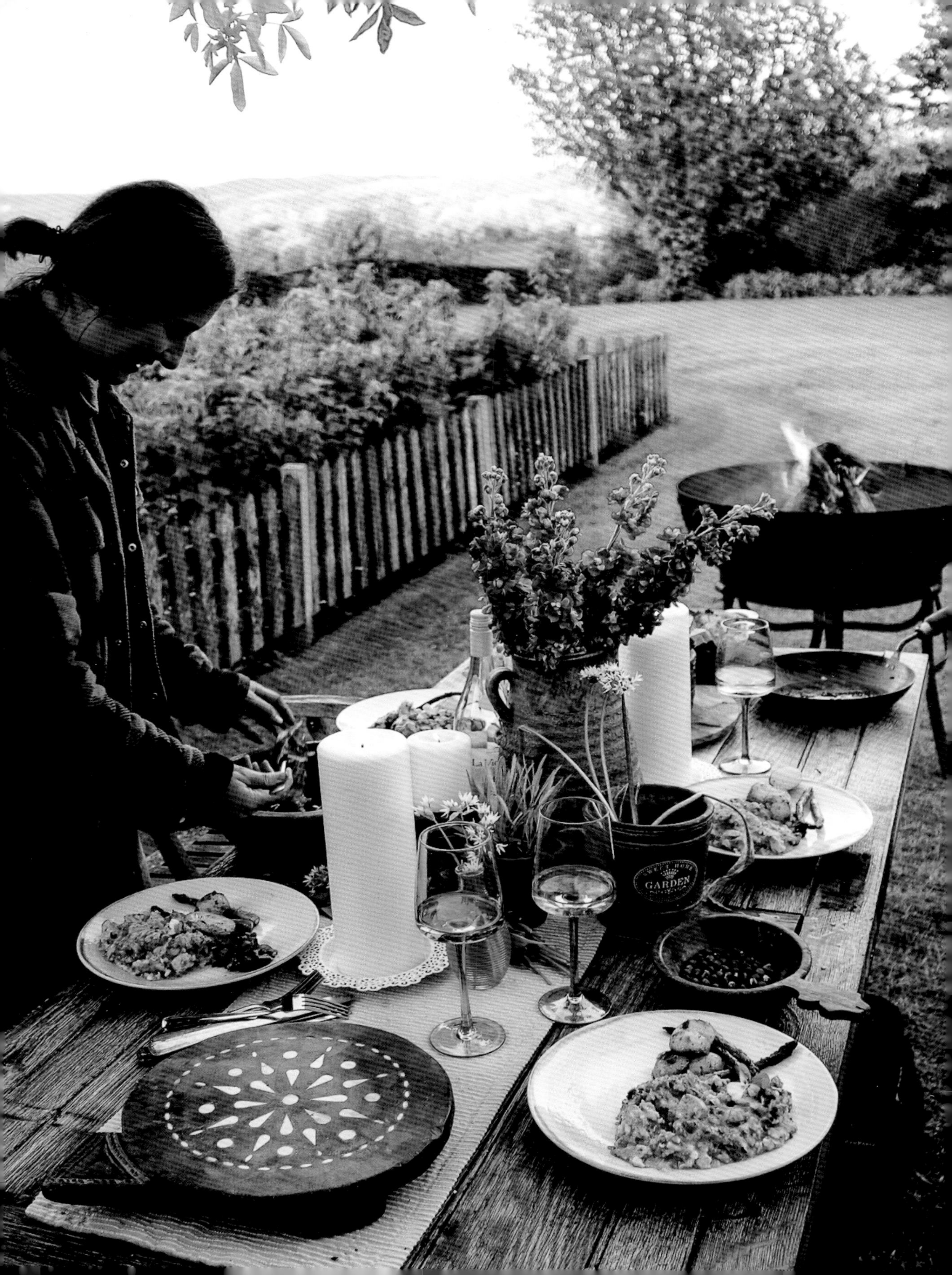
GARDEN

Introduction

This cookbook is a celebration of all things fire and food. Born from the love of being outdoors, entertaining on long summer evenings and simply just barbecuing, a Kadai inspires all, from the barbecue novice to the professional live-fire chef.

The versatility and clever use of multi-level cooking means there is now more choice than ever when it comes to what to barbecue; gone are the days of charred sausages and dry burgers. Created with a rustic aesthetic in mind, the Kadai is not about obtaining perfection, but about embracing the social 'togetherness' that time around the fire can bring.

This book has been compiled as a guide from our own experiences, successes and learning from our mistakes, as well as drawing on knowledge from other sources. We are constantly evolving and improving our skills, open to new ideas and ways of doing things. The word 'guide' is used here in the most literal sense, as the best way to learn is to practise and experiment to see what works best for you.

Cooking times depend on the fuel type, where the heat source is directed and weather conditions, but the more you cook the better the understanding gained.

A question you may ask whilst reading this book is whether grilling is barbecuing? This depends on who you ask and where in the world you are asking. Some argue barbecuing is slow cooking, using live fire with a low heat and smoke to flavour the food, whilst grilling uses a far higher dry heat for searing food quickly. We talk more about direct and indirect cooking techniques with barbecuing used as a general term but, as you read on, you will see there is so much more to it.

We have included some handy tips, facts and fantastic recipes by combining many different cooking styles, such as grilling, pan-frying, roasting, dirty cooking and more, using many different Kadai accessories. The recipe sections have been grouped for different times of the day and various lengths of cooking times to help inspire you.

However, the most important point of this book is to assist in your enjoyment of your Kadai and being in the great outdoors.

Getting started

Kadai kits come in various sizes, ranging from 60cm to 120cm, which are supplied with the Kadai Bowl, Holi Grill, Kadai Beads, Tongs, Wire Brush and either a High or Low Stand. Having both stands is the ultimate kit, using the High Stand for cooking, then transferring to the Low Stand for use as a firebowl. Tongs are an essential part of the kit as they are equally important for moving pans and adjusting the fire. Most recipes in this book were cooked on either a 70cm or 80cm Kadai on a High Stand.

As a Kadai looks beautiful in the garden, even when not in use, we recommend leaving it out on its Stand during the summer months with a Shield to keep the Kadai Beads dry. To use a Kadai for cooking or as a firebowl, place the Stand on level ground and add 10cm of clean Kadai Beads to the bowl.

Kadai Beads are unique to Kadai and are important as they are free-draining, allowing any rainwater to easily pass through to the filter fitted in the base of every bowl. The Beads also store the heat during cooking, insulate the ground beneath the bowl and protect the base of the bowl from hot ash.

A fire will always burn better on a non-metallic surface like the Beads, where the heat is not being conducted away. The Kadai Beads are made from super-heated clay to form a lightweight 100% natural aggregate.

We suggest trying to use good cuts of meat, fresh vegetables and sustainably sourced seafood. Buy ingredients locally where possible or see what is growing in your own vegetable garden. Nothing tastes better than really fresh veg from plot to plate. Get to know and support your local butcher, who will always share their thoughts on the best cuts of meat and the approach to cooking them. After all, they are the experts in their craft, so don't be afraid to ask them to de-bone a chicken or prepare a leg of lamb.

If you do not have a specific ingredient listed in a recipe, improvise with what you do have; play with the quantities; change what you're cooking or how you cook it, it's all part of enjoying your Kadai. This book is intended as a guide to inspire experimentation and creativity, such as encouraging you to come up with your own new tasty recipes.

PLANNING AHEAD

The key to creating a relaxed, calm, enjoyable environment for you and everyone else involved, is to plan before you cook. Have everything you are going to need ready in advance, including all the accessories, ingredients, seating, lighting and music. This helps relieve any pressure and rushing around fetching or searching for things, especially if you have guests arriving. Apart from the Kadai kit, most barbecuing will require:

from left to right:

Chimney Starter – the simplest method to get charcoal to temperature quickly and efficiently. **Blow Poker** – for increasing oxygen flow into the heart of a fire. **Kadai Gloves** – heat-resistant gloves are essential when handling hot cookware. **Chopping Boards** – important for keeping raw meat separate from cooked meat or vegetables. **Temperature Probe** – when cooking any meat, knowing the internal temperature is really useful. **Great music** – a key ingredient to any perfect evening, so compile your playlist and crank up the volume.

Charcoal or wood?

Generally, charcoal is used as a longer-lasting heat source and whilst it will provide a char-grilled taste, it is mostly smokeless. If you're looking to use smoke as part of the flavour of your dish you will need to either cook solely over wood, add small chunks of hardwood, like oak, to the bed of charcoal or use a Smoker Box (see pg. 29).

Both materials have a time and a place when cooking with fire, and it really depends on what you're cooking and how. For example, charcoal is better when using the Kadai Lid as it has a long slow burn, and wood when using the Asado Cross to build an indirect fire as high as possible (see pg. 34 for more information on these products). For prolonged barbecuing, we often start on a bed of charcoal to form a hot core, then add wood throughout the cook.

To light either, we recommend using natural wood wool firelighters made from wood shavings dipped in wax. These are 100% natural and readily available from most garden centres or hardware stores.

The magic of charcoal

Essentially, charcoal is wood that has been heated in the absence of oxygen to drive out the impurities and gases, leaving pure carbon. Good lumpwood charcoal should be light, brittle and still recognisable as once being wood. There is no substitute for good quality, sustainably produced charcoal from a local supplier.

You can make your own in the Kadai Charcoal Maker (*see left*) and learn how this chemical process works. Simply fill the Charcoal Maker with dry hardwood, place it in the fire and leave for a couple of hours to allow the gasification process to convert the wood magically into charcoal.

How to light charcoal

The easiest way to get your charcoal going is with a Chimney Starter. Light three natural firelighters in the middle of your Kadai, place the Chimney Starter over them and fill to the top with charcoal. After about 15 minutes check to see if the charcoal is glowing red halfway up the chimney. Using heat-resistant Gloves, pour out the charcoal so that the unburnt pieces are buried under the red-hot coals. You can then cook straightaway on a moderate heat with a store of unburnt charcoal underneath ready to ignite.

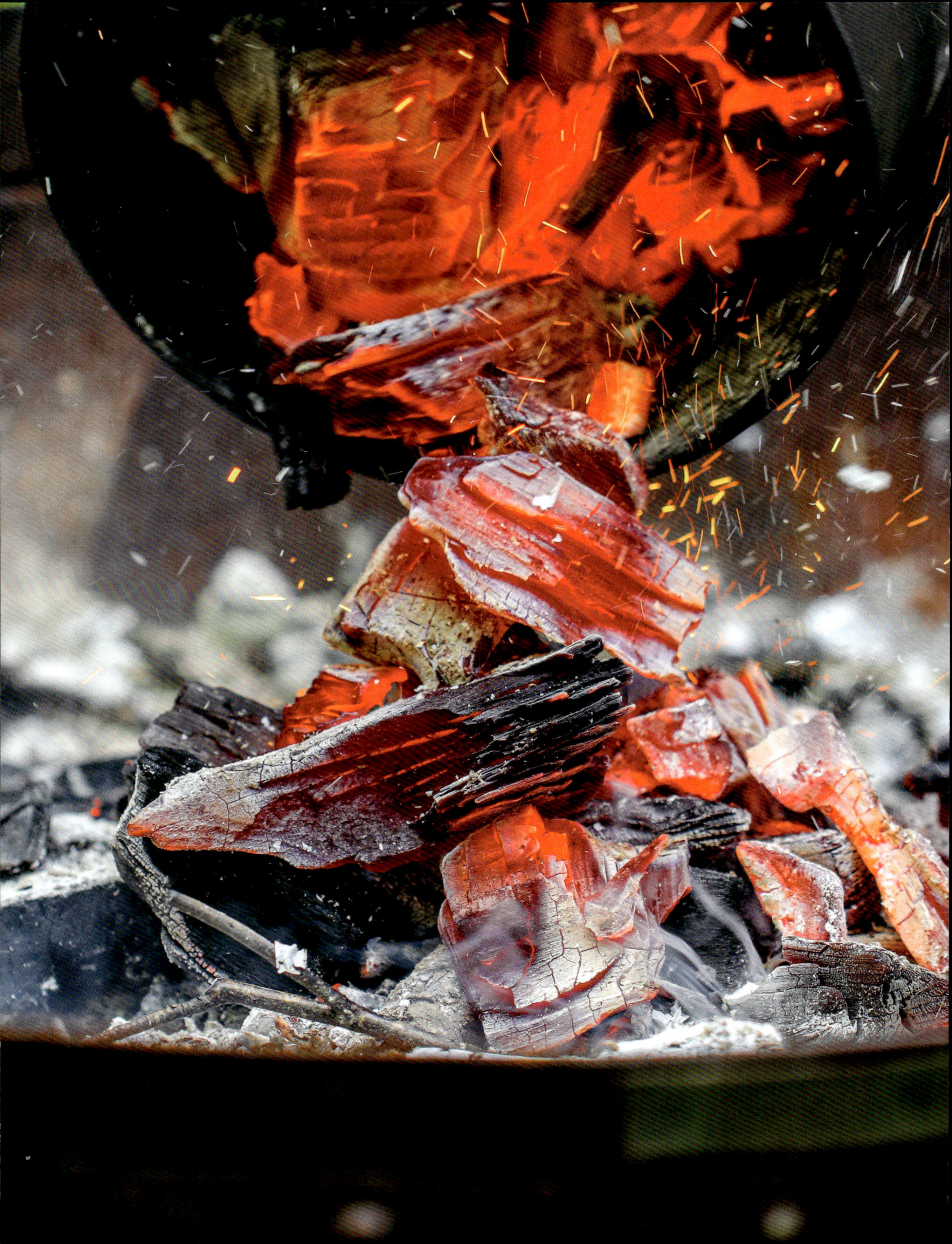

What charcoal to use

Charcoal briquettes are made from sawdust and wood by-products, with additives to bind them together when compressed into pillow-shaped lumps. This form of charcoal burns consistently and slowly, but it's worth checking if chemical additives have been used. Never use instant-lighting charcoal, as this is impregnated with lighter fluid that will make your food taste of spent fuel. Our preference is always locally sourced, lumpwood charcoal, as you know the type of wood species and you can trace exactly where it comes from. This form of charcoal is 100% natural, lights easily and has a more intense heat.

Often charcoal sold in supermarkets and garages is imported from overseas and is likely to be from an unsustainable source. We advise purchasing charcoal only from manufacturers that provide information on the wood source. If this information is not provided, there is no guarantee that the company will have the same commitment to natural, sustainable production as other local suppliers.

We are blessed with having Caradoc Charcoal just down the road from us who use large cast-iron retorts (*see right*) to make their lumpwood charcoal.

Cooking with charcoal

Apart from the simple pleasure of cooking with a grill over glowing charcoal, there are other exciting methods to try. The Caveman technique of cooking directly onto hot coals generates an intense heat that sears steaks, giving them a smoky, charred finish with wonderful aromas. Dutch Ovens are generally designed with a lid to sit red-hot coals on; (*see left*) this surrounds the pot to thoroughly tenderise meat for slow-cooked stews. Or try the South Asian Dhungar method of cooking Dhal; place a small bowl of hot charcoal and ghee in the centre of the pan to infuse the dish with a smoky, buttery flavour.

If you need extra charcoal during cooking, add a few pieces to one side of the bowl, alongside the already glowing coals, but away from the food. Alternatively, to make a new batch, fill the Chimney Starter with more charcoal and place over lit firelighters on a level non-flammable surface, such as old bricks. Add the hot coals to the bowl when they are ready. Avoid adding lots of fresh charcoal whilst cooking because this will dampen the heat and give off acrid smoke at the start of its burn, thus giving the wrong kind of flavour to your food.

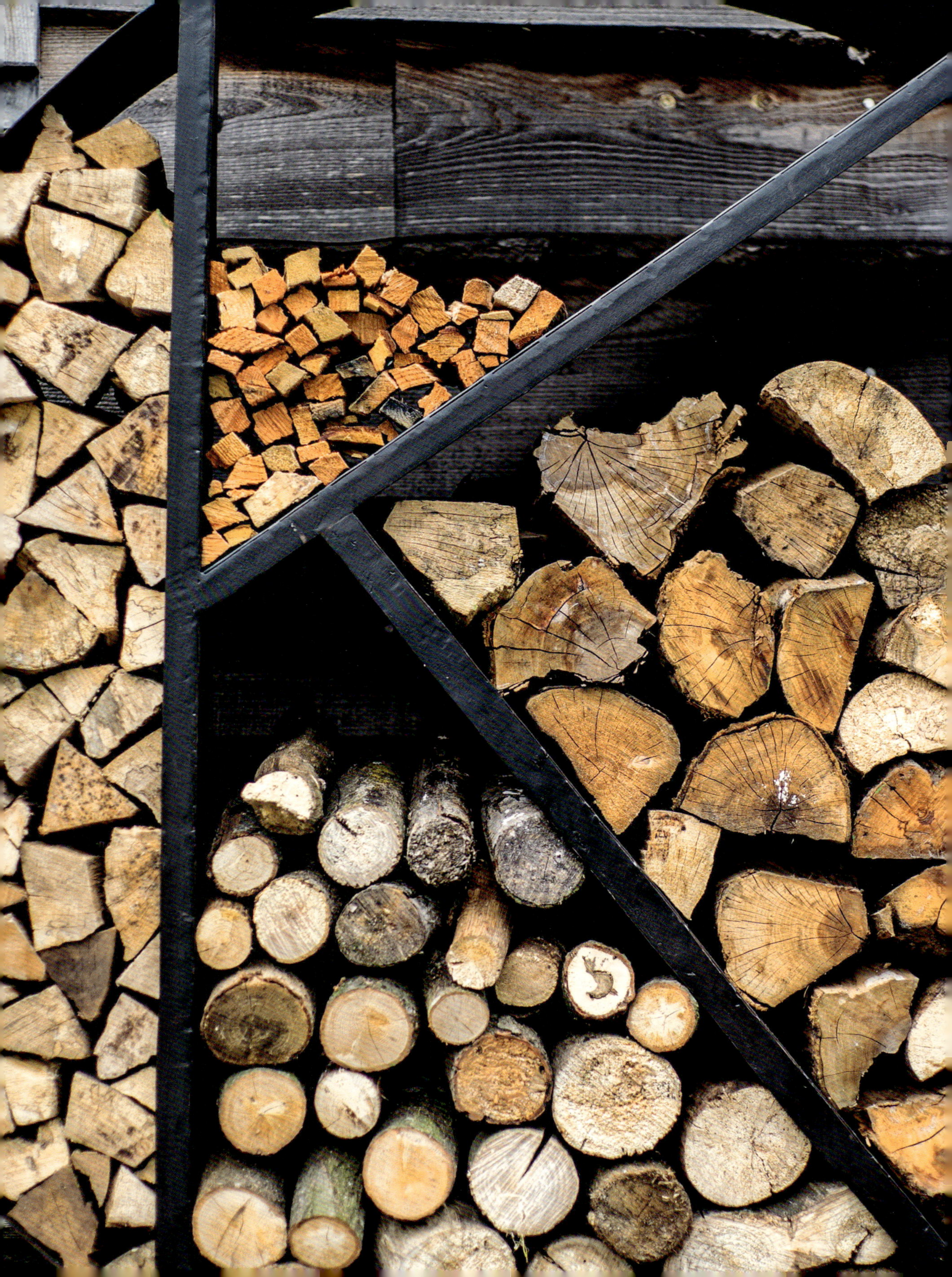

The beauty of wood

As with charcoal and cooking, using wood is as much about the quality of ingredients as it is the technique. No matter how skilled a firepit master you are, wet, poor quality wood will be your downfall. Below are some explanations of different woods and how to use them to avoid any frustrations.

What wood to use?

Softwoods, such as pine or cedar are evergreen and reproduce with fir cones. These trees keep their leaves through winter and are fast growing with an open-cell structure. Softwood burns quickly and has a high resin content. This is perfect for starting a fire or building the fire up after barbecuing for impressive roaring flames. However, it is not recommended for cooking over, due to the resin giving a bitter taste to food when burnt.

Hardwoods, for example, oak, chestnut, beech and all fruitwoods are deciduous, reproducing with flowers. They contain organic compounds known as carbonyls that, when burned, give meat a sweet, caramelised exterior and delicious smoky flavour.

Hardwood is ideal for cooking and making a fire last. When it burns down, it forms hot coals with glowing embers, giving an intense heat that's perfect for direct or indirect cooking.

Seasoned wood means it has been left for at least a year to air-dry undercover. 'Kiln-dried' means it has had moisture forced out in a huge oven for several days. Kiln-dried is generally dryer with under 20% moisture but is a little more expensive.

Remember the drier the wood, the better it burns, and the less smoke it will give off.

HOW TO BUILD A FIRE

You should begin with softwood kindling then move on to seasoned hardwoods which have a denser carbon content that burns hotter, leaving a deep, even heat. The key to lighting a good fire is to start with small pieces, then gradually add slightly larger bits. Remember, oxygen is a vital ingredient to a successful fire, so maintain lots of air gaps and avoid smothering the flames with too much wood.

A simple technique for creating the perfect fire is to build a tower of softwood kindling in a criss-cross pattern, then light a firelighter in the middle. This structure allows maximum oxygen flow to feed your fire. Once the kindling has caught, you can start adding small pieces of split hardwood logs in a pyramid shape, remembering to leave air gaps. Once these have taken, gradually add slightly larger pieces of wood as required, only adding a few pieces at a time to allow the new wood to catch fire.

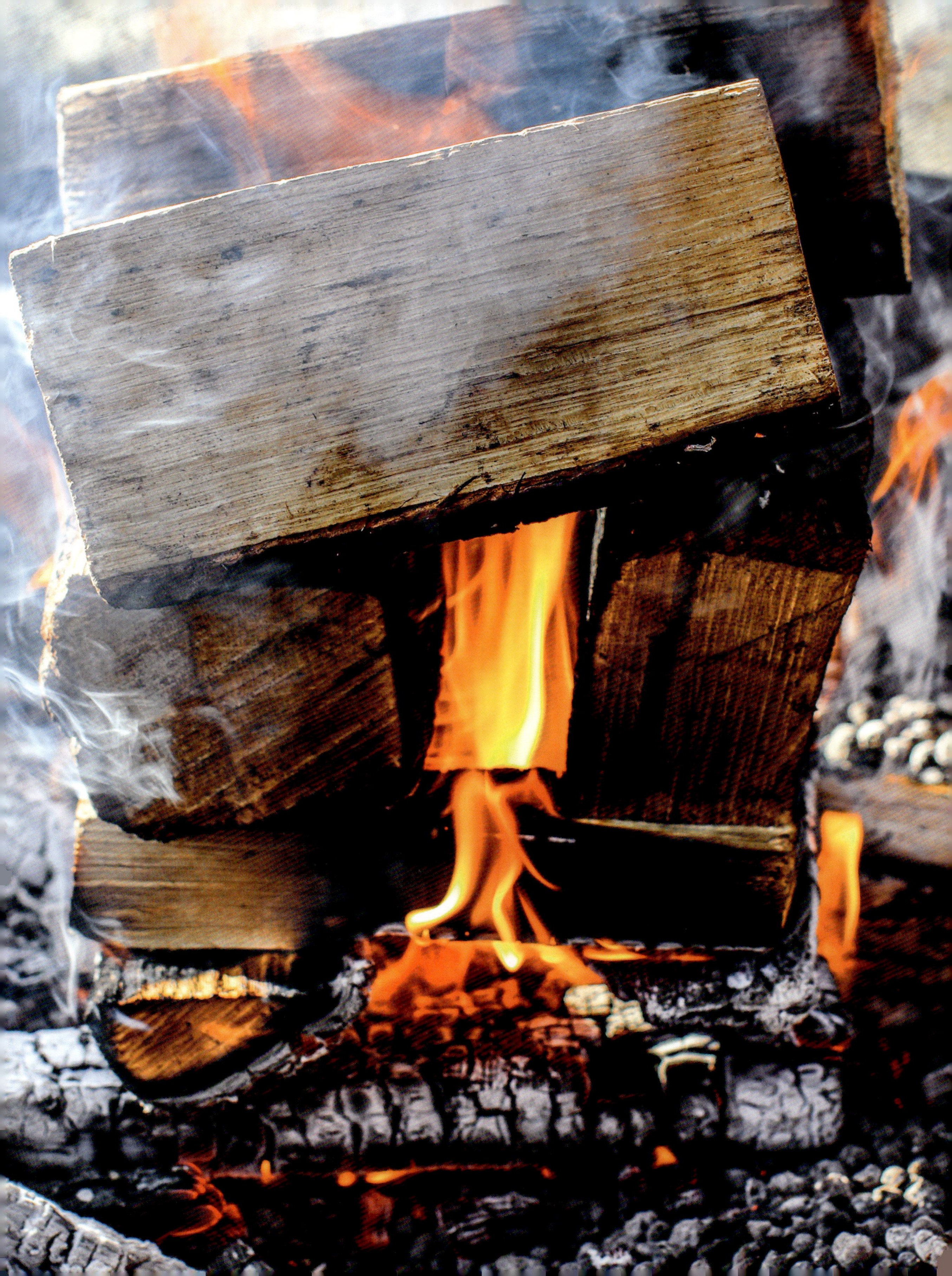

Maintaining your fire

Whether cooking with charcoal or wood, it is important to consider how long you would like the fire to burn, how intense you need the heat, and finally, where you need the hot coals or wood to be. Once the charcoal or wood is ready, using the Tongs, move the fire within the bowl as necessary, then even it out or build it up.

One load of hot, good quality charcoal from the Chimney Starter should give off enough heat for 45 minutes, before needing to be 'topped up'. Hardwood logs generally take about 30 to 45 minutes to reach cooking temperature, as hot glowing coals form and the flames subside. After about 30 minutes, as the embers die down, top up with a few split logs.

After cooking, lift out the Grill and use the Kadai handles to move the bowl onto the Low Stand to enjoy your Kadai as a firebowl. Gradually add a few small pieces of wood to the smouldering embers to build up a fire. If your fire has died down, use a Blow Poker (*see left*) to give a blast of concentrated oxygen into the middle of the fire.

Wood is beautiful and there is something very satisfying about sitting around a Kadai after a delicious feast, watching the flames dance up a skilfully-built fire. The art is to keep your friends and family warm around the light of flickering flames, as the evening rolls on...

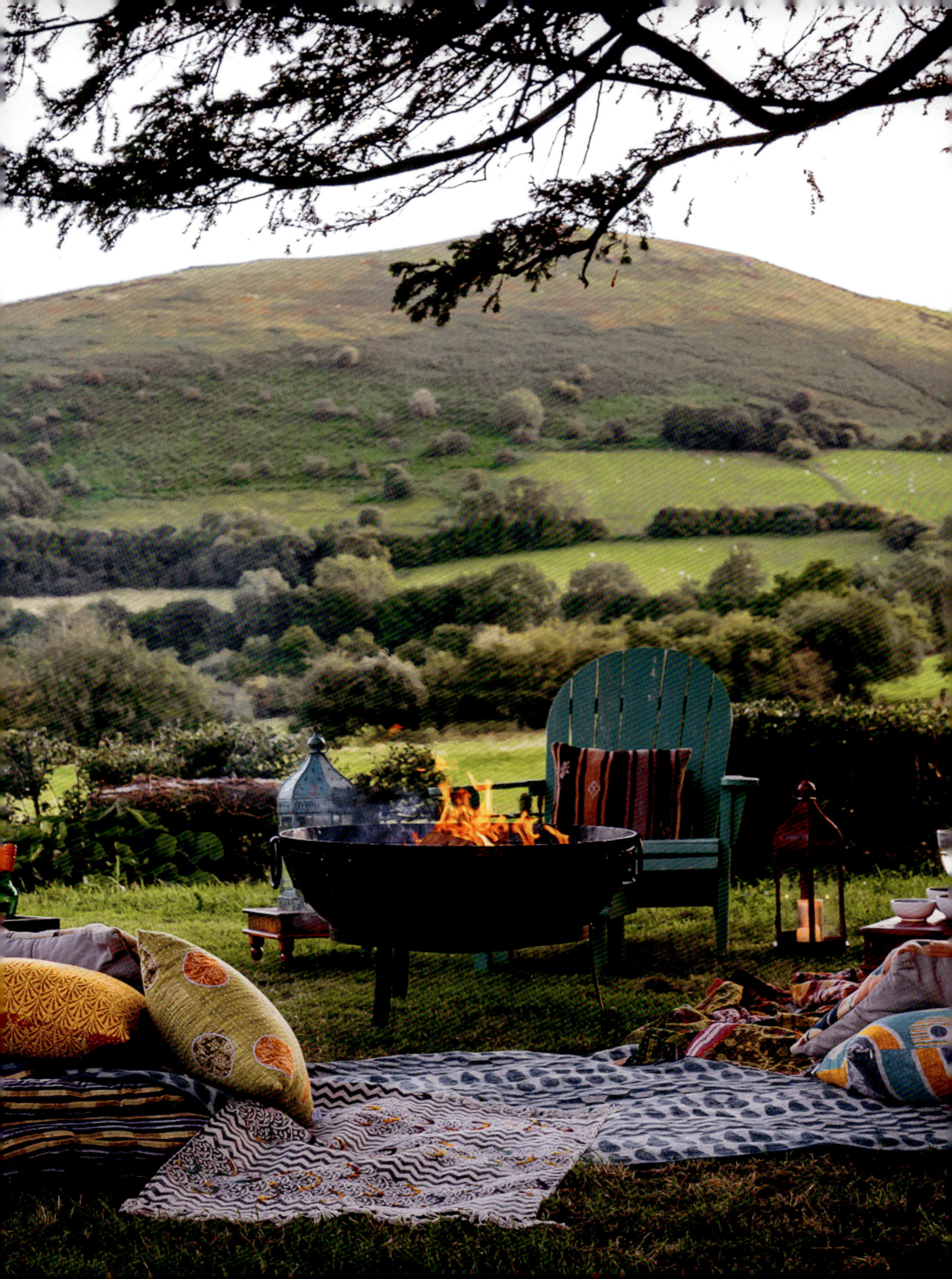

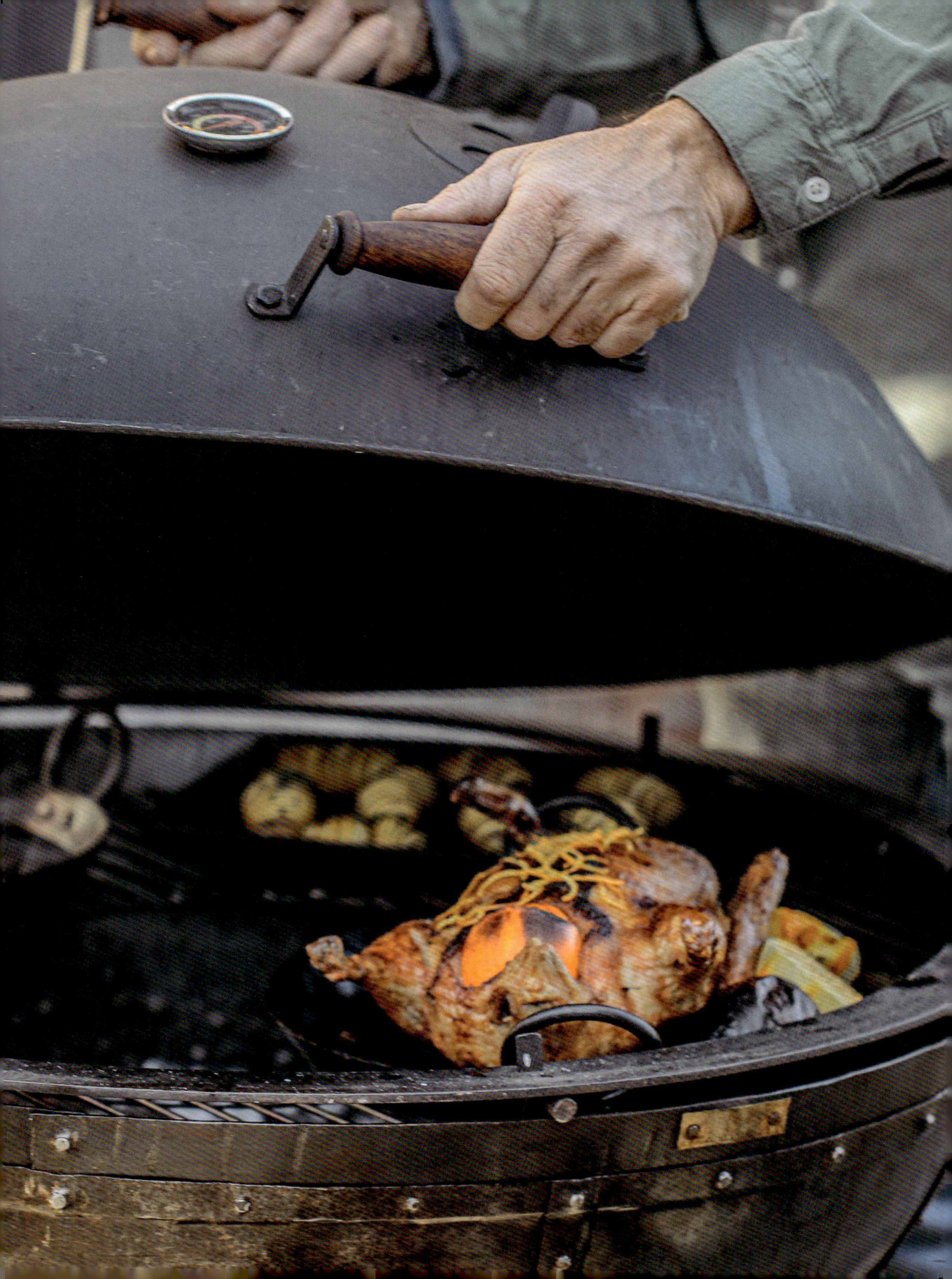

Cooking temperatures

No temperature gauge can tell you when an open fire is ready to cook on; it's a question of judgement and practice. To begin with, you may find there are times when the fire is too hot for what you are trying to cook, or it cools too quickly, and you need to add more fuel. Bear in mind, however, that if you add any fuel, the fire will immediately cool down until this has properly caught. Allow for this or add the new fuel to one side and avoid cooking over freshly added fuel.

With good quality charcoal you can start cooking once the coals have stopped giving off smoke. With wood, wait until the flames have died down to a decent bed of embers. Do bear in mind, wood will smoke a little but this is what gives the food its delicious flavour.

In each recipe we have recommended heat levels and cooking times required, but cooking over a fire is never an exact science. For meat, the most important temperature to consider is the internal temperature to check it is cooked how you like it, and that it is safe to eat.

THE HAND TEST

The hand test, performed with care and respect for the fire, is a simple indicator of how hot your fire is. Starting a sensible distance away, slowly bring your palm towards the coals, letting your hand register the change in temperature before moving closer. If you can hold your hand about 10 to 15cm (6 inches) over the hot coals for various lengths of time, you can then roughly gauge the heat of the fire on the Grill as follows:

High Heat	2-4 seconds	240 - 210°C
Medium Heat	5-7 seconds	210 - 170°C
Low heat	8-10 seconds	170 - 120°C

Broadly speaking, this means that if you can comfortably hold your palm over the hot coals for 2 to 4 seconds, this is perfect for searing steaks as the fire will be around 220°C (430°F). Anything over 10 seconds is a low heat, around 120°C (250°F), which is the ideal heat for slow cooking.

Meat

INTERNAL TEMPERATURE

There are various probes on the market that record the temperature of meat, allowing you to check if it is cooked properly. These probes vary from basic digital probes, to having advanced features that connect to your phone via an app. The temperature of your Kadai is hard to control exactly, so using a good quality probe will help you judge when meat is done. Always cook to temperature and not to time, for perfect results.

Insert the probe into the thickest part of the meat away from the bone, fat or gristle as these can give a false reading. For chicken use the middle of the breast.

Poultry
74°C *(165°F)*

Lamb
60°C to 70°C *(140°F - 158°F)*

Beef
60°C to 70°C *(140°F - 158°F)*

Steaks (Rare to well done)
50°C to 65°C *(120°F - 150°F)*

Burgers
71°C *(160°F)*

Venison (Medium rare)
60°C to 65°C *(140°F - 150°F)*

Pork
62°C *(140°F)*

Fish
62°C *(145°F)*

It is difficult to give exact temperatures at which meat should be cooked, as we all like our food cooked differently (e.g., steak). The temperatures shown give you a guide to ensure that meat is safe to consume. Also, remember that on average, for large cuts, the internal temperature of meat could rise by 6 to 8°C after resting.

Rest & relax

Like us, all cooked meats benefit from relaxing and having a rest after a stint on the barbecue. This allows you to finish off any vegetables, prepare sauces and lay the table, whilst the juices combine as they are reabsorbed. You should aim to remove the meat from your Kadai before the optimum temperature is reached (see pg. 24), as the residual heat will continue the cook. Depending on the cut, this could be a couple of minutes for rare steaks to 30 minutes for larger joints. To allow your meat to rest, place it either on a warmed plate away from the fire or on the Warming Rack, covered with foil to keep the heat in.

Fish generally needs only a few minutes to rest and firm up, which gives you enough time to plate up and serve.

Ways to cook

The art of direct & indirect cooking

Fortunately, Kadais are relatively unique in that they can perform both direct and indirect cooking with ease. In a nutshell, direct means the heat source is immediately underneath the cooking area, whether searing meat, using the Cooking Tripod accessories or grilling food quickly. Indirect means the heat source is placed away from the food you are cooking, such as on opposite sides of the Kadai, or around the edge of the bowl. This cooking process relies more on radiant heat and is the perfect method for long, slow barbecuing.

DIRECT COOKING is the more traditional concept most people are familiar with when it comes to barbecuing; cooking over a high heat for short periods of time to give meat, fish and vegetables an intense chargrilled flavour and transform them into something special. This method is most suited to the Skillets, Frying Pan and cast-iron Sizzling Plate that can be placed on the Grill for fast frying. The Cooking Tripod and accessories, such as the Tripod Skillet or Cooking Bowl, can be used for other quick cooking techniques, like stir frying.

INDIRECT COOKING is the perfect method for thicker, fattier cuts of meat that are better cooked more slowly, at a lower temperature. Using this radiant heat stops them drying out and the fat dripping onto the hot coals causing flare ups. The fire is built to one side of your Kadai, and this works well with the Asado Cross, Tripod Roaster or Oak Cooking Plank. The Kadai Lid also uses this method as it allows the heat to circulate over the food and out through the adjustable vent.

This indirect fire on one side of your Kadai bowl provides different heat zones to grill over. Therefore, this gives you more control than just having hot coals in the centre, and the versatility of moving food, Skillets or Pans to cooler areas of the grill.

Another method is to form the hot coals in a ring around the edge of the bowl, allowing the food to cook indirectly from all sides.

GRILLING Generally, when one thinks of having a barbecue, grilling is traditionally the most common method since it is relatively quick and easy. Meat, fish and vegetables can all be laid straight on the Grill over the coals or, for delicate and small items, in the perforated Grill Trays.

When cooking meat directly on the Grill, especially large cuts, the trick, once you have obtained the initial charring, is to keep turning it regularly. Removing it from the heat and then placing it back on lets the outside cool a little, allowing the residual heat to cook the food through perfectly. Black grill lines on steaks look wonderful but it's not actually what you are looking for. Instead, you should aim for a more even charred crust to caramelise the surface, bringing out wonderful complex flavours that are unique from live-fire cooking.

PAN-FRYING As well as cooking directly on the Grill, you can also use the Skillets, Frying Pan, Paella Pan and Hot Plate to cook different dishes at the same time on top of the Grill. Since Kadais have a large grill area, this works perfectly. By having the hot coals to one side rather than in the middle of the firebowl, you can use both Direct and Indirect methods at the same time, by creating varied cooking heat zones. This broadens the scope of what you can cook and how, such as pan-fried vegetables in olive oil, burgers on the grill or a full English breakfast in the morning. For more options, try using the 36cm Cooking Bowl in the Holi Grill centre for a tasty stir-fry dish. Alternatively, the Chapati Pan can be used directly in the coals for an intense heat to cook pancakes and other delights.

Hanging a leg of lamb from the Cooking Tripod or a chicken from the Tripod Roaster for a few hours will pick up unique aromas, as well as cooking them to perfection. The Asado (see pg. 34) is another classic Low and Slow method, plus a great way to pass the afternoon tending the fire with some friends and a beer.

LOW & SLOW is similar to roasting in the barbecue world and is another way that Kadai distinguishes itself from the traditional barbecue. Not only does this method produce succulent, tender meat from even the toughest cuts, but the low heat helps retain nutrients that might be lost at higher temperatures.

Build an indirect fire suitable for a long cook by having a good core of charcoal to hold the heat. Be prepared to make additional batches of charcoal or place well-seasoned larger pieces of hardwood to plan for the long haul. Depending on what you are cooking, temperatures will need to be around 95°C to 120°C (200°F to 250°F).

The varied range of Kadai accessories are perfectly suited to slow cooking. When using the Kadai Lid, this method also gives food a distinctive smoky flavour.

SMOKING meat, fish or vegetables is a technique used by barbecue chefs to bring new levels of complexity and flavours to the food. Only use hardwood, which falls into two groups: fruitwood like pear, cherry and apple or nutwood such as hickory, pecan and oak. All these woods have wonderful distinctive characters that are worth exploring.

The easiest way to smoke your food is using wood chips in a Smoker Box. Put the wood chips directly into the Smoker Box and close the lid. Place the Smoker Box next to a bed of hot coals in your Kadai and close the Kadai Lid. After about 5 minutes the Smoker Box will start releasing a light blueish smoke. Immediately move it to a cooler part of your Kadai, allowing the wood chips to smoulder slowly and not burn. The perforated holes will then release the smoke through to your food. If the smoke is white in colour, the wood chips are burning which is not what you want as this will taint what you are cooking.

Here is a guide to woods commonly used as smoking chips:

> **CHERRY**: Fruitier flavour for poultry and pork.
>
> **APPLE**: Mild and sweet flavour for chicken, pork and game.
>
> **HICKORY**: Savoury and sweet aroma for beef and pork.
>
> **PECAN**: Rich and very sweet flavour for red meats.
>
> **OAK**: Heavier smoky flavour for beef, chicken and seafood.
>
> **OLIVE**: Sweet and mild flavour for beef, pork and lamb.
>
> **VINE ROOTS**: Fruity rich aroma for game and fish.

It is worth noting that the Kadai Lid is an essential piece of equipment in this process, holding the aroma inside the bowl to flavour the food. Once the chips have completely blackened, remove the Smoker Box from your Kadai. For a more intense smoke flavour repeat this process.

Most important of all is to just enjoy playing with these smoke-infused flavours and see what your favourite turns out to be.

BAKING is probably not the first cooking method you think of when it comes to barbecuing. However, for thousands of years our ancestors have baked food directly in the fire using a process now known as the Maillard Reaction. The main principle of baking is to have a dry heat which typically comes from cooking in a clay oven or over hot ashes.

For this, the Wood Fired Oven (see pg. 37) is ideal for baking as the fire beneath gives off the perfect dry heat, whilst the clay exterior locks it in. Smoke from the fire below circulates around the Wood Fired Oven to give a unique flavour to your food. To bake food effectively, temperatures need to be between 150°C to 180°C (300°F to 350°F), but note that a pizza requires far higher temperatures. Both the Kadai Lid and Cookware Lid are other great accessories for baking on a Kadai.

There is a diverse range of food you can bake on a Kadai from frittatas to meat pies to pizzas; however it is not all about savoury. Sweet treats are often missed from a barbecue, but, thankfully, Kadais are ideal for creating those guilty pleasures. Get those taste buds going and discover the delightful twist a smoky depth brings to delicious summer fruit crumbles or scrumptious, sweet pumpkin pies.

OAK PLANK COOKING This method is inspired by Northwest Native Americans for cooking wild salmon caught during the annual migration. This brilliant idea slow-cooks a large, filleted fish on a plank opposite a wood fire to add a beautiful smoky aroma.

We use rustic waney-edge oak that is about 30cm (12 inches) wide and 69cm (27 inches) long, pre-drilled for nailing or wiring the fish to. Submerge the Oak Cooking Plank in water for about 8 hours before use with heavy weights. This helps protect the wood from the heat and also steams the fish preventing it from drying out. Lay the fish skin side down on the Oak Cooking Plank, leaving about 15 to 20cm from the bottom and fix it into position using either nails or wire pushed through the holes. Stand the board almost vertically against the Oak Cooking Plank Frame, or the Asado Oak Plank Bar to hold it in place. To slow-cook the fish, you need an indirect wood fire placed on the opposite side of the bowl to the Oak Plank. See inspirational recipes on pg. 140 and 147.

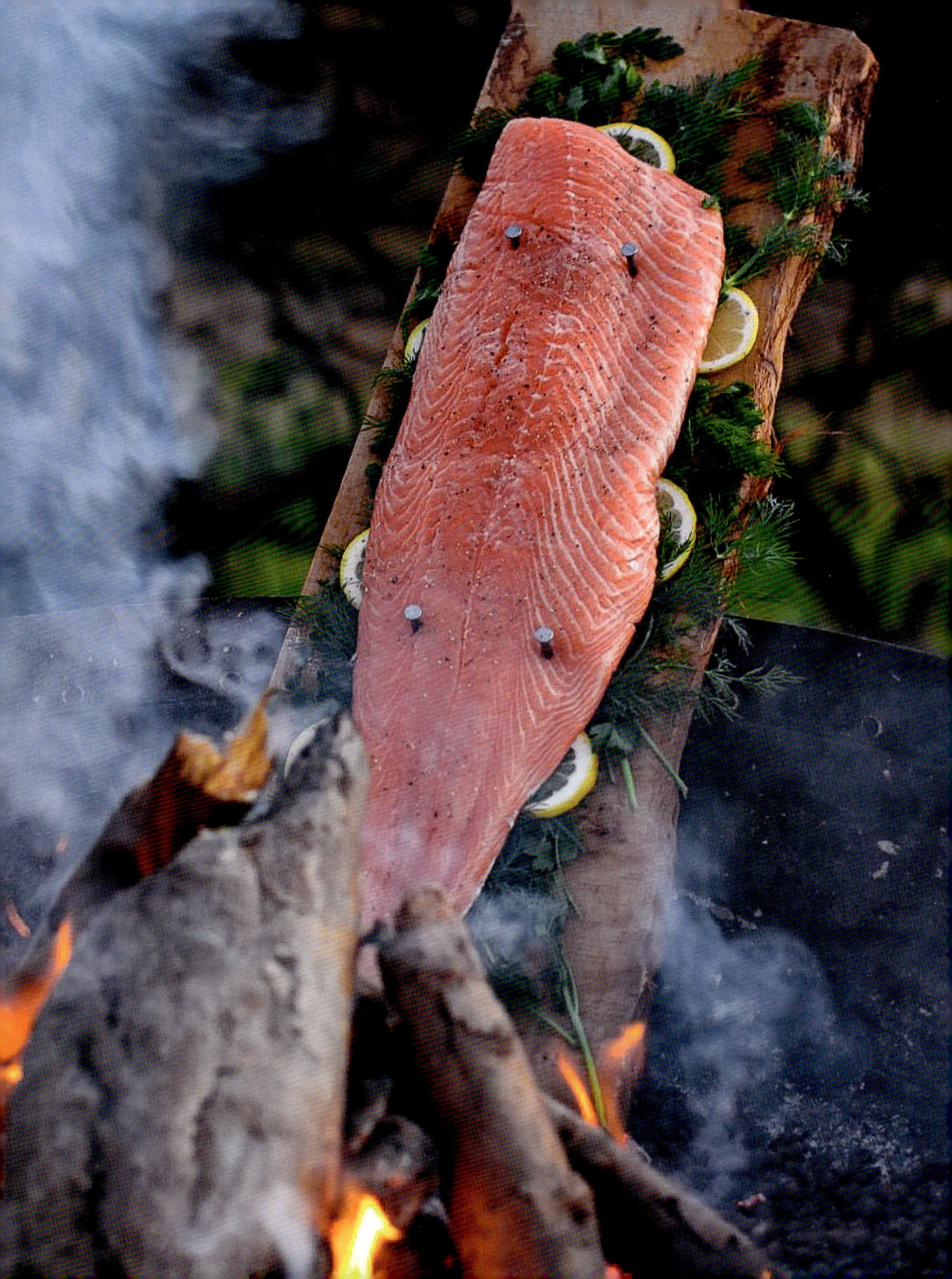

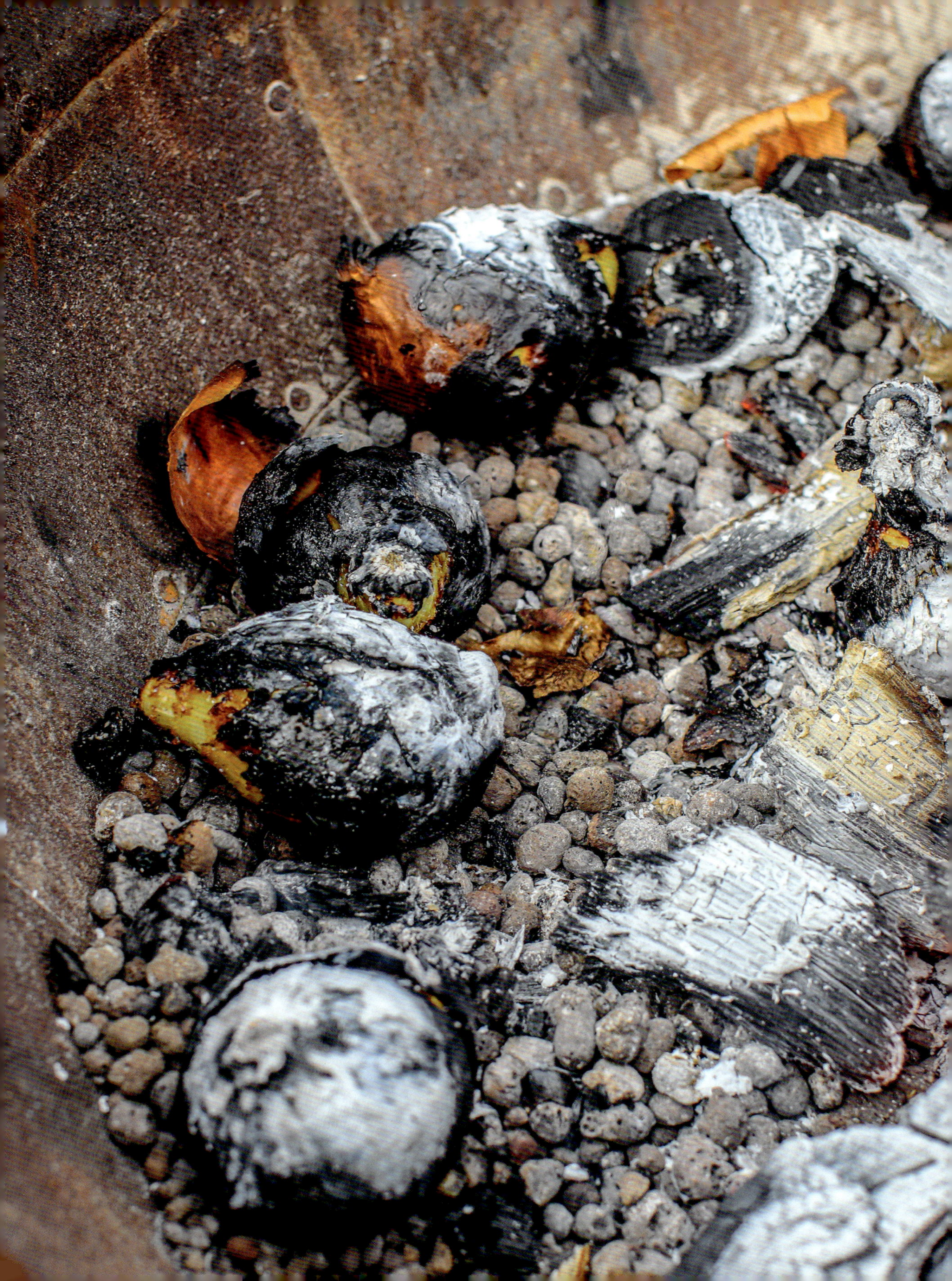

DIRTY COOKING is an alternative or complementary method to other more traditional barbecue techniques and is one of the most exciting. It is an expression that refers to cooking food directly on the hot coals or within the hot embers of a fire. Over the past few years this cooking style has been embraced by professional live-fire chefs, but it is actually how our cave-dwelling ancestors would have discovered the delights of cooked meat.

A Kadai is perfectly suited to dirty cooking with the Holi Grill allowing easy access to the hot coals and the Kadai Beads. Ensure the beads are clean and note that you might need to add extra beads to give more depth for dirty cooking. Timings can be a bit hit and miss, but when you get it right, dirty cooking is guaranteed to impress any guest as you dig dinner out from beneath the fire.

No matter what you are dirty cooking, start with a good base of white-hot coals and make sure you blow away any ash before placing your food in the Kadai. Steaks can be seared directly on the embers for a fantastic, charred exterior but with a beautifully flavoursome inside which is pink and juicy. Barbecue scallops and oysters directly in the fire, using their shells as the vessel for a delicious sauce (see recipe on pg. 80). Try caramelised onions or peppers for a deeper, sweeter, smokier texture or bake sweet potatoes by burying them under clean Kadai Beads.

Kadai Cookware

COOKING TRIPOD One of our favourite accessories is the Cooking Tripod that converts the Kadai into a multi-level barbecue and can be used with or without the Grill.

To fit a Cooking Tripod, first hold the ring letting the three legs dangle down, with the straight leg in the centre and the two cranked legs one on each side. Then position each leg on the rim of your Kadai with the hand-forged feet holding it in place. Move the legs so that they are an equal distance from each other and hang the chain from the tripod hook. The chain length can be easily adjusted by changing the link on the tripod hook to vary the cooking height.

Cooking Tripod accessories include the Cooking Bowl, Tripod Skillet, Stone Griddle Plate, Swing Grill, Dutch Oven and the Tripod Roaster. You can also simply hang a leg of lamb or other joints of meat directly from the hook for a truly spectacular roast (see pg. 135). Most Cooking Tripod accessories require direct heat in the centre of the Kadai, except the Tripod Roaster where indirect heat works better.

ASADO CROSS This accessory is based on the Argentinian drover's method of slow cooking large joints or whole beasts, wired onto a unique frame and held on an incline away from the direct heat. In Argentina, the 'asador' is appointed the task of cooking the meat, a task of huge responsibility and, for this reason, performed with great care and expertise.

The Asado Cross fits on either a 70cm or 80cm Kadai bowl rim using butterfly bolts to clamp it securely in position. Into this, the central rod with two adjustable cross frames can be fitted once the meat has been secured. There are four slots to choose from to alter the angle of incline and to spin the spit through 180 degrees to cook both sides of the meat evenly. As this principle relies on Indirect Cooking, build a wood-based fire on the opposite side of the Kadai to the Asado, with medium-sized logs raised to a height of about 30cm/12 inches. This fire will need occasional maintenance during the cook so that the radiant heat slowly brings the meat to perfection. Spread the fire out and lower the Asado spit on its lowest setting to finish charring the meat for a mouth-watering caramelised crust. See pg. 144 for a recipe using this alternative barbecue style to cook a whole muntjac deer.

A tip is to place a larger log as a heat shield in the middle of the Kadai and put a Skillet pan directly under the meat to catch any dripping fat which can be used for gravy or to baste the meat.

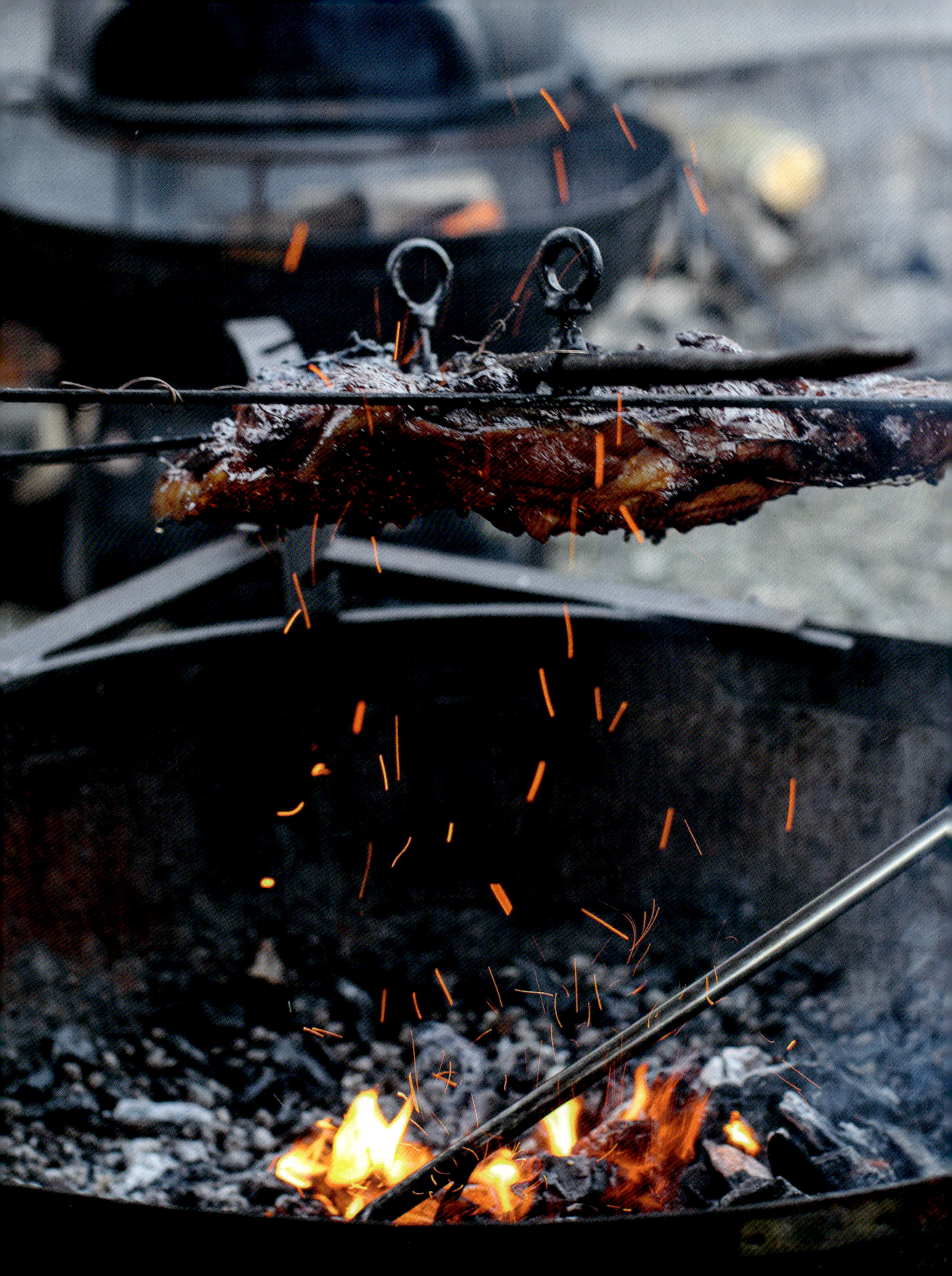

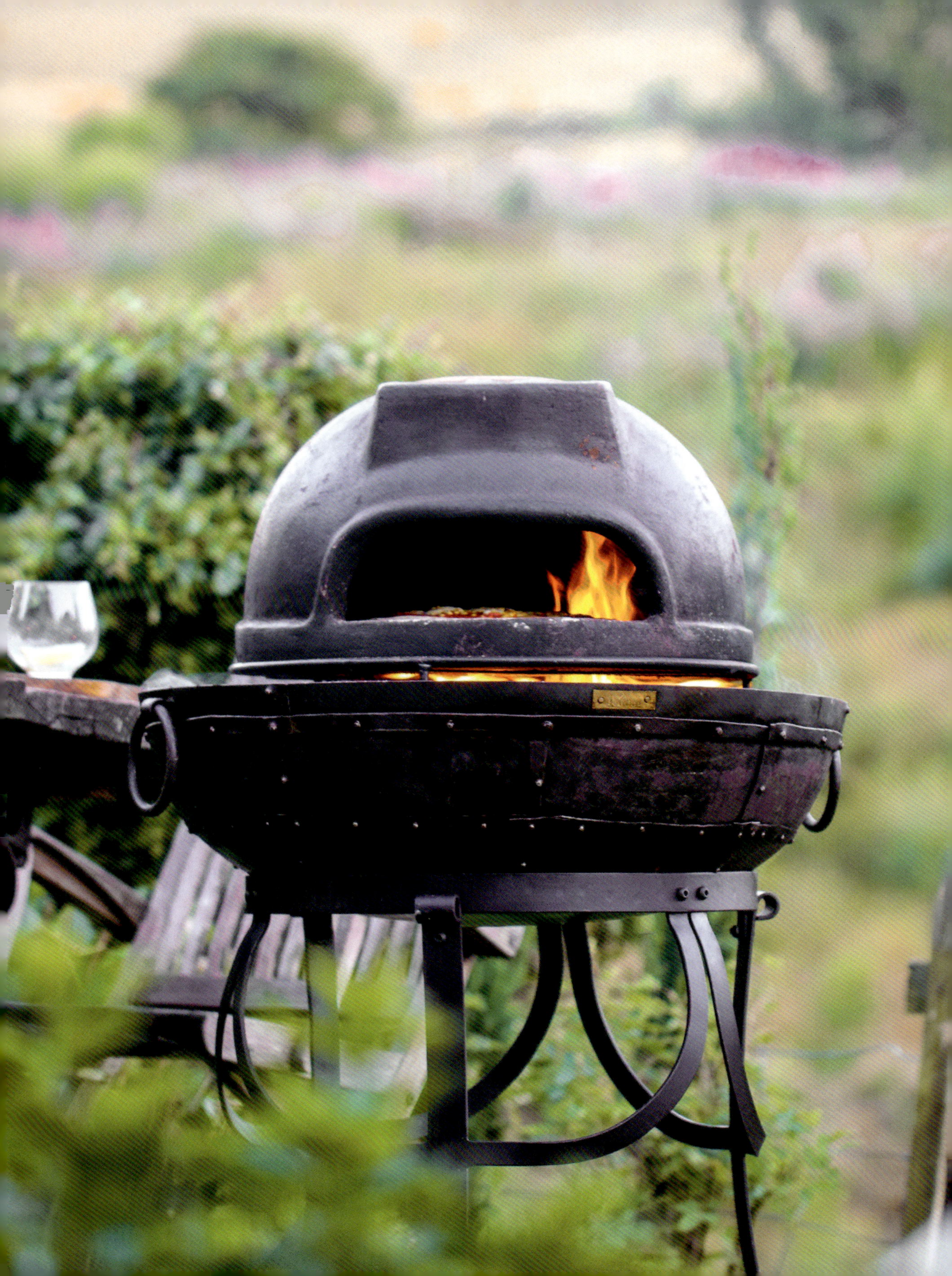

WOOD FIRED OVEN When considering how to cook a pizza on a Kadai, we came up with the idea of taking a Mexican clay oven, re-shaping it and cutting a slot in its base. This unique concept not only cooked the best pizza we have ever tasted, but also led to our using the oven to cook more than just pizza.

To set up the fire for your Wood Fired Oven, build a hot base of charcoal and push it to the back of the Kadai. Place the oven stand in the middle of the Kadai with the handles on each side and the single leg at the front, away from the coals (this allows an open space for adding wood at the back). Lower the oven onto the stand, with the mouth at the front and build up the fire with small 5cm thick pieces of split hardwood. You are aiming to get as many flames to flicker though the oven slot as possible in order to heat the oven. Add more wood gradually, focusing on positioning the flames under the slot, and remember to use small pieces of wood, whilst keeping the fire at the back of the oven.

This will take about 30 minutes. You want the internal temperature to reach between 220°C and 260°C. To check this temperature without a gauge, carefully hold your hand near the oven mouth but take care not to touch the clay oven. You are aiming for the 2 second hand test (see pg. 23 for 'hand test' guidance). If you are cooking a pizza, place a small piece of dough in the Oven. If it cooks in two minutes, then your Oven is hot enough to use.

KADAI LID This is brilliant for indirect cooking, roasting, smoking and using as an oven. Build your fire at the back of the Kadai on the opposite side to the Lid's vent so that the heat and smoke pass over the food. This also creates variable heat zones under the Lid. Large joints of meat can be placed on the cooler side by the vent with the heat and smoke passing over the top for a slow cook. Another method is to push the hot coals to form a ring around the edge of the Kadai, then place food in the centre to give a 360 degree cook. Adding some smoking chips in the Smoker Box (see pg. 29) will give a delicious smoky flavour to the meat or fish and enhance the flavours of your food.

If you are using the Kadai Lid for a long, slow cook, keep an eye on the temperature gauge to maintain an even heat, adding fuel as necessary. When adding more charcoal during the cook, we recommend utilising our Chimney Starter (see pg. 13) set on bricks. This avoids any acrid smoke from the initial burn of the charcoal being introduced to the cooking process. Avoid fully opening the Kadai Lid unnecessarily: this will prevent the heat from escaping.

Kada

Kadai Care

As with all equipment, a little care goes a long way when looking after your precious Kadai kit. Once you have finished cooking and everything has cooled down, it's well worth taking the time to ensure everything is ready for your next barbecue.

SEASONING COOKWARE All new metal cooking utensils and implements need washing thoroughly in hot soapy water, then seasoning with cooking oil before their first use.

Grill Trays, Frying Pans, Skewers and the like are all made from mild steel, so after washing and drying, put them on the hob on a medium to high heat to force any moisture out. Remove from the heat and whilst still hot, use a cotton cloth or kitchen roll to apply a very thin coat of vegetable oil; wipe off any excess and leave to cool.

Skillets, Cooking Bowls, Sizzling Plates and pans without wooden handles benefit from a deeper seasoned non-stick finish. Apply a thin coat of vegetable oil and place them upside down in a hot oven for 30 minutes. Curing these in an oven will ensure a more overall finish as the heat will radiate around the pan, ensuring the oil is absorbed evenly. This might smoke a little until the curing process is complete. Wooden handled items (such as the Chapati Pan) can be left on the hob on a high heat for this curing process but keep moving the pan around the hob to distribute the heat. The resulting polymerised non-stick finish is worth the effort for years of continued use and can be repeated whenever you feel it is necessary.

KADAI MAINTENANCE An annual clean with a light abrasive pad, followed by a thin coat of Owatrol oil or other rust inhibitor, will maintain the appearance of your Kadai, as well as protecting it from the elements and heat.

This oil can also be applied to the Kadai Stands, Cooking Tripod and other mild steel non-cooking accessories (such as the Kadai Shield, Kadai Lid or Log Store).

Kadai Beads are made from super-heated clay and can be sieved with the Riddle, either dry or wet. When riddling dry, simply scoop out the dirty Beads into the Riddle, using the Kadai Shovel and shake from side to side over a large bucket. Any unburnt pieces of wood or charcoal can be left with the Beads, but remove other debris. Tip the clean Beads into another bucket and repeat until your Kadai is empty. Once done, check the Kadai filter is not clogged and rinse out the bowl with clean water before replacing the Beads. The ash can be spread over a compost heap to neutralise the acidity or added to your green waste bin. If the Beads are wet, use a hose over the Riddle to wash the Beads, but be mindful where the ash waste is going. The Beads can be re-used indefinitely and topped up as required.

The Kadai Shield (*see below*) is an excellent accessory to keep your Kadai Beads and bowl dry and ready for use. It also helps to protect the Kadai Bowl from corrosion and can be used as a snuffer at the end of the evening.

CLEANING COOKWARE AFTER USE

To clean your seasoned pans, use warm soapy water and a sponge, but avoid abrasive wire scourers that could damage the non-stick finish. Hand-dry immediately and heat on the hob or your Kadai to expel any moisture. Apply a thin coat of vegetable oil while the pan remains hot, wiping off any excess and leaving to cool. Wire brush the Holi Grill or use the wooden Grill Scraper for any hardened burnt bits and apply a very thin coat of vegetable oil.

Looking after your Kadai cookware will give years of continued use. Make sure always to store them in the dry away from moisture. See Kadai.com for more information about care and use of your Kadai products.

COOKING WITH KADAI *kadai care*

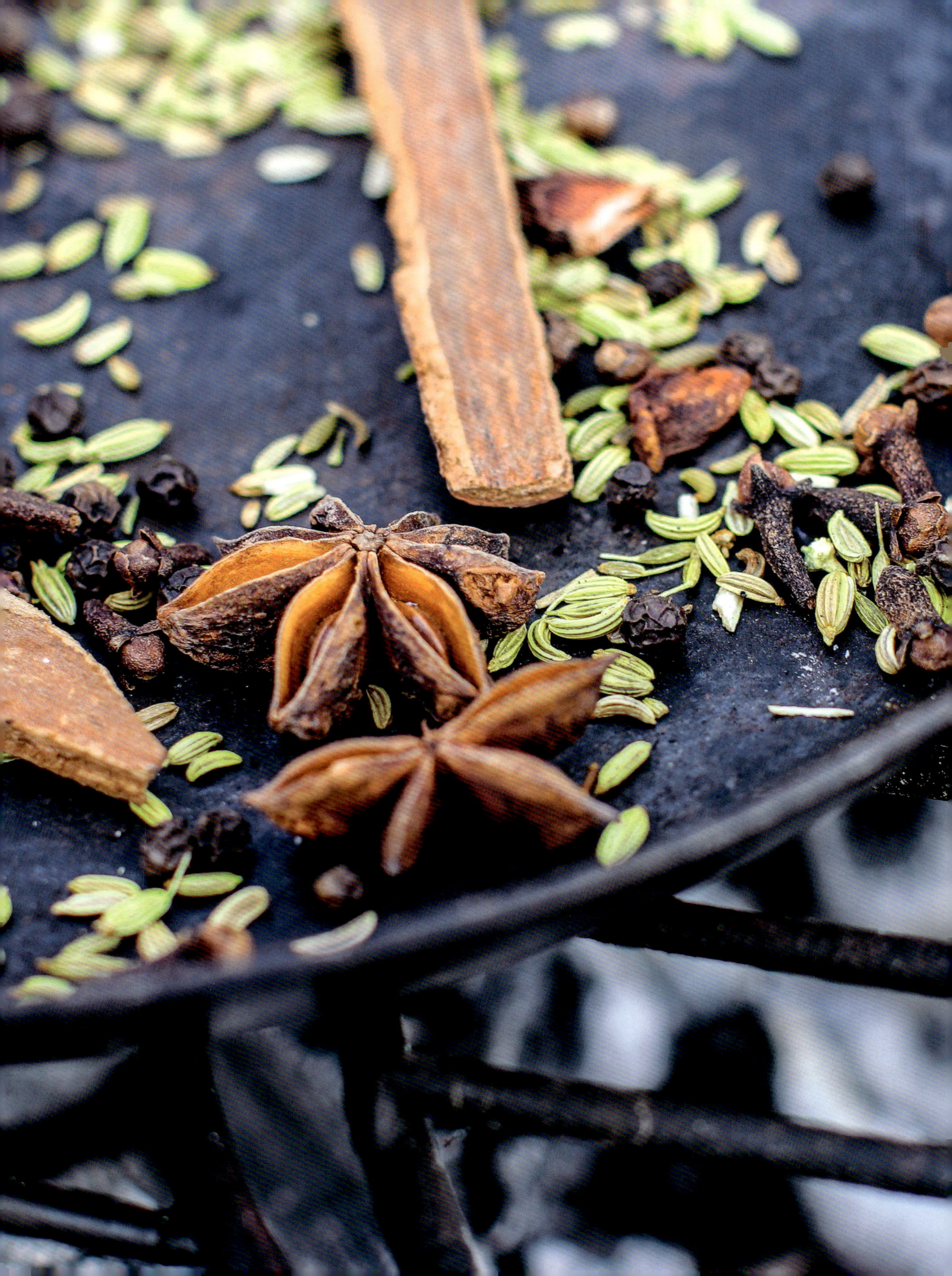

How to spice things up

Barbecuing is all about flavour. Experimenting with various herbs, spices and condiments can help to elevate your outdoor food to another level. Read on to discover the world of seasoning. We have included recipes for some of our favourite rubs, marinades and sauces, but creating your own is all part of the fun of cooking.

There are many different oils available, but we tend to use a good quality, extra virgin olive oil, as the richness of flavour and added health benefits make it a great choice. British rapeseed oil is another option, especially for cooking at higher temperatures. Alternatively, try some infused oils, like chilli, truffle and garlic, for added flavour.

Seasoning with different salts can help to intensify flavour, especially flavoured sea salts or seasoned salts. There is now a huge variety of salt available, so we suggest experimenting with different options until you settle on your salt of choice.

We always recommend using freshly ground black pepper, as recently ground spices and seasoning will offer a more intense flavour than pre-ground. Buy whole seeds/spices to grind at home using a pestle and mortar, then store in an air-tight container to keep them fresh. Only buy small amounts at a time to ensure your spices don't become stale.

We enjoy adding extra 'heat' to our barbecue food, by using fresh chillies (or powder). Try out different varieties available and discover the 'heat' that works best for you, (although we would recommend 'going easy' on the Carolina Reaper variety as they pack a very intense punch).

Barbecue food can be as simple or complex as you like, depending on what you want to achieve. Our recipes offer a variety of inspiration from the simple to the more technical, but all are full of flavour.

We have put together a 'herb & spice' list for you to experiment with. All the herbs and spices blend well with the meat in question and can create some wonderful combinations. (See pg. 46 for specific rubs to get you started.)

BEEF

Basil, Bay Leaf, Black Pepper, Cayenne, Chilli Powder, Coriander, Cumin, Curry Powder, Dry Mustard, Garlic, Green Pepper, Onion, Oregano, Paprika, Parsley, Rosemary, Sage, Tarragon, Thyme.

FISH

All Spice, Bay Leaf, Cardamom, Cayenne, Celery Seed, Chives, Cloves, Curry Powder, Dill, Dry Mustard Powder, Fennel, Garlic, Ginger, Lemon Zest, Marjoram, Mint, Onion, Paprika, Parsley, Red Pepper, Saffron, Sage, Sesame Seed, Tarragon, Thyme, Turmeric.

LAMB

Basil, Cinnamon, Cumin, Curry Powder, Dill, Dried Lemon Peel, Garlic, Marjoram, Mint, Nutmeg, Onion, Oregano, Parsley, Pepper, Rosemary, Sage, Savory, Sesame Seed, Thyme.

POULTRY

Basil, Bay Leaf, Black Pepper, Cayenne, Cinnamon, Coriander, Curry Powder, Garlic, Ginger, Lemon, Lime, Mace, Marjoram, Mint, Onion, Oregano, Paprika, Parsley, Rosemary, Saffron, Sage, Savory, Tarragon, Thyme.

PORK

All Spice, Basil, Bay Leaf, Caraway, Celery Seed, Chilli Powder, Chinese Five-Spice, Cloves, Coriander, Dry Mustard Powder, Fennel, Garlic, Ginger, Juniper Berries, Lemon Pepper, Marjoram, Onion, Oregano, Paprika, Parsley, Rosemary, Sage, Savory, Thyme.

Following on are some of our favourite go-to recipes for rubs, marinades and sauces to start you on your flavour journey.

Rubs

Rubs are a mix of dried herbs and spices that can be used to keep meat or fish tender by locking in juices and adding a delicious light crust. It is best to do this at least half an hour before cooking. Pat the food first with a paper towel to remove any moisture, coat with olive oil, then generously sprinkle the rub over both sides, rubbing it in well with your hands. Rubs can also be made with liquid ingredients to form a paste. You can buy pre-mixed rubs, but they are easy to make yourself and any discerning barbecue chef should have a few signature house rubs up their sleeve. Try to make a little extra to store in a sealable jar for later use.

For beef

Prep time: 5 minutes

50g brown sugar
1 tsp salt
4 tbsp smoked paprika
2 tbsp coarse black pepper
1 tbsp oregano
1 tbsp cumin
1 tbsp onion powder
1 tbsp garlic powder
1 tsp cayenne pepper

Makes enough for 1 large beef joint

Mix the ingredients together in a bowl and rub evenly onto your beef before cooking. This will infuse the meat leading to enhanced flavour and colour.

For pork

Prep time: 5 minutes

2 tsp brown sugar
1 tsp chilli powder
2 tsp paprika
1 tsp garlic powder
1 tsp dried thyme
1 tsp onion powder
1 tsp salt and pepper

Makes enough for 4 portions of pork (450g)

Mix the ingredients together in a bowl and rub evenly onto your pork before cooking. This will infuse the meat leading to enhanced flavour and colour.

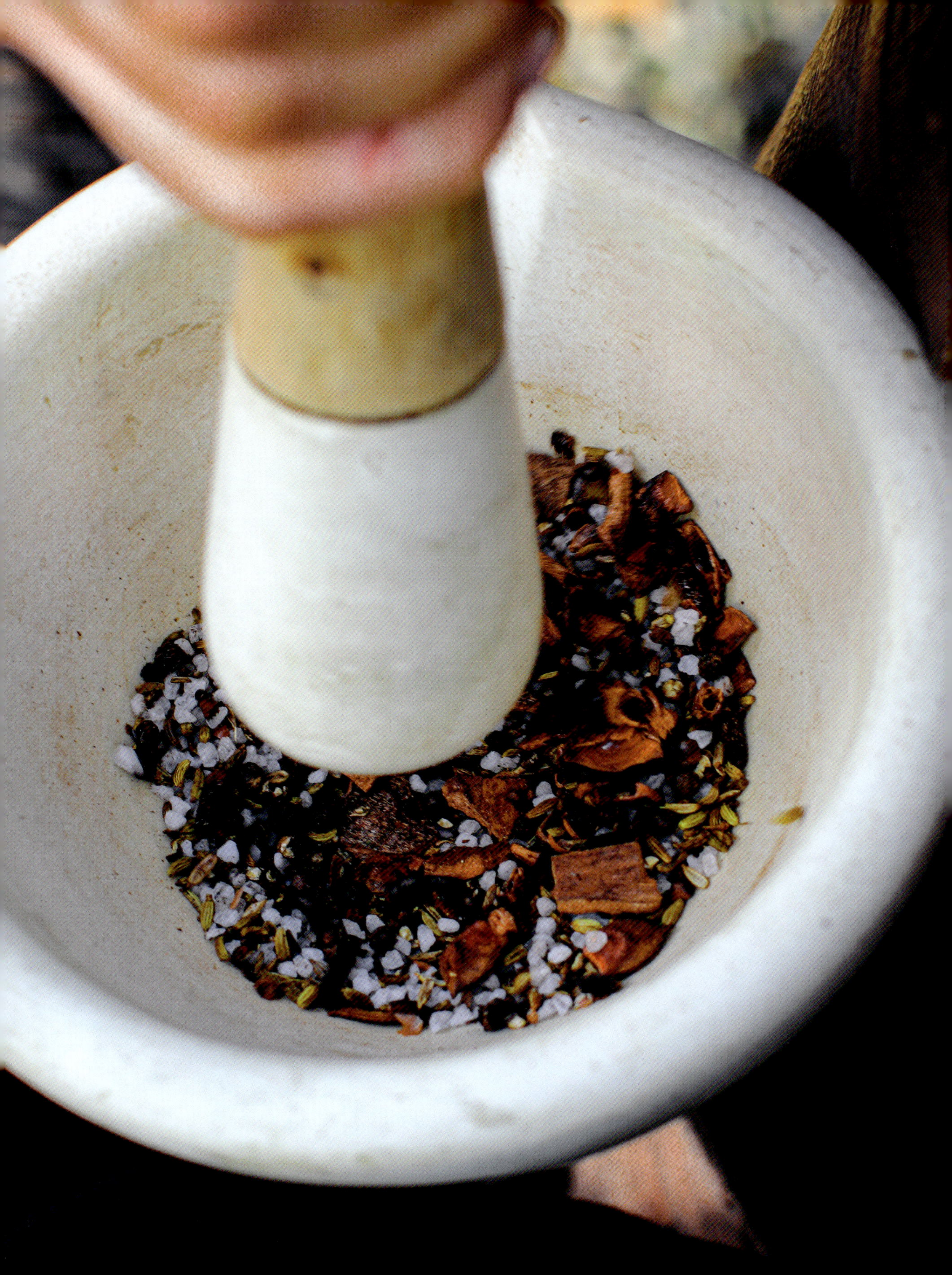

Rubs

For lamb

Prep time: 5 minutes

1 tsp garlic powder
1 tsp sea salt
1 tsp dried rosemary
1 tsp dried oregano
1 tsp dried basil
1 tsp freshly ground black pepper
1 tsp dried parsley
½ tsp dill weed
½ tsp dried marjoram
1 tsp ground nutmeg

Makes enough for 1 large leg of lamb

Mix the ingredients together in a bowl and rub evenly onto your lamb before cooking. For extra flavour, make small cuts in the uncooked meat and push garlic cloves into them.

....

For chicken

Prep time: 5 minutes

50g brown sugar
2 tbsp paprika
2 tbsp onion powder
2 tbsp garlic powder
1 tbsp ground coriander
1 tbsp dried oregano
1 tbsp dried parsley
1 tbsp ground ginger
1 tbsp cayenne pepper

Makes enough for 1 whole chicken

Mix the ingredients together in a bowl and rub evenly onto your chicken before cooking. This will infuse the meat leading to enhanced flavour and colour.

For fish

Prep time: 5 minutes

½ tsp mustard powder or ginger powder
1 tsp smoked paprika
1 tsp allspice
½ tsp cloves
1 tsp cayenne
½ tsp ground cardamom

Makes enough for 4 fillets of fish

Put the ingredients into a mortar and grind together with the pestle. Spread the rub evenly over raw fish. The longer the rub is left on the fish before cooking, the tastier it will become.

For vegetables

Prep time: 5 minutes

2 tbsp harissa paste
2 garlic cloves, finely chopped
½ preserved lemon, finely chopped
2 tbsp lemon juice

Makes enough for 500g prepared vegetables, such as courgettes, aubergines, peppers or cauliflower florets.

Combine the ingredients in a bowl and whilst grilling vegetables, brush them with the mixture.

Marinades

Marinating is a way of infusing your food with different flavours before you cook it. We would always recommend that marinating overnight in the fridge is the best option as this will allow the flavours to penetrate deep into the food, resulting in more delicious dishes. But, if you are short of time, usually, 2 to 3 hours should suffice. Cover the meat in the marinade and pop it into a sealable plastic bag. Shake the bag a little to cover all the surfaces of the meat and then leave it in the fridge until you are ready to start cooking.

For pork

Prep time: 5 minutes

50g white sugar
2 tsp salt
1 tsp Chinese five-spice powder
½ tsp sesame oil
4 tsp rice wine
4 tsp soy sauce
4 tsp hoisin sauce
2 tsp black treacle
½ tsp red food colouring (optional)
3 cloves of garlic, crushed
2 tbsp honey
4 tsp hot water

Makes enough for 1.5kg of pork

Combine all the ingredients in a bowl. Mix until smooth, then smother over the pork. Leave to marinate in the fridge for at least 3 hours before cooking.

For lamb

Prep time: 5 minutes

1 tsp ground allspice
100g tahini
1 garlic clove
2 tbsp pomegranate molasses
3 sprigs of rosemary

Makes enough for 4 portions of lamb (360g)

Put all the ingredients into a mini food processor and blend until smooth, then remove. Rub onto the lamb, cover and leave to marinate in the fridge for at least 3 hours before cooking.

For a rustic texture, remove the rosemary leaves from the stem, put all ingredients in a bowl and blend by hand with a pestle and mortar.

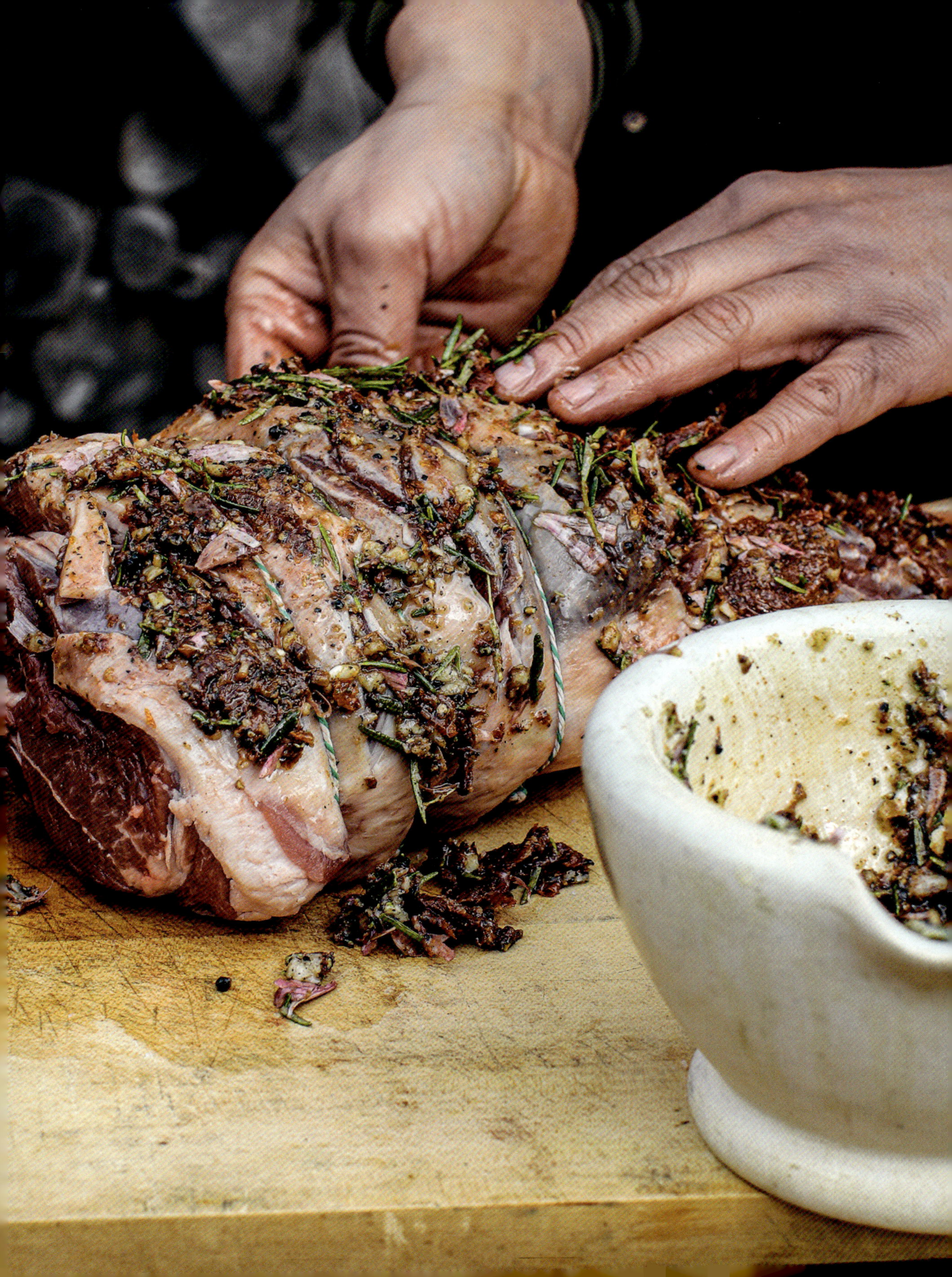

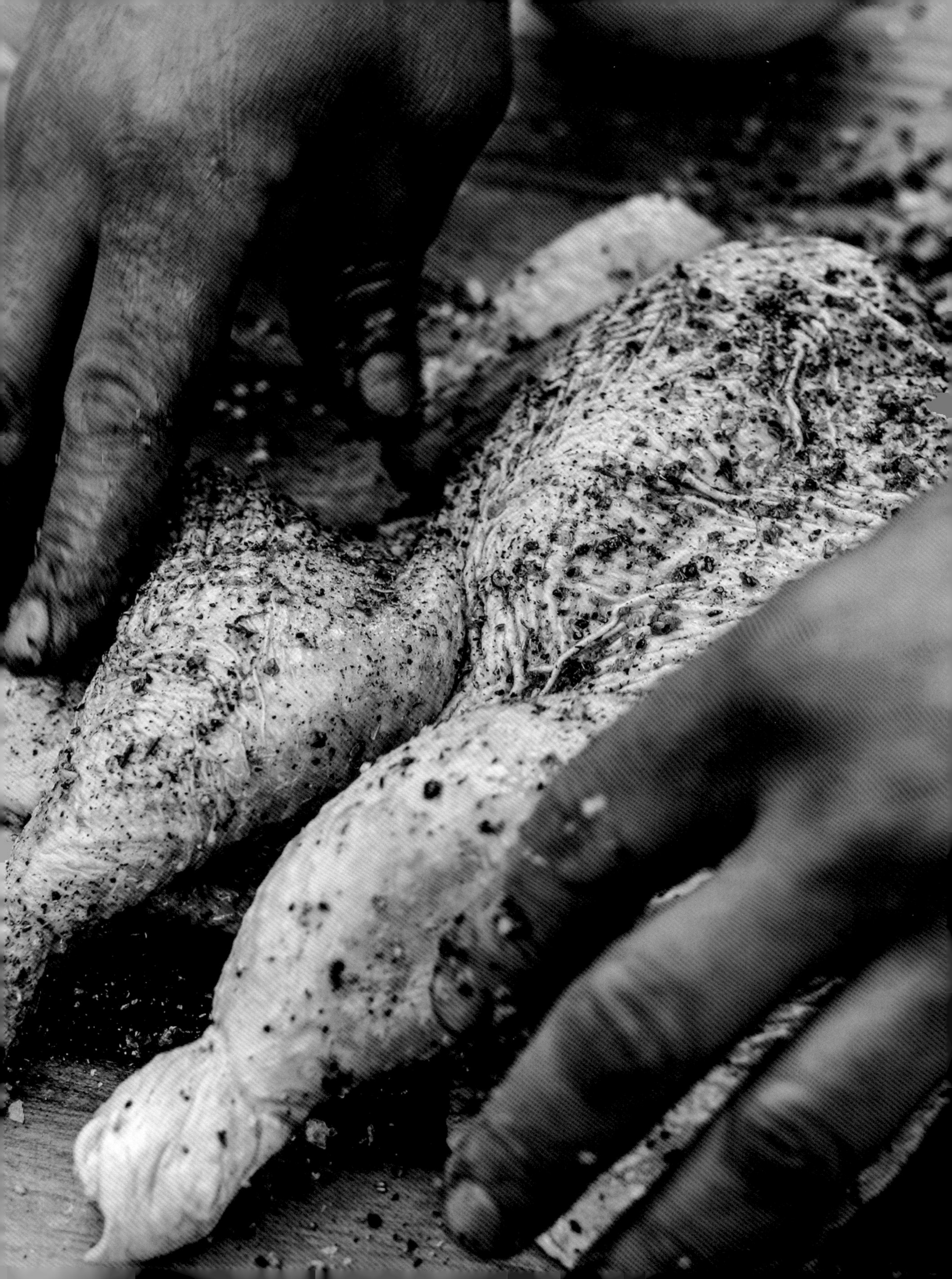

Marinades

For chicken

Prep time: 5 minutes

2 lemons, juiced
1 tbsp salt
250ml plain natural yoghurt
2 tbsp garlic purée
1 tbsp ginger purée
1 tbsp ground cumin
1 tbsp ground coriander
1 tbsp fresh ground black pepper
1 tsp turmeric
2 green chillies, finely chopped
Handful of fresh coriander leaves, chopped

Makes enough for 1 whole chicken

Mix all the ingredients together in a bowl until smooth. Rub onto the chicken, cover and leave to marinate in the fridge for at least 3 hours before cooking.

....

For fish

Prep time: 5 minutes

4 tbsp Thai fish sauce (Nam Pla) (an oriental ingredient found in delis)
1 red chilli, deseeded and very finely chopped
1 tbsp fresh coriander, very finely chopped
4 tbsp lime juice

Makes enough for 4 fillets of bass, or other fish with the skin on

Mix all the ingredients together, then brush on the fish before barbecuing or baking in the Wood Fired Oven.

Sauces

Sauces can give meat and vegetables a delicious flavour, adding a sweet or spicy coating. It is important to note that most barbecue style sauces contain sugar, which will burn above 130°C. Hold off basting this type of sauce onto your food until about 10 minutes before it is ready, to give enough time for the sauce to be absorbed and heat for caramelisation. Baste a few coats on until your dish is cooked and remember to leave a little extra for you to enjoy when served.

Kadai's Barbecue Sauce

Prep time: 5 minutes
Cooking time: 50 minutes
Recommended heat: Medium

30g salted butter
1 large white onion, diced
4 garlic cloves, finely chopped
475ml Guinness
120g ketchup
60g dry mustard powder
120ml molasses (sugar cane)
120ml apple cider vinegar
220g brown sugar
120ml honey
2 tbsp Worcestershire sauce
1 tsp paprika
½ tsp ground cinnamon
½ tsp salt
½ tsp red pepper flakes

Makes about 10 servings

Place the Cooking Tripod on a lit Kadai and attach the Cooking Bowl (see pg. 34).

Melt the butter in the Cooking Bowl. Add the onion and garlic and cook for about 10 minutes until the onion starts to caramelise (this step adds to the sweetness of the sauce).

Add the remaining ingredients to the Cooking Bowl, mix thoroughly and bring to a gentle boil. Leave to simmer for about 40 minutes, stirring occasionally.

Remove from the heat and allow to cool. Use a blender to combine the ingredients until smooth. Store in an airtight container in the fridge for up to 2 weeks.

Equipment:
Cooking Tripod, Cooking Bowl

Chimichurri

Prep time: 10 minutes

Handful of fresh coriander, finely chopped
Handful of fresh parsley, finely chopped
1 red chilli, finely chopped
1 tsp dried oregano
3 tbsp rapeseed oil
5 tsp red wine vinegar
1 lime, juiced
1 tbsp honey
1 tsp salt

Makes 4 servings

Combine all the ingredients together in a bowl and allow 30 minutes for the vinegar and salt to work into the herbs.

....

Pesto

Prep time: 5 minutes

150g fresh basil, chopped
150g parmesan, grated
100g pine nuts
100g ground almonds
2 garlic cloves, chopped
150ml olive oil

Makes 4 servings

Combine the basil, parmesan, pine nuts, ground almonds, garlic and half the olive oil in a mini food processor.
Pulse several times, adding the remaining oil halfway through. Once the ingredients form a paste consistency, remove from the processor.

TIP: For a delicious dressing or pasta sauce add more olive oil.

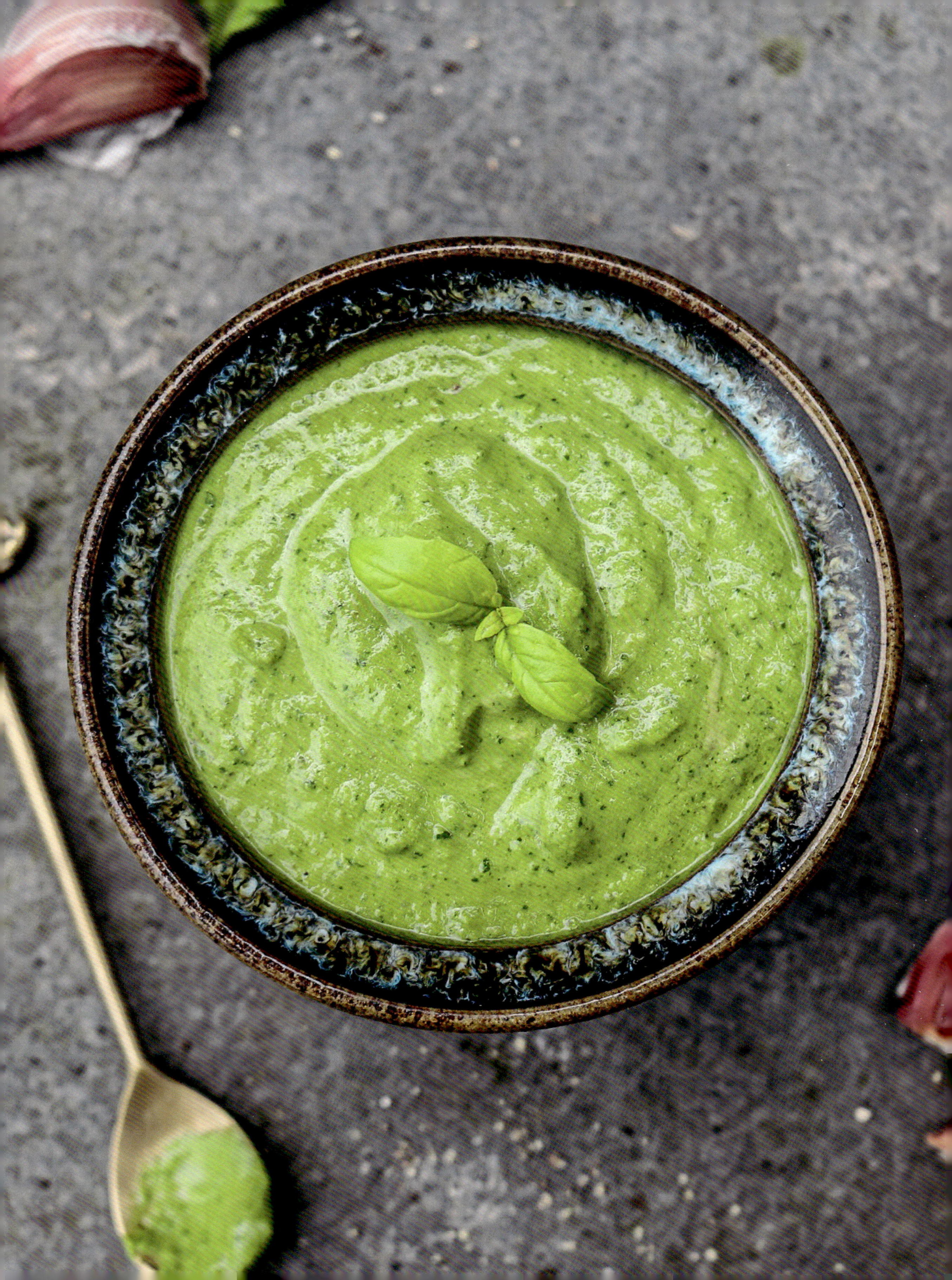

Sauces

Salsa verde

Prep time: 5 minutes

2 garlic cloves
25g fresh parsley
25g fresh basil
10g fresh mint
2 tbsp capers
2 tbsp gherkins, chopped
6 anchovy fillets, in olive oil and drained
1 tbsp Dijon mustard
3 tbsp red wine vinegar
8 tbsp olive oil

Makes 4 servings

Combine all the ingredients in a mini food processor. Mix until smooth, then remove.

TIP: Salsa Verde can be used as a dip, a sauce or drizzled over barbecued fish or vegetables.

Mojo rojo

Prep time: 10 minutes

1½ large sweet red peppers, chopped
2 red chillies, chopped
5 garlic cloves
100ml extra virgin olive oil
2-3 tbsp sherry vinegar
1 tbsp smoked paprika
1 tbsp ground cumin
Salt to taste

Makes 4 servings

Add all the ingredients to a mini food processor. Blitz on high power until the mixture is a vibrant, orange-coloured, smooth sauce.

TIP: Perfect for serving with any type of potatoes, steak or fish.

A few notes on herbs...

Many of the recipes in this book use fresh or dried herbs. Fresh herbs can be a great addition to barbecue food, either homegrown or shop bought. Use as a topping, once the food is cooked, for added flavour, garnish or add to recipes. A herb brush can also be used to baste your food during barbecuing which further enhances flavour (see pg. 59 for more information).

What is the difference between fresh and dried herbs? Quite simply, dried herbs have gone through a drying process that helps preserve them. They can then be crushed down into powders which makes them more potent with a concentrated flavour. The higher water content in fresh herbs makes them less strong-tasting than dried but adds beautiful, vibrant colours and incredible smells to any meal.

A substitution can be made in any dish so long as you bear in mind dry herbs are much stronger in taste than fresh herbs. As a rule of thumb, when swapping dry herbs into a recipe, use 1/3rd of the quantity stated for fresh herbs.

GROW YOUR OWN Growing your own herbs at home is a great way to have a regular supply and be sustainable. Herbs are often sold in single-use plastics, wasting unnecessary resources and harming our natural environment. Growing herbs at home is free and easy, offering a good yearly supply.

There are two types of herbs - annual/biennial and perennial. Annual or biennial herbs such as basil, coriander and parsley are fast growing, best planted at intervals throughout spring and summer. This will produce a fresh and continual supply.

Perennial herbs like oregano, mint, thyme and sage are slow growing, needing a more permanent home to survive. Herbs are best grown in raised flower beds, borders and pots, ideally where it is sunny and sheltered with well-drained soil. It is possible, however, to plant into heavy clay soil by incorporating some coarse grit or organic matter into the mix to improve drainage. The best pH-level for growing herbs is neutral to alkaline.

HOW TO MAKE A HERB BRUSH

Herb brushes will add a punch of flavour to your barbecue recipes. You can choose either a single herb or a small collection of your favourites, fastened into one brush. Start by choosing the herbs that best complement the dish you are cooking. You will need full stems and not just the leaves, so choose sturdier herbs such as sage, rosemary, oregano or thyme. Each piece should be 15 to 25 cm (6 to 10 inches) in length.

For the base of the brush, you need a wooden spoon, chopstick, or thin garden stick. Grasp the herbs and create a bundle in your hand. Take your chosen wooden base and push it directly into the middle of the herb stems by 5 to 8 cm (2 to 3 inches). Tie the herbs to the base with some twine, very tightly, and wind it around several times to create a thick handle. Cut off the excess twine, then baste away using your very own herb brush to bring fantastic, fresh flavours to your meat, fish or vegetables.

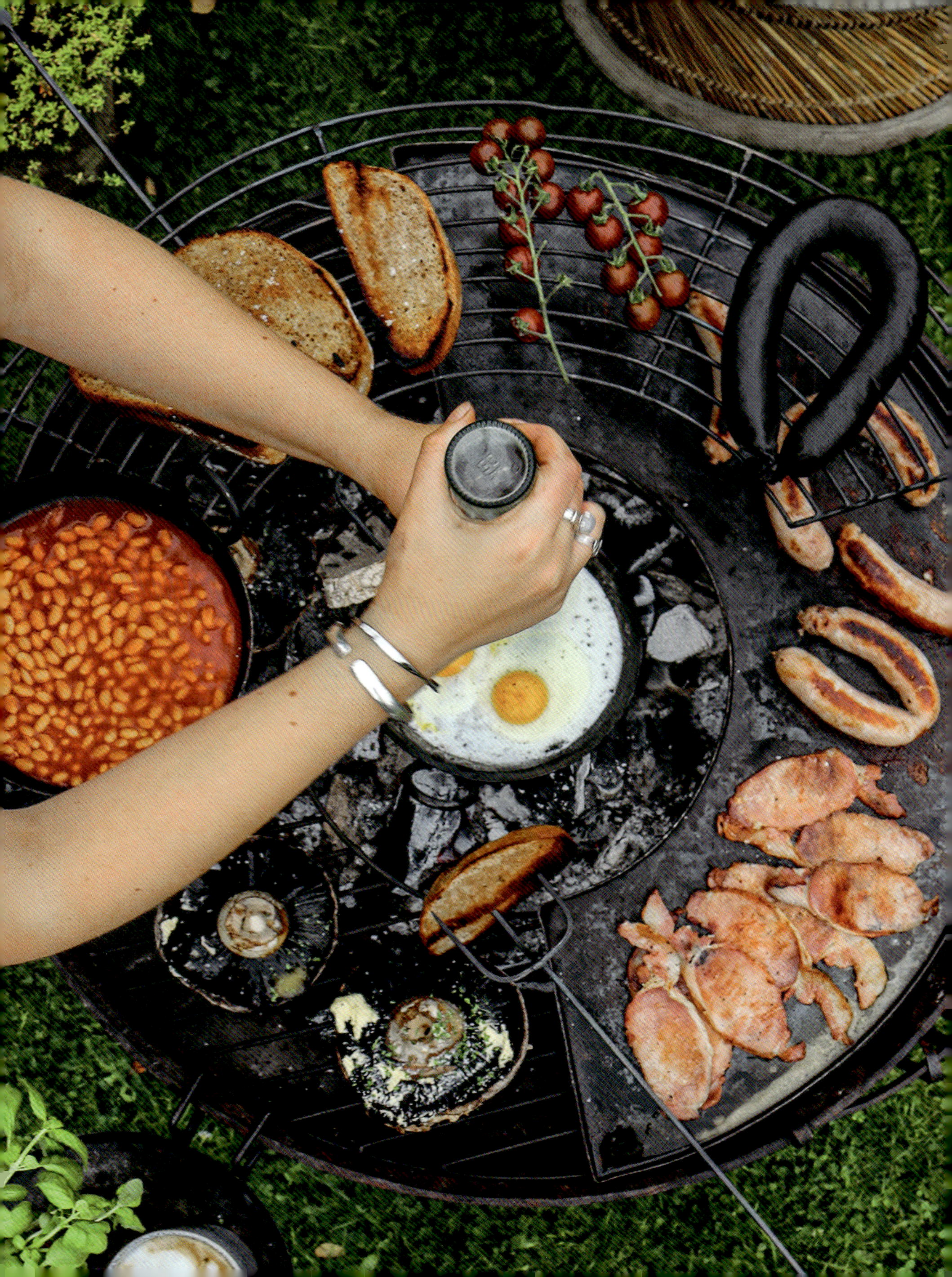

Lazy mornings

Breakfast is the most important meal of the day, but what's the one trick to make it even better? Cook it on the Kadai. With the coffee brewing, cook everyday classics like a full English or experiment with something more adventurous like Shakshuka. Harness the smoky flavour of barbecuing for a scrumptious and flavoursome breakfast that is worth getting up and outside for. For those late risers, try these morning delights as the perfect brunch.

MAPLE BACON BAGELS with SMASHED AVOCADO

Mix up the traditional breakfast bagel with this zesty, smoky and creamy recipe. Try these delicious flavours, certain to get that fire burning. This simple favourite is great cooked on your Travel Kadai when camping or for a quick breakfast on a larger bowl.

Prep time: 5 minutes
Cooking time: 20 minutes
Recommended Heat: Medium

2 ripe avocados, fleshed out
1 lime, juiced
8 cherry tomatoes, chopped
½ -1 red chilli, deseeded and finely chopped (optional)
4 tsp maple syrup
12 rashers bacon
Drizzle of olive oil
4 free-range eggs
4 bagels, sliced
4 knobs of unsalted butter
Salt and freshly ground black pepper to taste

Serves 4

First make the avocado smash by smashing the avocados with the lime juice, salt and pepper. Stir in the cherry tomatoes and chilli, then set to one side.

Lay the bacon rashers on the Grill Trays and brush with the maple syrup. Cover with the Cookware Lid and grill until crispy, about 4 to 5 minutes on each side.

Heat a little oil in a Skillet and fry the bagel tops and bottoms, cut side down. Toast for a few minutes, until a golden colour, then remove from the Skillet. Spread the bagel tops and bottoms with butter.

Crack the eggs into the Skillet and fry until cooked to your preference. Layer each bagel with the avocado smash on the bottom, 3 rashers of bacon, one fried egg, season with salt and pepper and complete with the bagel top.

Equipment:
Set of 3 Grill Trays, Cookware Lid, Set of 3 Skillets

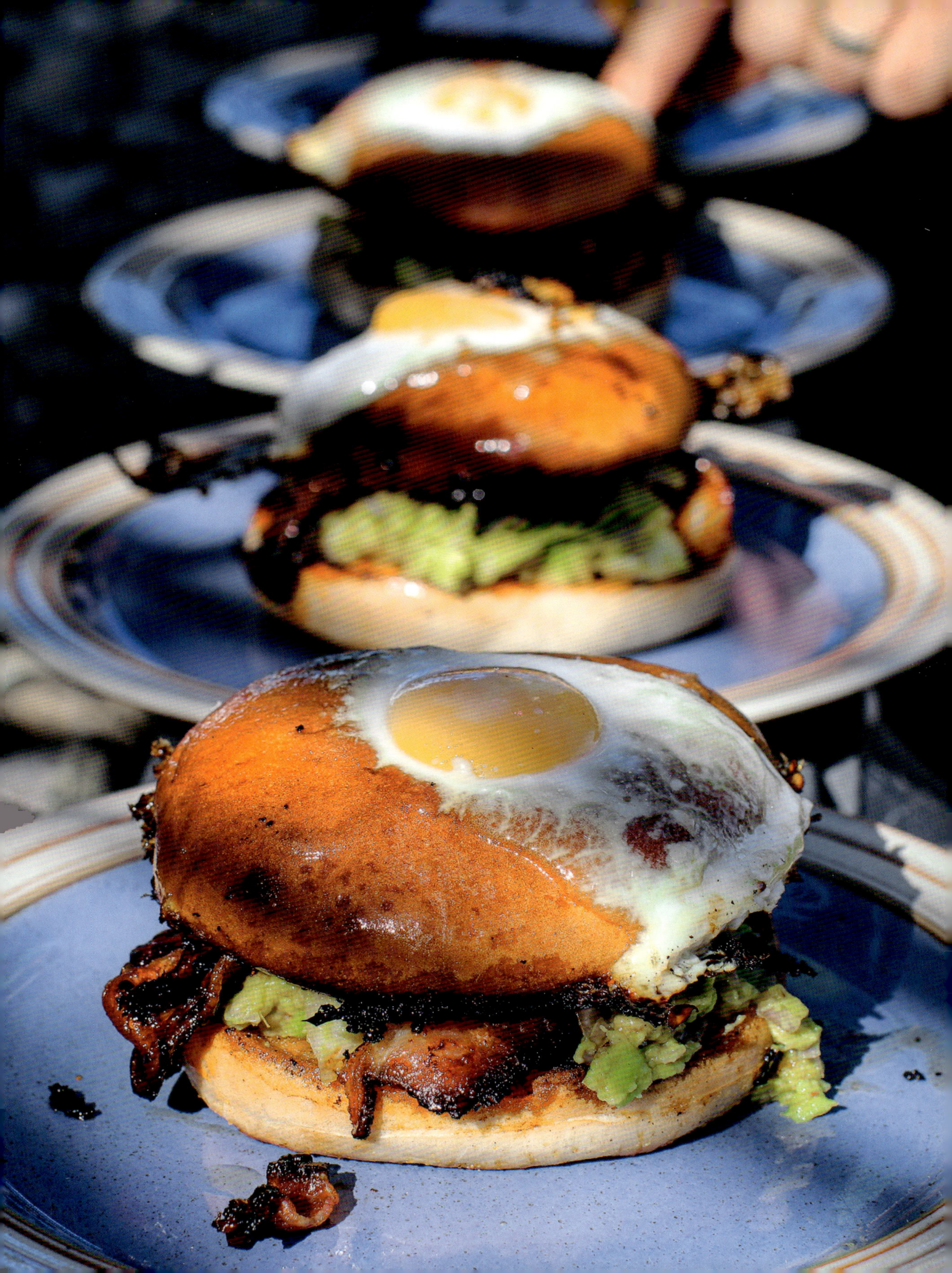

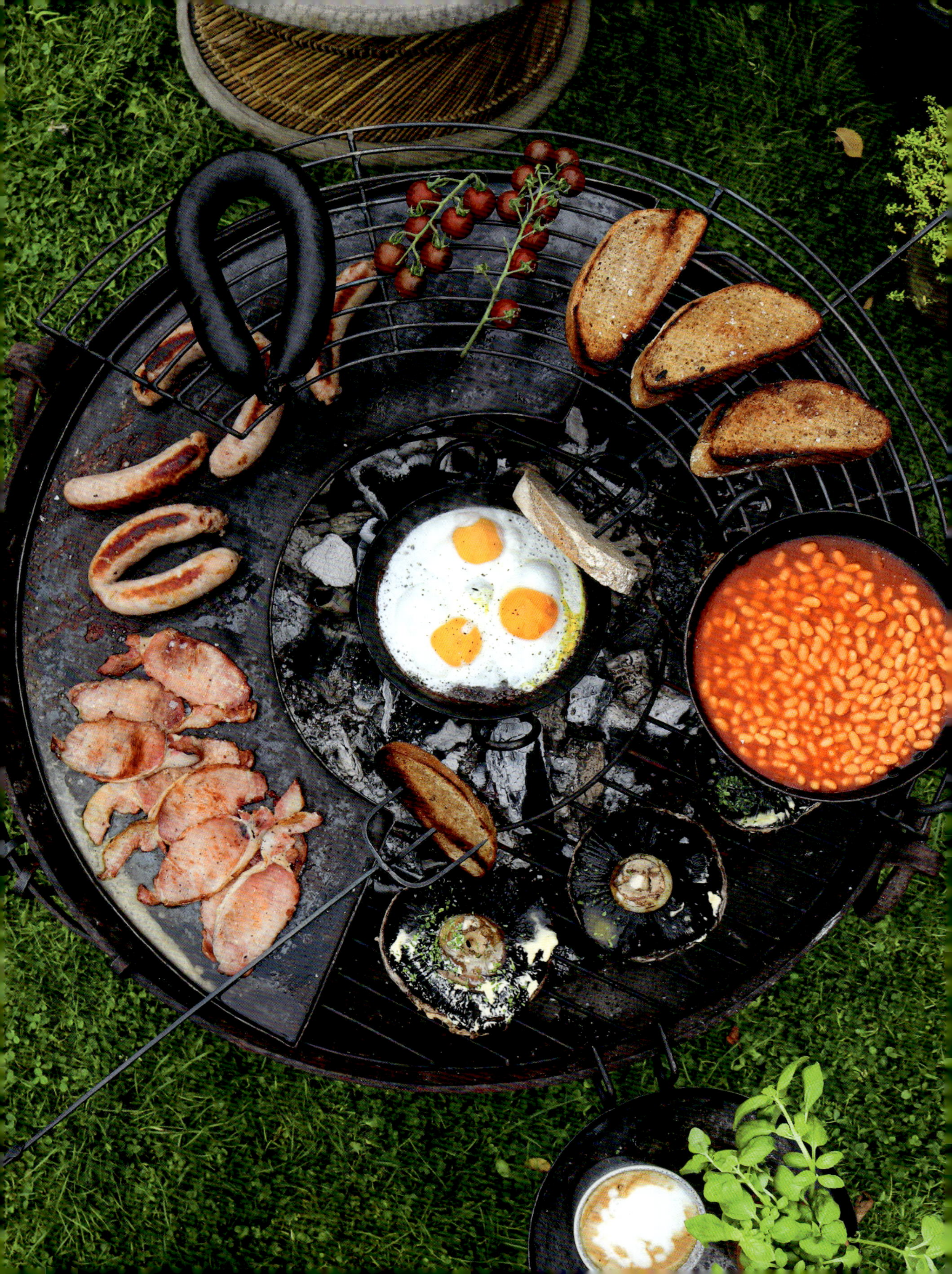

LAZY DAY ENGLISH BREAKFAST

A favourite among friends and family, bring the flair to a lazy weekend with our complete Full English Breakfast. Enjoy our take on this traditional feast using the clever pairing of Hot Plate and Warming Rack to discover your own ultimate breakfast combination.

Prep time: 5 minutes
Cooking time: 20 minutes
Recommended Heat: High

8 Cumberland sausages
1 black pudding sausage, sliced
4 large portobello mushrooms
Cherry tomatoes, on the vine
8 rashers bacon
Sourdough bread, sliced
400g tin baked beans
4 free-range eggs

Serves 4

Place the Hot Plate onto one side of the Grill and leave for a few minutes to get hot.

Fry the sausages for about 5 minutes before adding the black pudding, turning both occasionally. The sausages will take about 15 minutes to properly cook through.

Place the mushrooms and tomatoes directly on the bars of the Grill and leave to cook.

After 5 minutes, add the bacon rashers to the Hot Plate and cook to your preference.

Move any cooked food onto the Warming Rack to keep warm, while cooking the remaining ingredients.

Place the sliced sourdough bread directly onto the Grill, turning often, for about 5 minutes or until toasted golden brown. Place on the Warming Rack to keep warm and continue cooking.

Pour the baked beans into the small Skillet and leave to warm on the bars of the Grill. Fry the eggs in the medium Skillet for 3 minutes, directly on the hot embers.

Once all the ingredients are ready, plate up and enjoy.

Equipment:
Hot Plate, Warming Rack, Set of 3 Skillets

FIRE-SMOKED KIPPERS *with* LEMON & PARSLEY

This incredibly easy, yet flavoursome dish has truly stood the test of time. Delicately smoked over an open fire, these kippers will perfectly complement your morning poached or scrambled eggs and a freshly buttered piece of toast.

Prep time: 5 minutes
Cooking time: 1 hour
Recommended Heat: Medium/Low

4 kippers, pre-smoked
Drizzle of lemon juice
Small handful of fresh parsley, chopped

Serves 4

Using a sharp knife, split the kippers in a butterfly fashion from tail to head along the dorsal ridge, keeping the heads intact.

Using food-safe metal hooks, attach the kippers by the heads, to the Asado Cross (see pg. 34).

Suspend the kippers over the heat until they are cooked through (approximately 1 hour). Check that the kipper skin is starting to separate, and the meat can be easily removed from the bones.

Remove from the heat and serve either whole or pull the meat off the bones. Flavour with a drizzle of lemon juice and a sprinkling of parsley.

For fresh, unsmoked kippers, follow the same recipe but cook for approximately 1 hour 30 minutes.

Equipment:
Asado Cross

TIP: For a complete, delicious breakfast, put the Grill on to toast some bread and cook some eggs in a Skillet to your liking. Then cover the toast in unsalted butter, layer the kippers and eggs, then season with lemon, parsley, salt and black pepper.

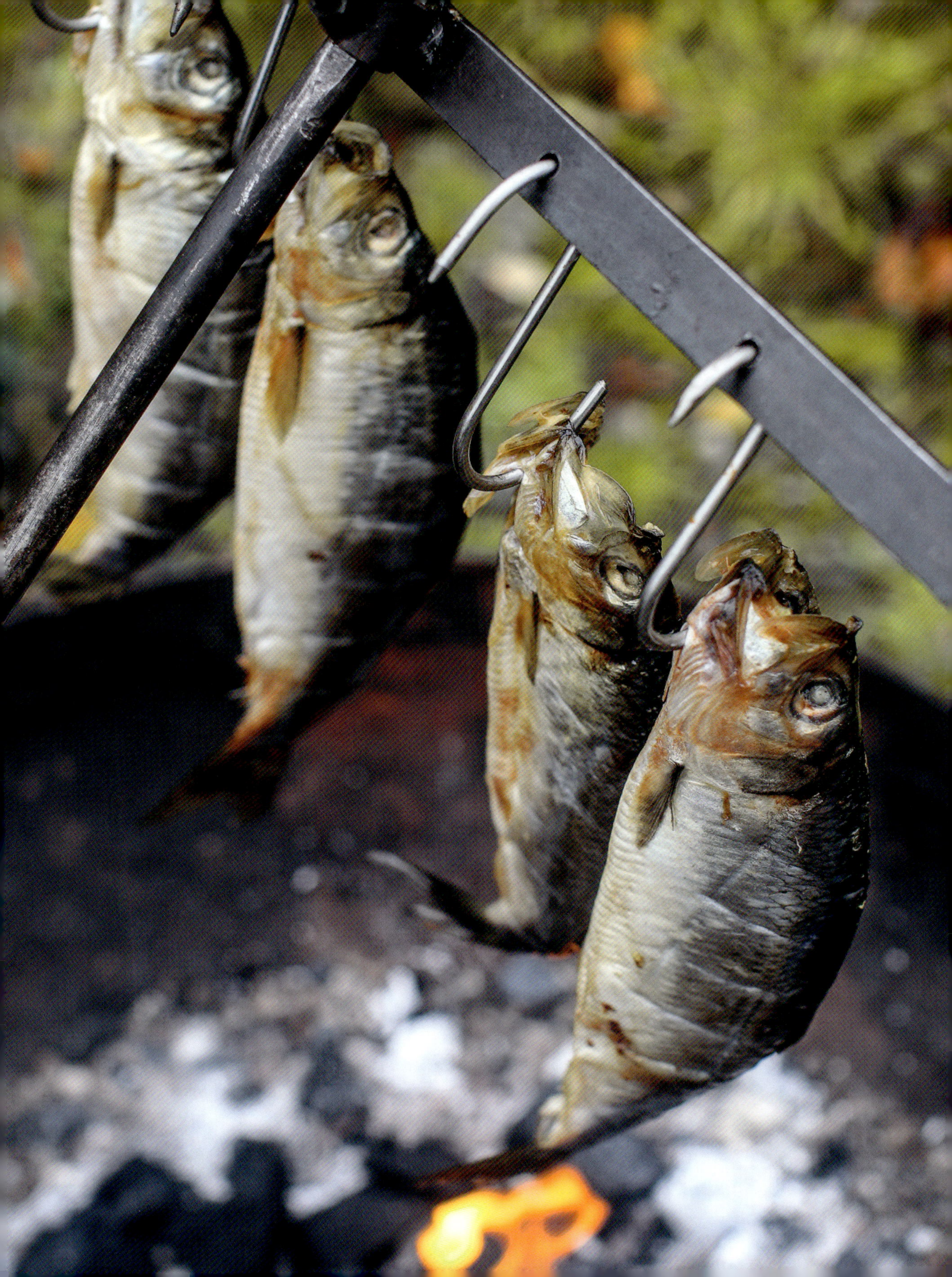

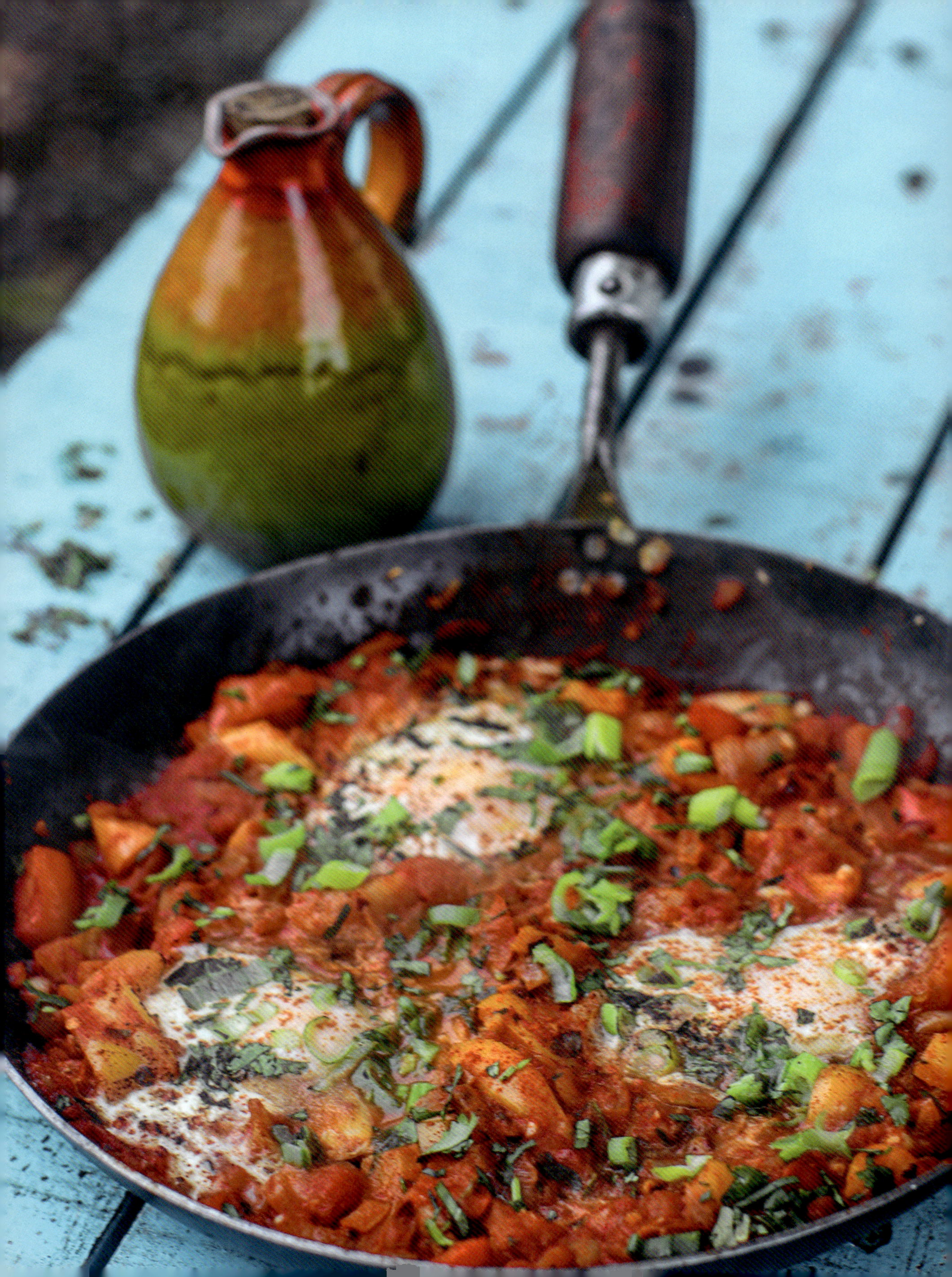

MIDDLE EASTERN SHAKSHUKA

Travel to the Middle East with this perfect balance of dried spices, rich tomato and gooey poached eggs. Shakshuka makes a scrumptious breakfast that is deeply warming and aromatic. Enjoy sharing this dish with crusty bread.

Prep time: 15 minutes
Cooking time: 30 minutes
Recommended Heat: Medium/Low

Drizzle of olive oil
1 large white onion, chopped
2 yellow peppers, sliced
4 garlic cloves, finely chopped
1 tbsp cumin
1 tbsp paprika
Sprinkle of crushed chilli flakes (optional)
2-3 fresh mint leaves, chopped
400g tin chopped tomatoes
4 free-range eggs
Small handful of fresh coriander, chopped
4 slices ciabatta

Serves 4

Heat the oil in a Frying Pan, then add the onions, peppers and garlic. Sweat over a medium heat for 5 minutes.

Mix the spices together in a small bowl and add them to the Frying Pan. Mix them with the onions and peppers. Fry for 2 minutes to ensure the flavours have a chance to infuse.

Add the tomatoes and simmer for 15 minutes until the tomatoes are soft and have thickened. Create 4 spaced 'wells' in the tomato mixture and crack the eggs into them. Place the Cookware Lid over the Frying Pan and cook the eggs to your preference.

Remove from the heat and sprinkle with the coriander. Serve with warmed, crusty ciabatta.

Equipment:
Frying Pan, Cookware Lid.

TIP: Add slices of chorizo with the diced onion for a 'smokier' filling.

COURGETTE FRITTATA
with FETA & MINT

This is our version of an Italian classic, bringing together fresh courgette ribbons, tangy feta and cooling mint. Delve into the Mediterranean flavours of the Wood Fired Oven to bake this gloriously fluffy and vibrant vegetarian dish.

Prep time: 20 minutes
Cooking time: 30 minutes
Recommended Heat: Low

2 courgettes
8 free-range eggs
Handful of fresh mint, chopped
Handful of fresh parsley, chopped
100g feta cheese
Salt and freshly ground black pepper to taste

Serves 4

Using a peeler, slice the courgettes into large ribbons and spiral them evenly around each other to form a rose like circle in the medium Skillet.

Create about 6 courgette spirals. Set the Skillet aside and prepare the egg mixture.

Crack the eggs into a bowl and whisk together thoroughly, adding a pinch of salt and pepper to taste.

Pour the egg mixture over the top of the courgette spirals in the Skillet.

Crumble the feta over the courgette and egg. Top with the mint and parsley.

Set up the Wood Fired Oven (see pg. 37). Ensure the fire is built up at the back of the bowl, with the flames coming up through the vent. Too much heat under the Wood Fired Oven will burn the Frittata base.

Place the Skillet into the Wood Fired Oven and cook until the egg sides have risen (much like an omelette), about 30 minutes. Bake low and slow, turning the Skillet occasionally to ensure an even cook around the edges.

Equipment:
Set of 3 Skillets, Wood Fired Oven

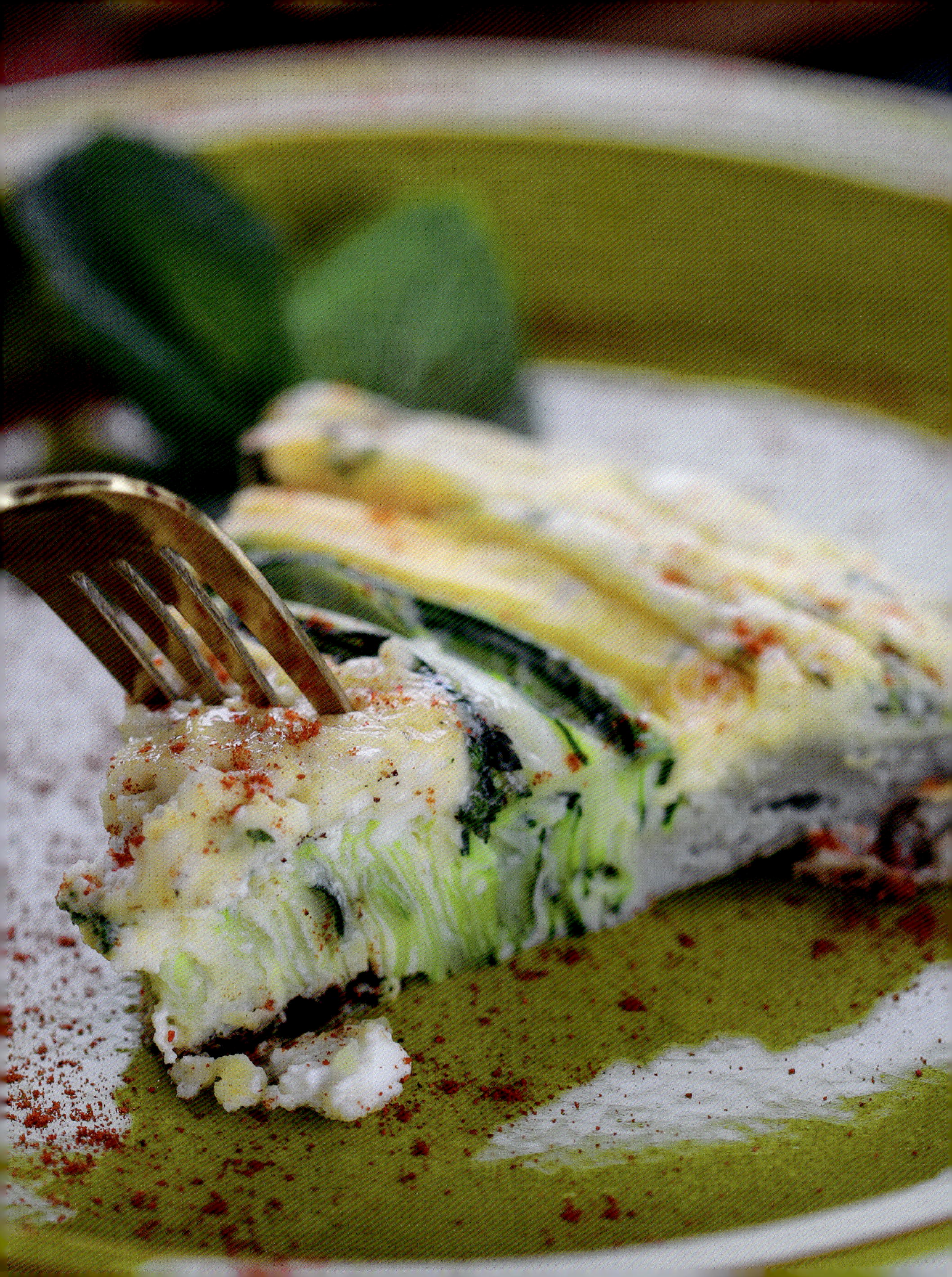

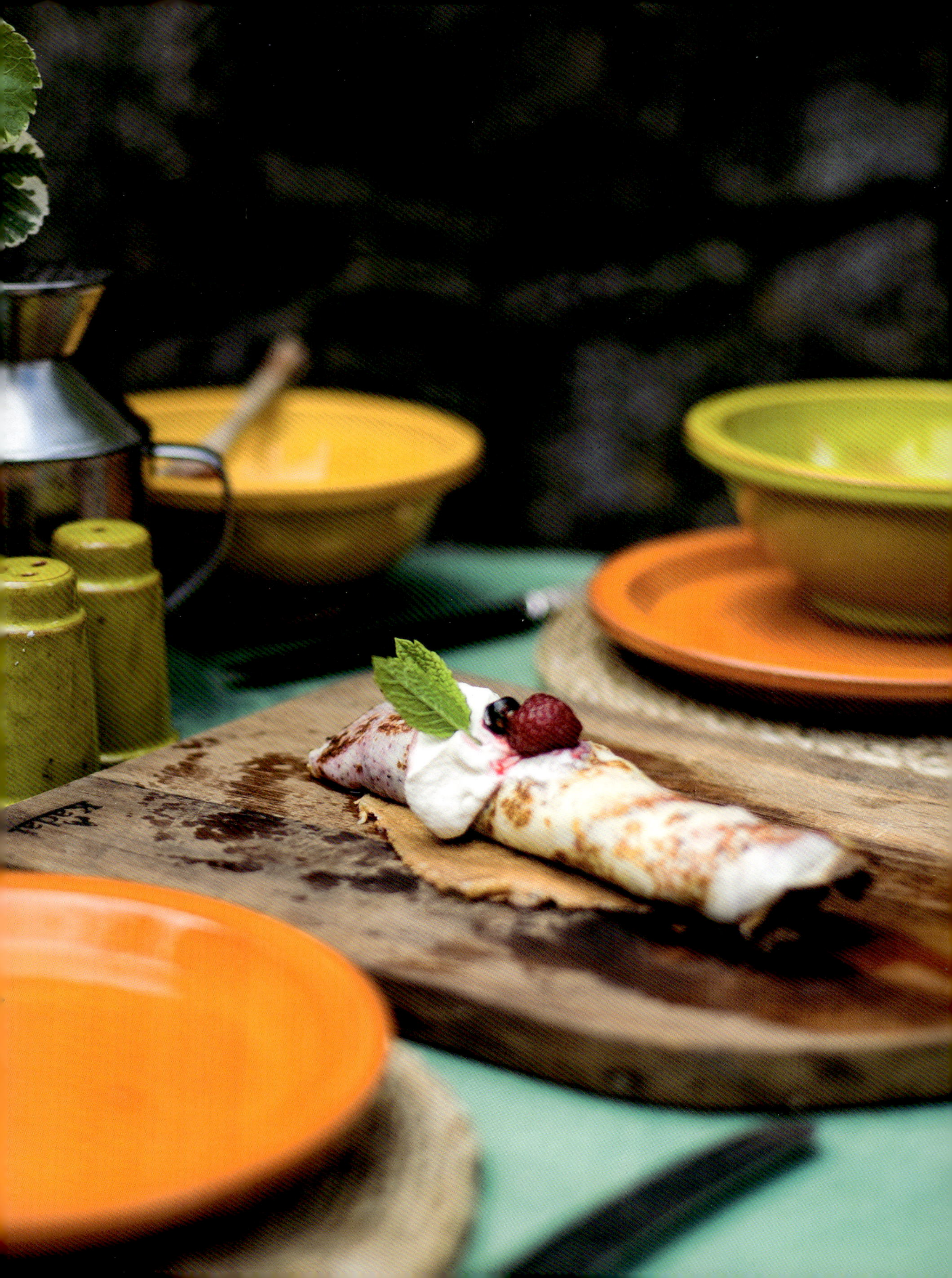

PANCAKES, CRÈME FRAÎCHE & FRESH BERRIES

Time to get the children involved, with this child-friendly and incredibly easy recipe. Grab your Chapati Pan to make some fluffy and delightful pancakes straight off your firebowl. Serve with the Kadai favourite of crème fraîche, fresh berries and maple syrup or just the classic lemon and sugar.

Prep time: 5 minutes
Cooking time: 6 minutes, per pancake
Recommended Heat: Low/Medium

For the pancakes:
100g plain flour
2 free-range eggs
275ml milk
50g unsalted butter

For the toppings:
Dollops of crème fraîche
Handful of fresh summer berries
Drizzle of maple syrup
Sugar and/or lemon juice

Serves 6 (2 per person)

Add the flour to a bowl and break in the eggs. Whisk in the eggs and then the milk to make the batter.

For the best results, let the fire in your Kadai die down. Use the Tongs to spread the warm charcoal around the base of the firebowl and place the Chapati Pan on top, leaving it to get hot.

For each pancake, add a knob of butter to the pan and move it around to the edges whilst it melts. Add a generous dollop of batter to the pan, swirling it around gently until evenly distributed.

Cook for about 2 to 3 minutes until golden brown then flip over and cook for another 2 to 3 minutes.

Serve each pancake on a plate smothered in crème fraîche, fresh berries and maple syrup. Repeat for the following servings.

Equipment:
Tongs, Chapati Pan

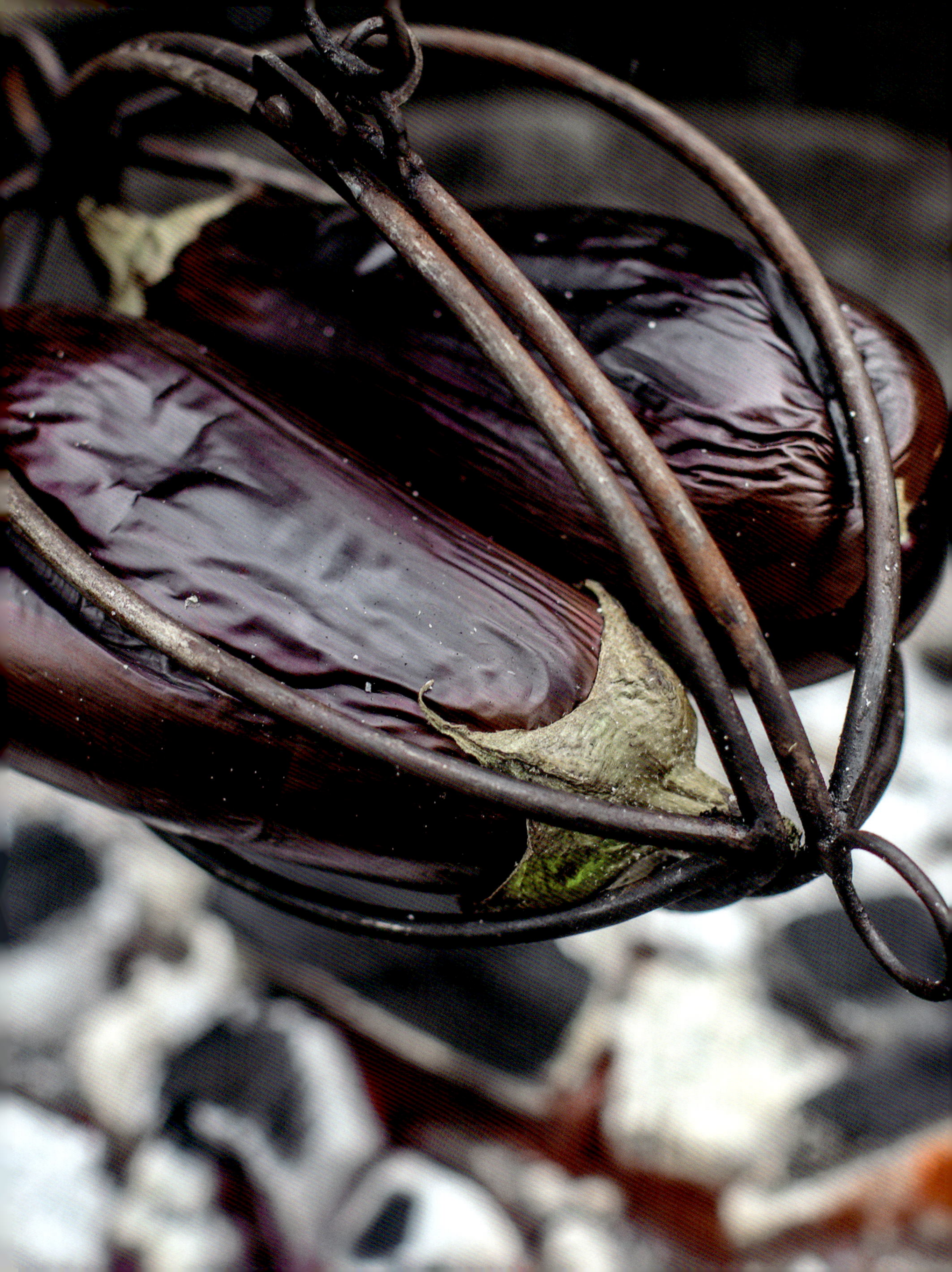

Nibbles & sides

Barbecue small bites are an essential part of any party to keep your guests entertained, whilst you get on with the business of cooking the main meal. There's no doubt that these recipe inspirations will satisfy all tastes, thanks to their simple, yet superb flavour and presentation. Alternatively, use these delicious recipes as sides to accompany your main dish.

CRISPY CALAMARI

Bring the taste of the sea to your garden with our fried calamari recipe. Add a smoky, Spanish twist to this classic combo with paprika and cayenne pepper, perfect for a night sharing tasty tapas.

Prep time: 10 minutes
Cooking time: 15 minutes
Recommended Heat: High

100g plain flour
1 tsp smoked paprika
½ tsp cayenne pepper
500ml rapeseed oil
500g prepared squid (calamari), sliced into rings
Lemon wedges
Salt and freshly ground black pepper to taste

Serves 4

Mix the flour with the paprika and cayenne pepper thoroughly in a medium bowl.

Carefully coat each calamari ring in the flour mixture. Make sure each piece is well covered and shake off any excess flour.

On the Grill, heat up the oil in a medium Skillet. Get the oil hot and bubbling before adding the calamari one piece at a time. We recommend doing only 4 to 6 at a time (depending on the size).

Fry each piece for 2 to 3 minutes or until golden and crispy, flipping them halfway through if needed.

Take each piece out with Tongs and place onto a tray lined with kitchen paper. Continue to cook the rest in the same way, until your tapas dish is full.

Season with lemon wedges, salt and pepper before serving.

Equipment:
Set of 3 Skillets, Tongs

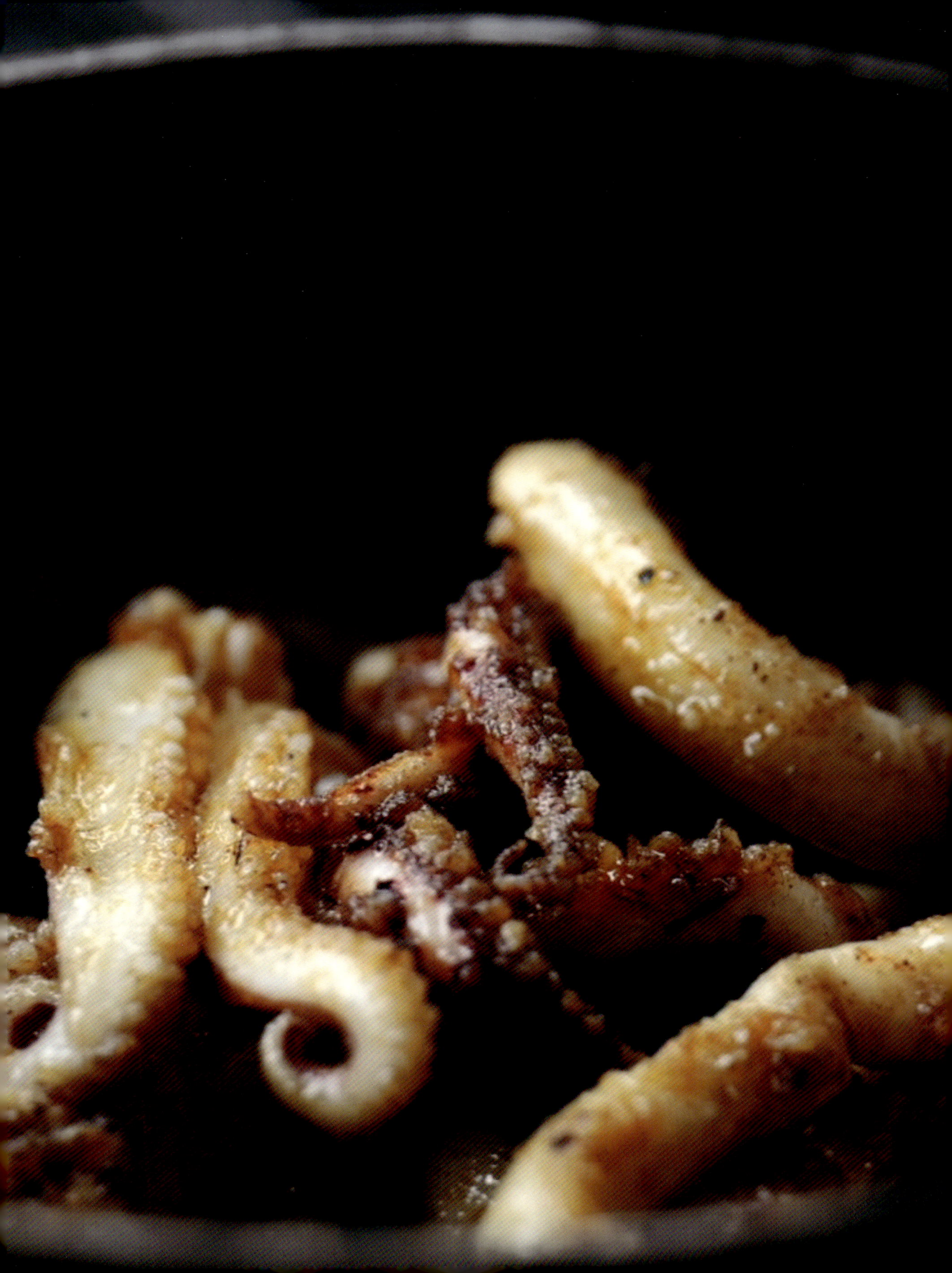

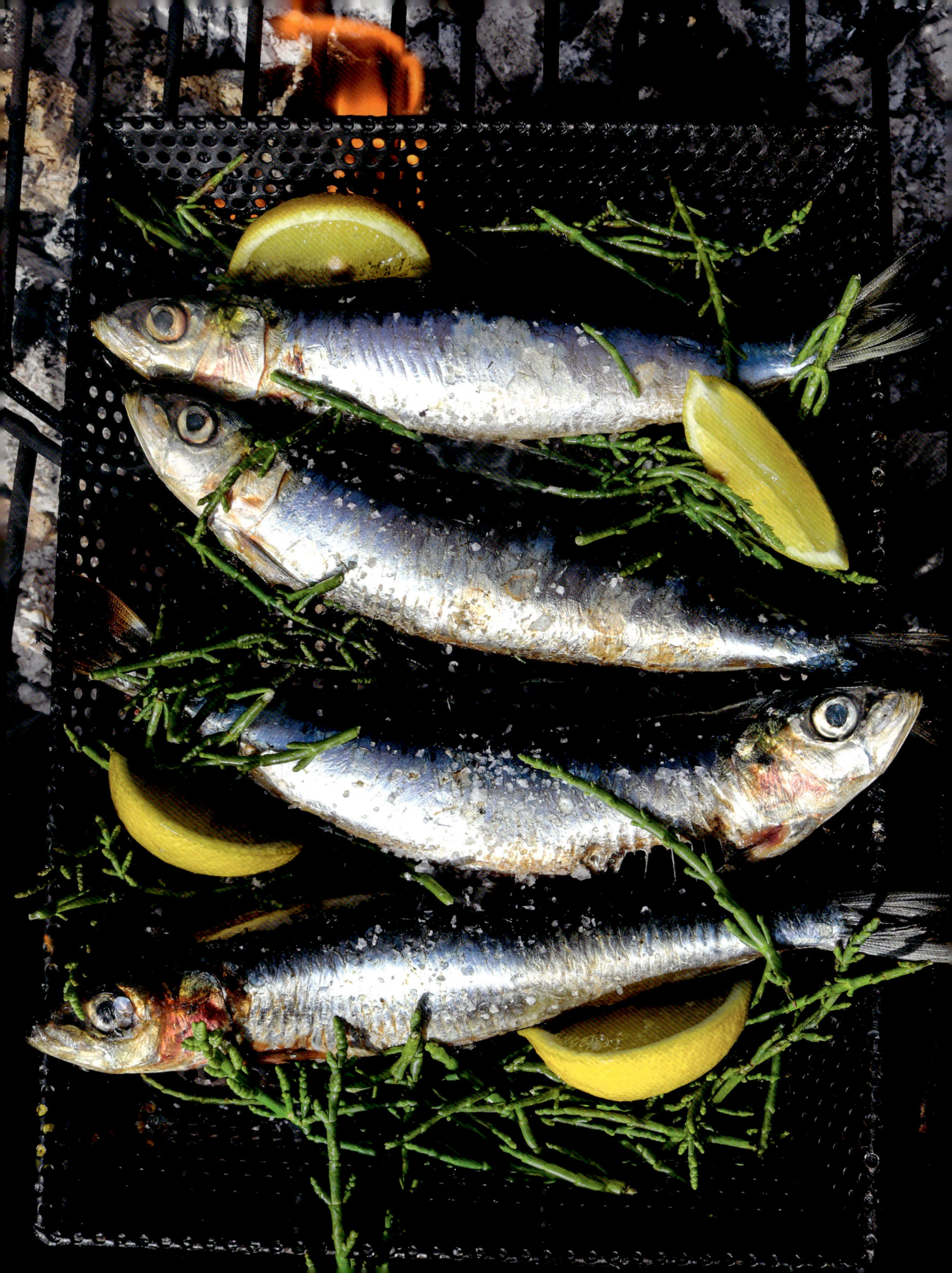

GRILLED SARDINES
with SEASONAL SAMPHIRE

Experience the unparalleled flavours of samphire in this beautiful seasonal recipe. One of the most delicious sea vegetables, samphire grows on mud flats and complements saltwater fish, like sardines, perfectly. Available between June and September, make the most of this summer pairing whilst you can.

Prep time: 10 minutes
Cooking time: 15 minutes
Recommended Heat: Medium

115g bag of samphire
12 large sardine fillets
Drizzle of olive oil
1 lemon, juiced
Handful of fresh basil or parsley
Lemon wedges
Salt and freshly ground black pepper to taste

Serves 4

Give the samphire a good wash and break up any larger pieces so they are all roughly the same size. Set to one side.

Lightly drizzle a Grill Tray with the oil, then place over a medium heat. Add the sardines, then a drizzle more of oil and a squeeze of lemon juice on top.

Gently grill the sardines for approximately 10 minutes, turning occasionally.

Add the samphire to the Grill Tray for the last 3 to 4 minutes, so it will start to wilt, then season with salt and pepper.

Serve the sardines and samphire with fresh herbs and lemon wedges.

Equipment:
Set of 3 Grill Trays

DIRTY OYSTERS

Impress your guests with these unusual dirty oysters. Here at Kadai we are all about seasonal food. With oysters this means the rule of R. For the freshest selection buy your oysters only in months with an R (September to April). A firm favourite, we serve them in their shells with garlic and hot sauce as a gourmet appetiser.

Prep time: 10 minutes
Cooking time: 5 minutes
Recommended Heat: Low

12 fresh oysters (from your local fishmonger)
4 tbsp unsalted butter
2 garlic cloves, finely chopped
1 tsp freshly ground black pepper
1 tbsp sea salt
2 tsp hot sauce, preferably tabasco (optional)
2 tbsp parmesan, grated (optional)

Serves 4 (3 per person)

Carefully prepare the oysters, prising them open with a small sharp knife. Then place each oyster in some ice until you are ready to grill them.

Once the charcoal is white hot, use the Tongs to flatten the pile for direct grilling.

Place the small Skillet on the hot coals and leave to heat up for a minute. Add in the butter and slowly melt, so as not to burn.

Add in the chopped garlic, black pepper, salt and a dash of hot sauce. Leave the sauce to sizzle until all the ingredients are mixed in. Remove from the heat.

Using a spoon, drizzle some of the butter sauce onto each oyster until they are close to being full.

Place the oysters directly onto the white-hot coals, shell side down. Leave them to cook for 3 to 4 minutes.

Carefully remove the oysters from the coals with the heatproof Gloves and leave to cool for 2 minutes.

Garnish with parmesan and serve.

Equipment:
Tongs, Set of 3 Skillets

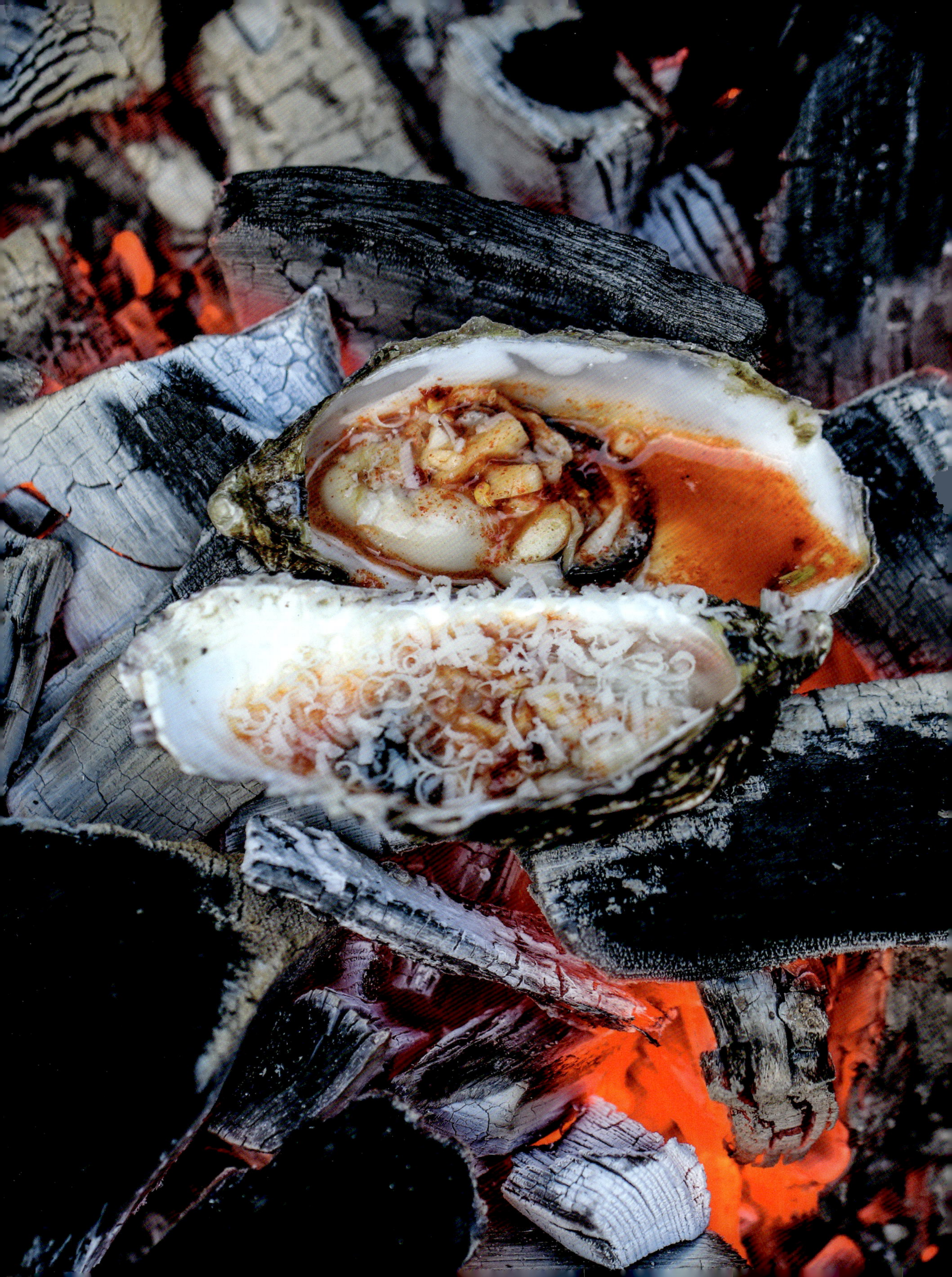

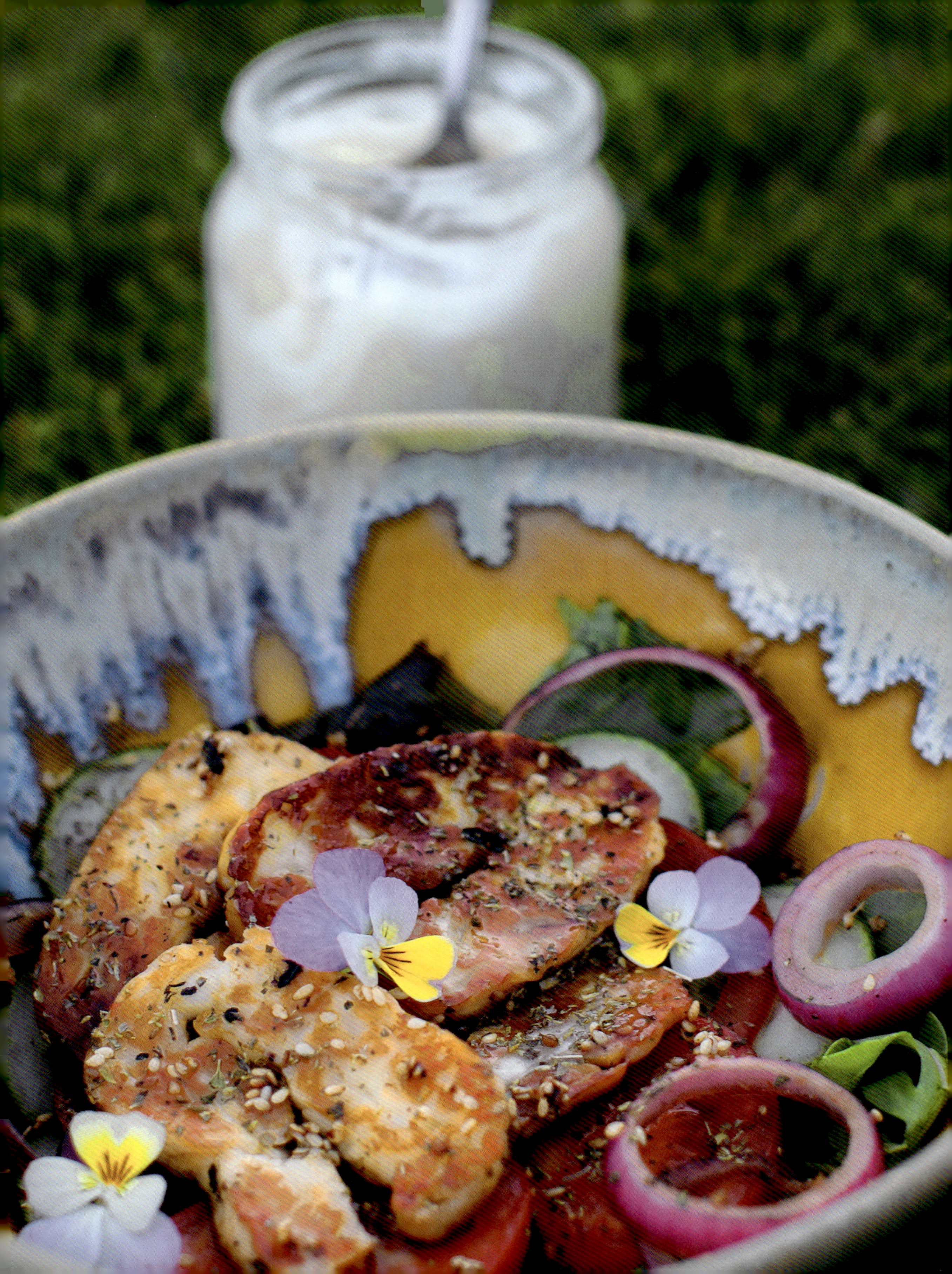

SUMMERTIME HALLOUMI SALAD

Indulge yourself in Mediterranean cuisine with this grilled halloumi salad, ideal for those summer days in the sun. Season this classic squeaky barbecue cheese with lemon, honey and oregano for a sweet and fresh salad topping.

Prep time: 5 minutes
Cooking time: 10 minutes
Recommended Heat: Medium

2 tbsp lemon juice

2 tsp honey

1 tbsp dried oregano

4 tbsp olive oil

100g salad leaves

2 cucumbers, sliced lengthways

4 tomatoes, sliced

½ red onion, finely sliced

160g kalamata or black olives

250g halloumi, cut into approx. 8 slices

Sprinkling of sesame seeds

Salt and freshly ground black pepper to taste

Serves 3

Whisk the lemon juice, honey, oregano and 2 tbsp of the oil together in a small bowl. Season to taste and leave aside for the dressing.

In the base of a large serving bowl add the salad leaves, followed by a layer of sliced cucumber, tomato and onion. Scatter the olives over the top.

Heat the remaining oil in a medium Skillet. Add the halloumi slices and cook until the water has evaporated and there is a brown charring on the outside.

Remove the halloumi from the Skillet and lay across the salad. Grab the dressing and drizzle all over.

Finish with a sprinkling of sesame seeds.

Equipment:
Set of 3 Skillets

BLACKENED BEETROOT & WHIPPED FETA SALAD *with a* SPICED OIL

Dirty-cooked beetroots are unbelievably delicious, brimming with a rustic and earthy flavour. Buried into the hot coals, each beet will have a crispy skin and soft centre. This makes for a well-balanced salad topped with whipped feta lemon and edible flowers.

Prep time: 10 minutes
Cooking time: 45-60 minutes
Recommended Heat: Low

For the salad:

6 medium beetroots, washed and leaves removed

200g feta cheese

2 tbsp Greek yoghurt

1 tbsp lemon juice

3 large handfuls baby salad leaves

Handful of seasonal edible flowers (optional)

Salt and freshly ground black pepper to taste

For the spiced oil:

100ml olive oil

½ tsp chilli flakes

1 tsp cumin seeds

1 tsp nigella seeds

1 tsp fennel seeds, lightly crushed

Serves 4

Nestle the beetroots down into the hot embers of the Kadai with a heat-proof Glove. Leave them to cook for 45 minutes to 1 hour, depending on their size. Turn regularly to ensure an even cook. Test if the beets are ready by piercing them with a skewer to see if they are soft. Remove them from the embers to a board and leave to cool.

Meanwhile, pour the olive oil into a small Skillet and leave it to warm on the Grill. Add the spices and leave to cook for 1 minute. Remove the Skillet from the heat and set to one side.

Crumble the feta into a blender, add the yoghurt and blend until smooth. Season to taste with the lemon juice, salt and pepper.

Once the beetroots are cool to touch, peel away and discard the charred skin and cut into wedges.

To serve, spread the whipped feta over a plate, add the beetroot wedges along with any juices and then scatter over the baby salad leaves and seasonal edible flowers.

Drizzle with spiced oil just before eating.

Equipment:
Set of 3 Skillets

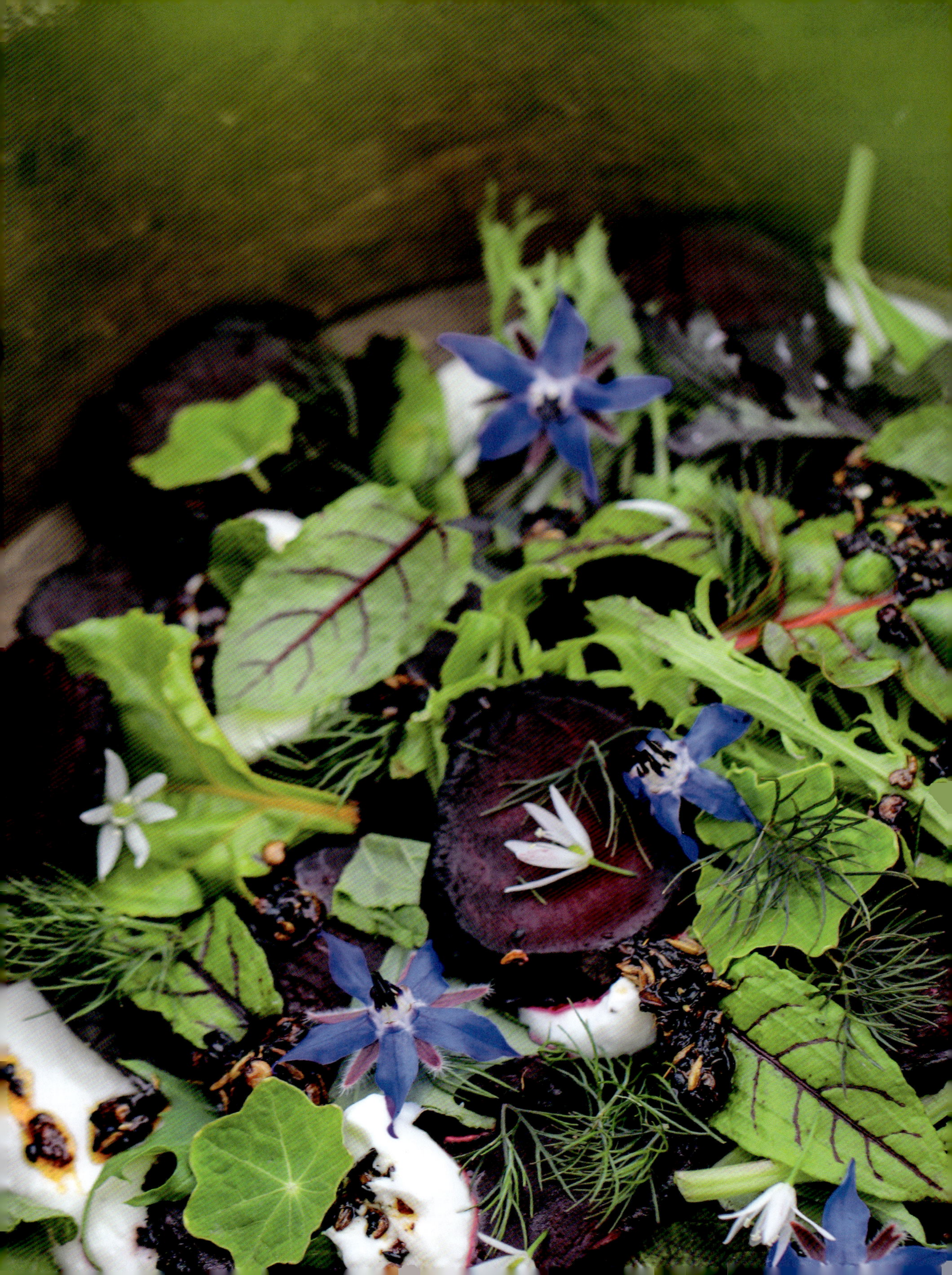

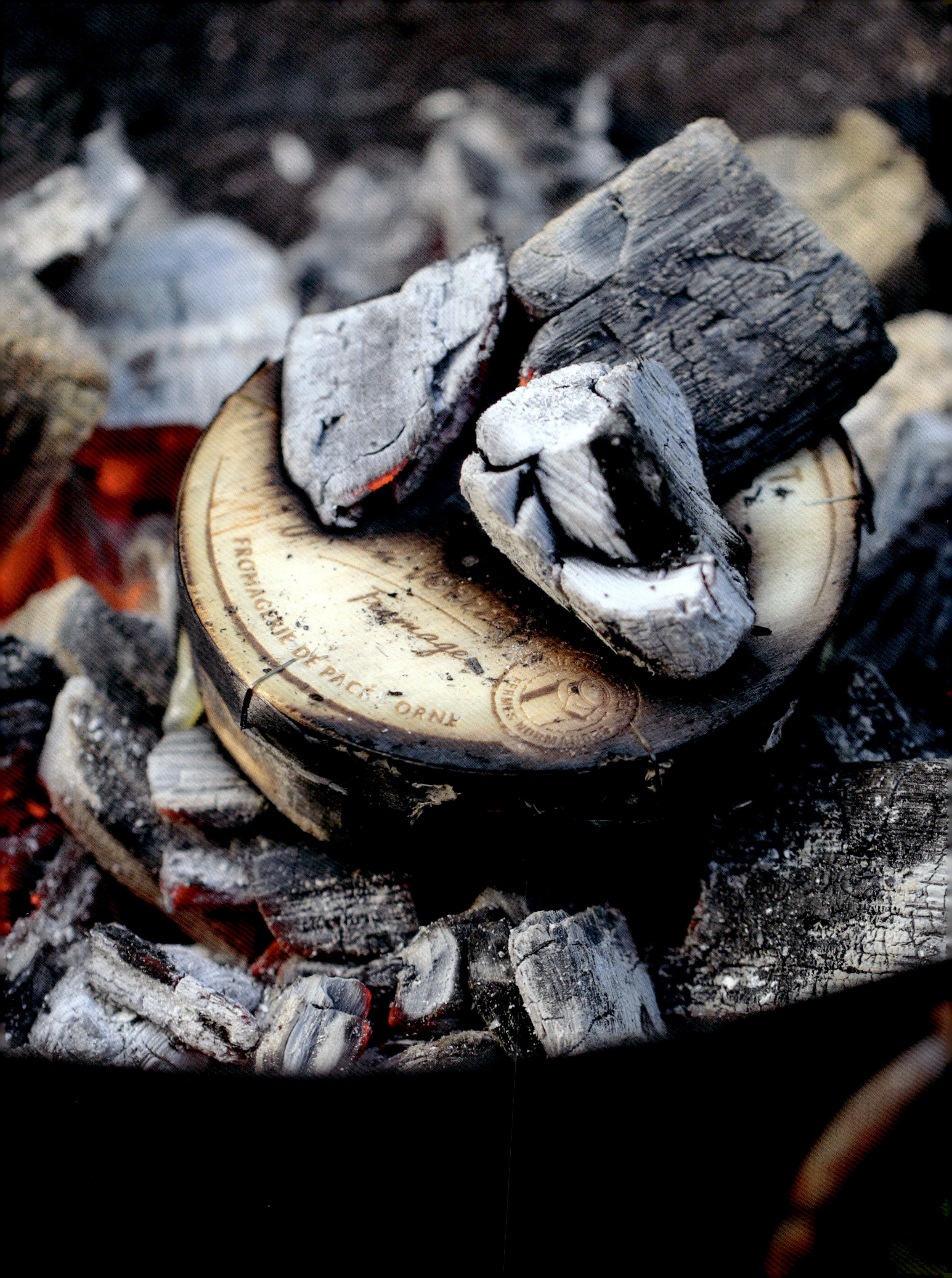
FROMAGERIE DE PACÉ ORNE
Fromage
FERMES NORMANDES

EMBER-BAKED CAMEMBERT

Small in size, big in flavour - harness the rich aroma of smoking charcoal by placing a box of camembert straight into the fire and baking to perfection. Prepare crusty bread on the side to sink into the gooey cheese.

Prep time: 5 minutes
Cooking time: 5 minutes
Recommended Heat: Low

1 wooden-boxed camembert

For serving:
1 loaf sourdough bread or 1 French baguette
2 carrots, sliced into sticks
8 cornichons
2 portions of new potatoes, boiled

Serves 2

Having removed the paper from the cheese, replace the cheese back into the wooden box.

Using the Tongs place the box onto the embers and rest a couple of pieces of lit charcoal on the lid.

Leave to cook for approximately 5 minutes until the cheese has become liquid inside its rind. Keep an eye out that the box doesn't over-char or catch fire.

Carefully lift the box out of the fire onto a heat-proof serving plate with the Tongs. Leave the box for a few minutes to cool.

Take the lid off the box and serve the cheese with bread, carrots, cornichons and potatoes for dipping.

Equipment:

Tongs

LEBANESE BABA GANOUSH
with PITTA BREAD

This deeply smoky baba ghanoush is adapted from Lebanese cuisine. Slowly smoulder the aubergine in the Tripod Roaster above open flames to uncover a soft and flavoursome filling. Smoothed into a creamy and hearty dip with spices, garlic, lemon and tahini, it is a must-have on every sharing platter.

Prep time: 5 minutes
Cooking time: 45 minutes
Recommended Heat: Medium

2 large aubergines
1 tbsp ground cumin
1 tbsp smoked paprika
1 large garlic clove, finely chopped
Handful of fresh parsley, chopped
1 lemon, juiced and zested
1 tbsp rapeseed oil
2 tbsp tahini
2 pitta breads

Serves 2 (as a dip)

Place the aubergines whole into the Tripod Roaster and suspend on the Cooking Tripod (see pg. 34) over a medium heat for approximately 30 minutes.

Slice the aubergines in half lengthways and place, cut side down, directly onto the Grill and cook until they are totally charred and soft in the middle.

Remove from the Grill and scoop out the soft aubergine flesh. Using a fork, mix the aubergines well to create a smooth paste.

In a bowl, mix the cumin, paprika, garlic, parsley, lemon zest and juice. Then add the oil and tahini, mixing thoroughly.

Scrape the aubergine paste into the seasoning mixture and combine well with a fork.

Toast the pitta breads on the Grill for a minute or so until nicely coloured on both sides. Then serve alongside the baba ganoush.

Equipment:
Cooking Tripod, Tripod Roaster

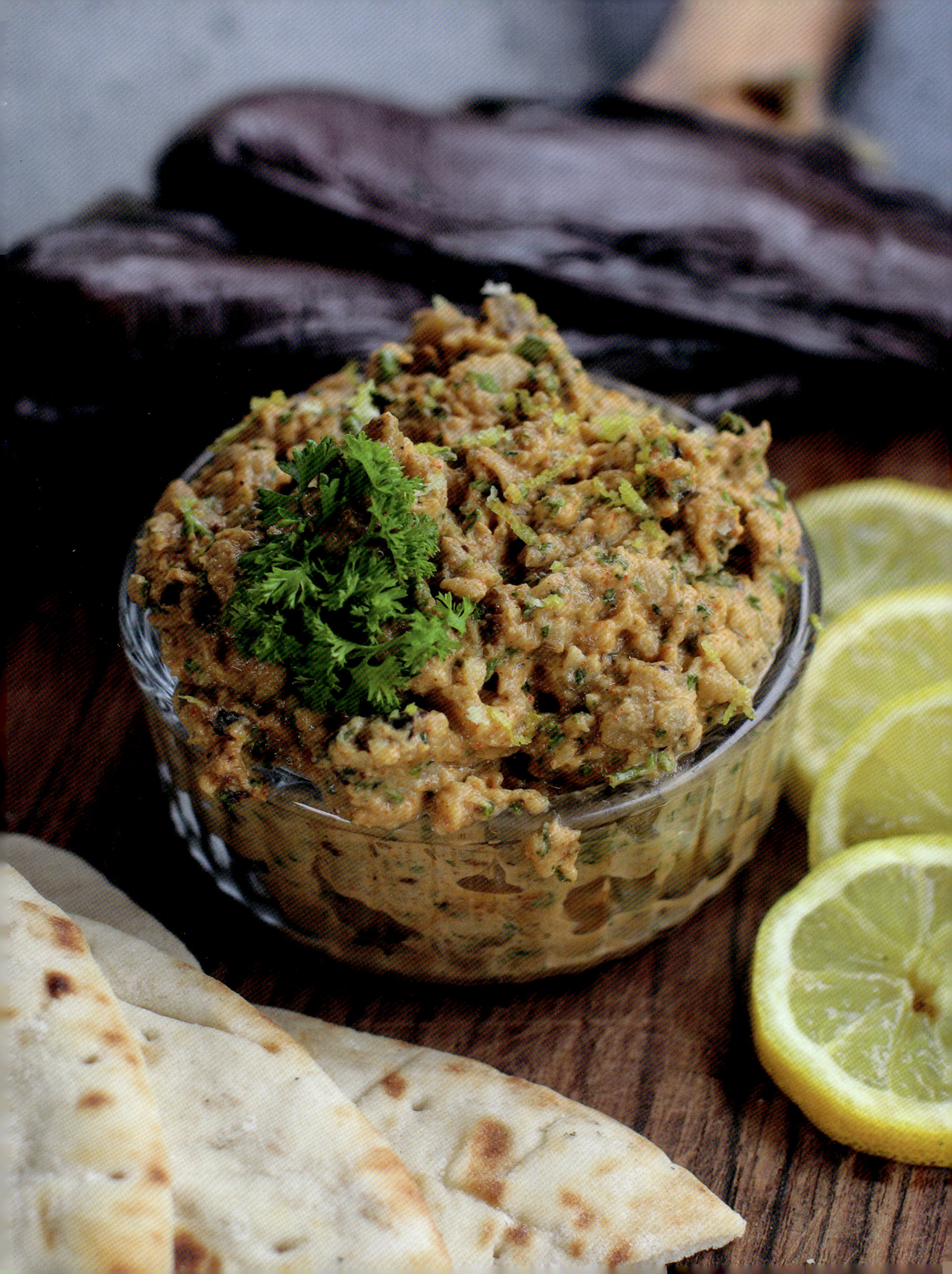

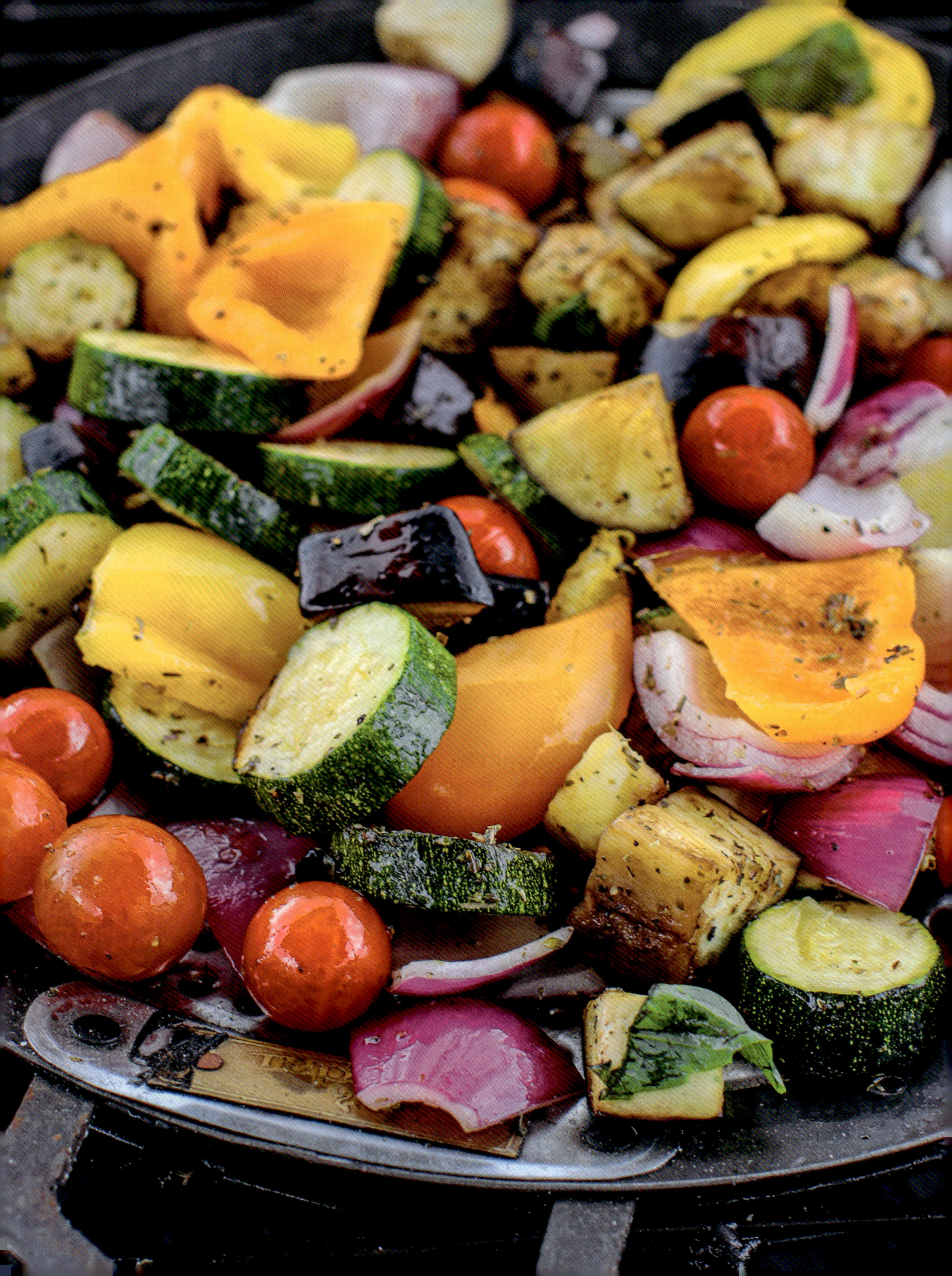

CHARRED VEGETABLES *with* HONEY GLAZE

Coating each vegetable in a honey glaze and charring them over on open fire with the Zhara Roasting Pan, creates a beautiful layer of caramelisation. Bursting with depth and colour, these vibrant vegetables will bring some fabulous flavours to your outdoor dining table.

Prep time: 10 minutes
Cooking time: 15 minutes
Recommended Heat: Medium/High

For the glaze:

2 cloves garlic, finely chopped
100ml honey
2 tbsp wholegrain mustard
1 lemon, zested and juiced
50g light brown sugar

For the vegetables:

2 large courgettes, cut into small, chunky pieces
2 peppers, deseeded and cut into small chunky pieces
2 aubergines, cut into small chunky pieces
2 red onions, cut into wedges
1 tbsp olive oil
Salt and freshly ground black pepper to taste

Serves 4

Combine the glaze ingredients in a small bowl, mixing thoroughly.

Place the courgettes, peppers, aubergines and red onions in a bowl. Pour over the glaze and coat evenly.

Brush the Zhara Roasting Pan with the oil and place on the Grill or directly on the hot coals to heat up.

Once the Zhara Roasting Pan is warm, add the vegetables. Leave to cook for 20 minutes, turning them occasionally until browned.

Once cooked, the vegetables can be kept warm on the side of the Grill until ready to serve.

Equipment:
Zhara Roasting Pan

ROASTED PEPPERS
stuffed with ITALIAN PESTO

A delicious duo, these pesto peppers are a healthy light bite that work beautifully with the Kadai Grill Trays. Lock in that smoky flavour with our perforated trays, for sweet and succulent peppers, brimming with fresh pesto.

Prep time: 10 minutes
Cooking time: 25 minutes
Recommended Heat: High

4 red peppers
1 quantity fresh pesto (see pg. 55)
150g cherry tomatoes
2 garlic cloves, finely chopped
Drizzle of olive oil
Salt and freshly ground black pepper to taste

Serves 4

Cut the peppers in half lengthways without removing the stem. This will keep the peppers intact with a closed shape for the filling.

Remove the seeds from each half and then place them, skin-side down on a Grill Tray.

Fill each pepper halfway with 1 large tbsp of pesto, 3 to 4 cherry tomatoes and a few slices of garlic.

Season the peppers well with salt, pepper and a generous drizzle of oil.

Place the Grill Tray into the Wood Fired Oven (see pg. 37) and cook for approximately 20 to 25 minutes.

About 5 minutes before the end, ensure the Wood Fired Oven flames are coming up the vent at the back and over the top of the peppers, to char the skins.

Equipment:
Set of 3 Grill Trays, Wood Fired Oven

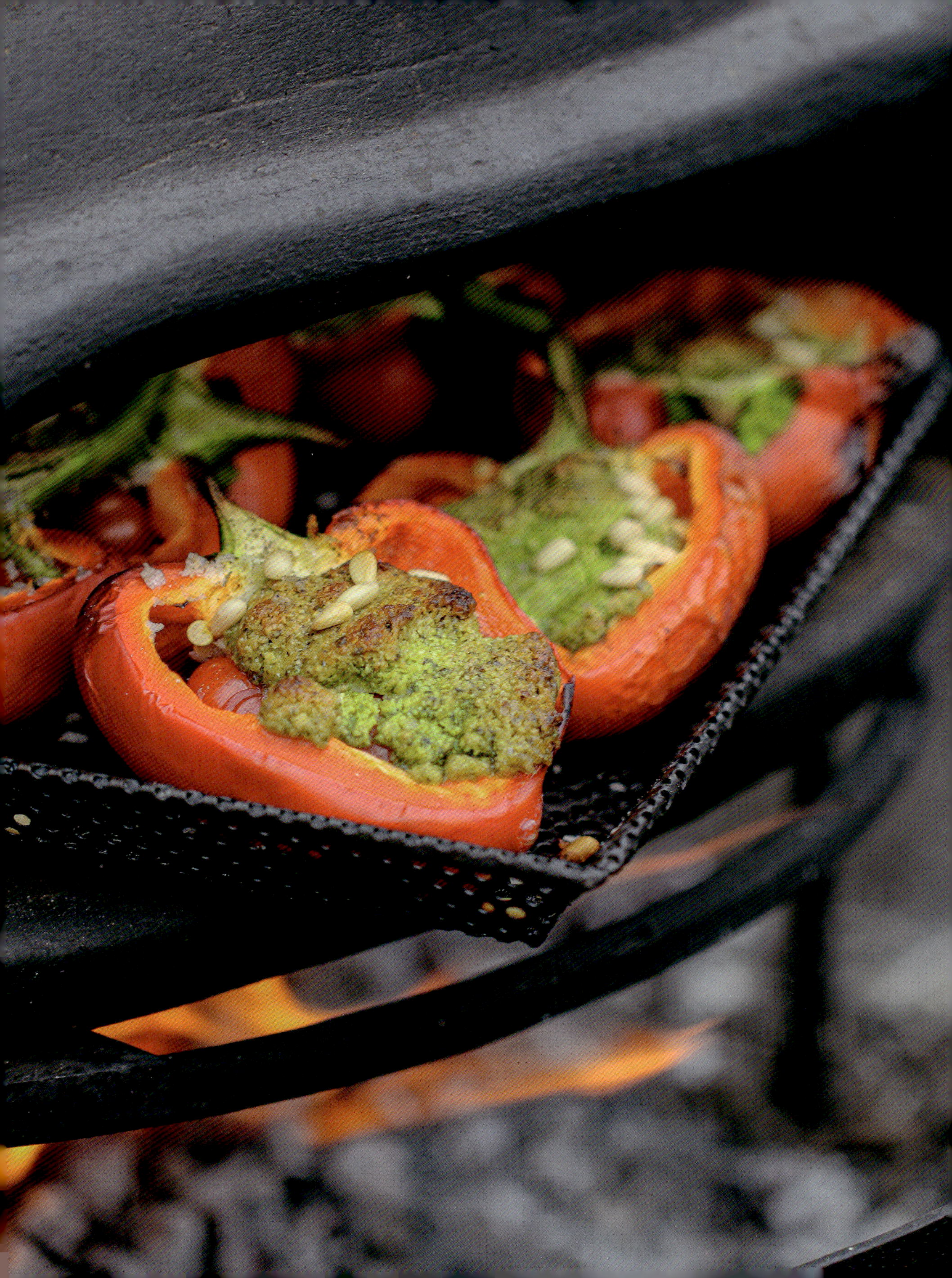

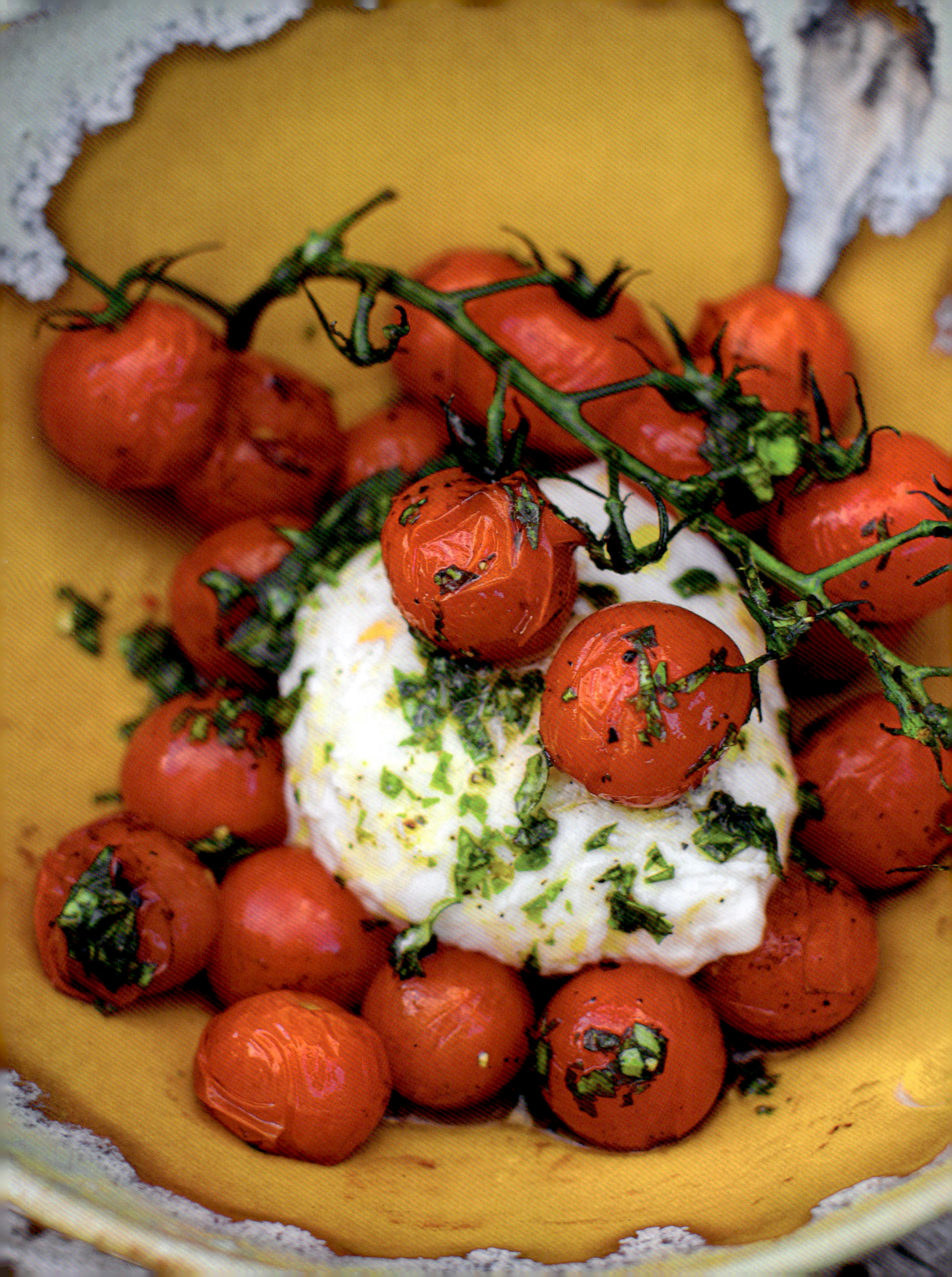

GRILLED TOMATOES
with a BASIL OIL DRIZZLE

Tomato, mozzarella and basil have always worked a treat together and this recipe is no exception. Bring the taste of Italy to your Kadai with this elegant appetiser. Juicy and sweet grilled tomatoes complement the smooth mozzarella and aromatic basil, best served with crunchy croutons or focaccia.

Prep time: 5 minutes
Cooking time: 8 minutes
Recommended Heat: Medium

For the basil oil:
Large handful of fresh basil leaves
125ml extra virgin olive oil, plus extra for drizzling

For the salad:
3-4 vines of cherry tomatoes
150g mozzarella, sliced
Sea salt and freshly ground black pepper to taste

Serves 2

To make the basil oil, either combine the leaves and oil together in a mini food processor or chop the leaves and simply mix them into the oil. Set aside in the fridge. Drizzle the tomatoes with a little oil and season with a pinch of salt and some pepper.

Place the tomatoes in a Grill Tray and cook gently for 5 to 8 minutes until charred and softened.

Arrange the tomatoes on a serving plate or in a salad bowl with the mozzarella cheese.

Drizzle the dish with generous spoonfuls of the basil oil, sprinkle with some sea salt to serve.

Equipment:
Set of 3 Grill Trays

TIP: Perfect with lightly toasted focaccia and a drizzle of balsamic vinegar.

CREAMY MUSHROOMS *on* TOASTED CIABATTA

The winning combination of mushrooms, white wine and a creamy garlic sauce is even better when cooked on a Kadai. Rustle up this leisurely light lunch with just a few familiar ingredients and serve with warm toasted bread.

Prep time: 5 minutes
Cooking time: 20 minutes
Recommended Heat: Medium/High

50g salted butter
1 white onion, finely chopped
500g mushrooms of choice (chestnut, portobello or oyster), sliced
250ml white wine
2 150g rounds of garlic Boursin
50ml double cream
4 slices of ciabatta
Salt and freshly ground black pepper to taste

Serves 4

Attach the Cooking Tripod and Cooking Bowl to the Kadai (see pg. 34).

Add the butter to the Cooking Bowl and melt. Then add the onions and sauté for 10 minutes until soft.

Add in the mushrooms and white wine, allowing the alcohol to cook out of the wine for 5 minutes.

Mix in the Boursin, allowing the rounds to melt into a sauce.

Pour in the double cream and simmer for 5 minutes until the sauce thickens.

Toast the ciabatta on the Grill a few minutes before the mushrooms are ready.

Plate up the ciabatta and pour the creamy mushrooms over the top. Season well with salt and black pepper.

Equipment:
Cooking Tripod, Cooking Bowl

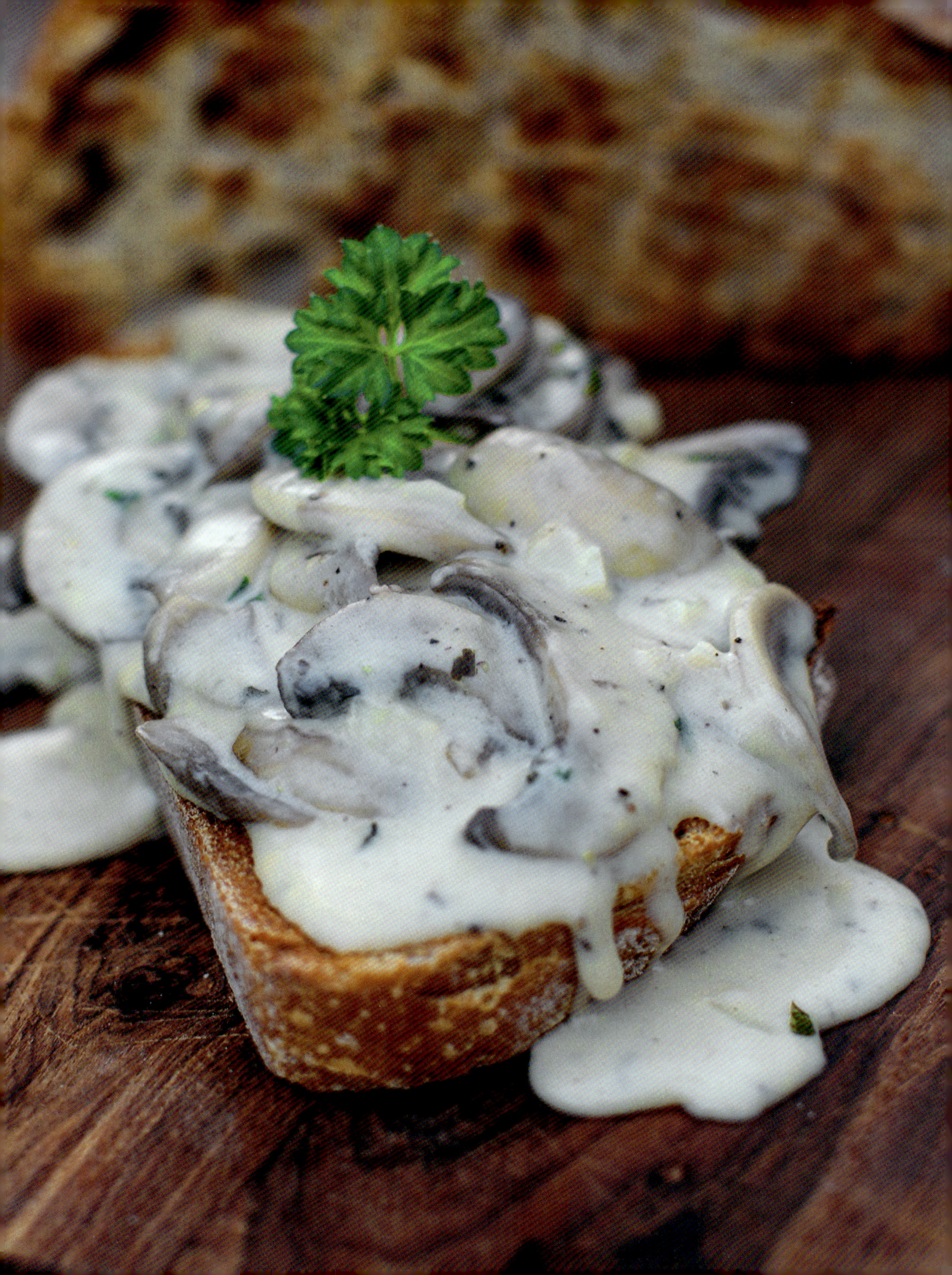

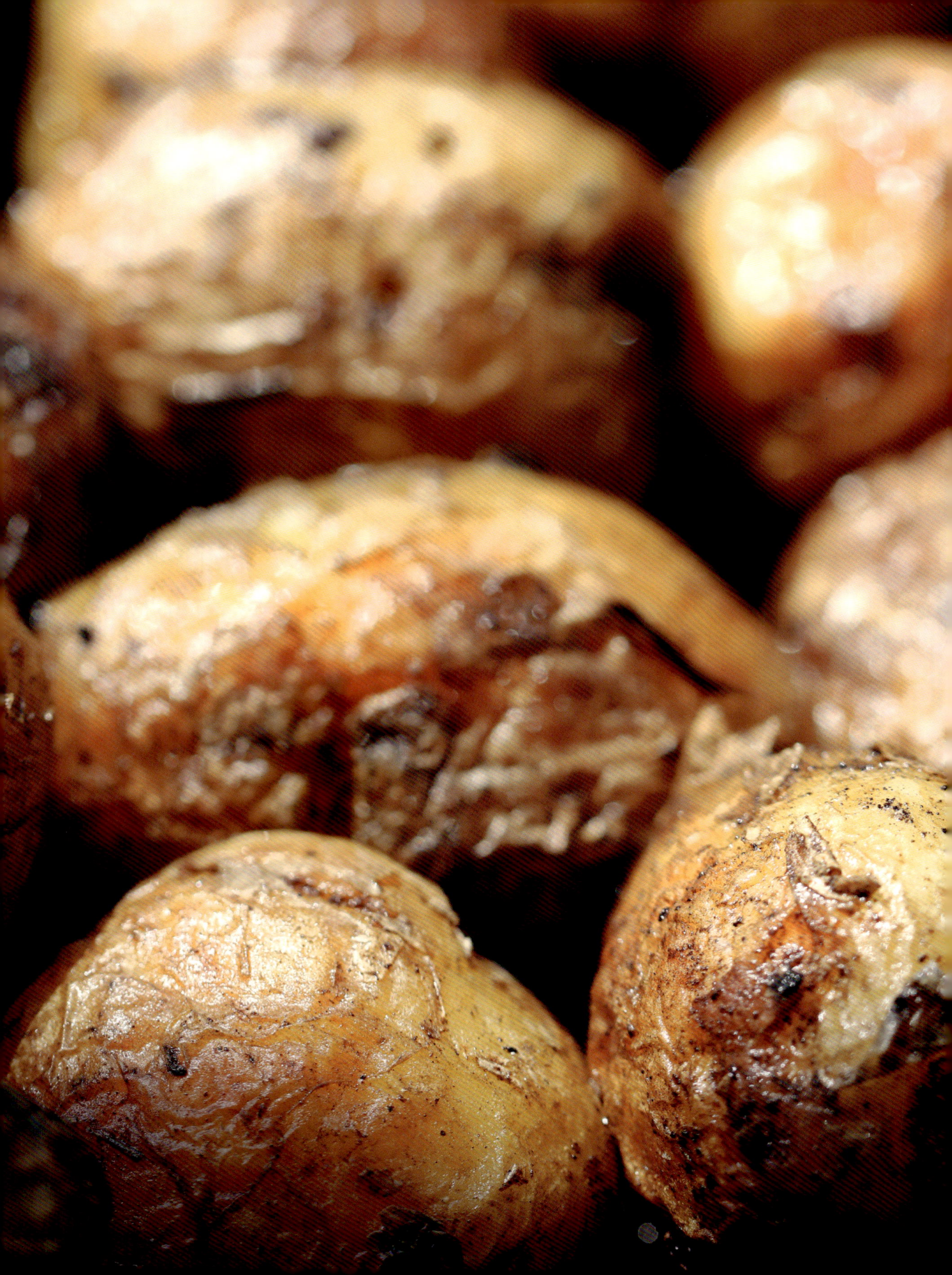

ROAST POTATOES

A real English classic, these wholesome roast potatoes are crisped to perfection with the Zhara Roasting Pan. They make a delicious accompaniment to any main dish or as a small sharing plate.

Prep time: 5 minutes
Cooking time: 35 minutes
Recommended Heat: High

1kg baby new potatoes, halved
Drizzle of olive oil or goose fat
1 whole head of garlic, left unpeeled
Salt and freshly ground black pepper to taste

Serves 4

Place a saucepan (suitable for the Kadai) of lightly salted water on the Grill and bring it to the boil. Add the potatoes to the boiling water, and par boil for approximately 8 minutes. Remove the pan from the heat and leave the potatoes in the water for 3 more minutes before draining.

Heat up the Zhara Roasting Pan on the Grill with the Cookware Lid on. Add the oil or goose fat to the pan of potatoes and leave to warm through before adding to the Zhara Roasting Pan. Season the potatoes with salt and pepper, re-cover with the Cookware Lid. Using heat-proof Gloves, hold the pan and lid firmly and shake the potatoes to break them up a little bit.

Add the garlic bulb to the pan. This will become gooey once cooked and is delicious squeezed out over the potatoes.

Add some extra charcoal to the fire and after a few minutes, push the embers to the outside of the firebowl, leaving a 20cm circular gap in the centre. Move the Zhara Roasting Pan above the gap and leave the potatoes to cook for approximately 20 minutes. Top up with charcoal every 5 minutes or so if necessary.

Once the potatoes are soft in the middle, build up the hot charcoal in the centre of the firebowl below the Zhara Roasting Pan. Cook the potatoes (shaking the Zhara Roasting Pan frequently) at this higher temperature until they are crispy on the outside. Season with salt and serve with the roasted garlic purée.

Equipment:

Zhara Roasting Pan, Cookware Lid

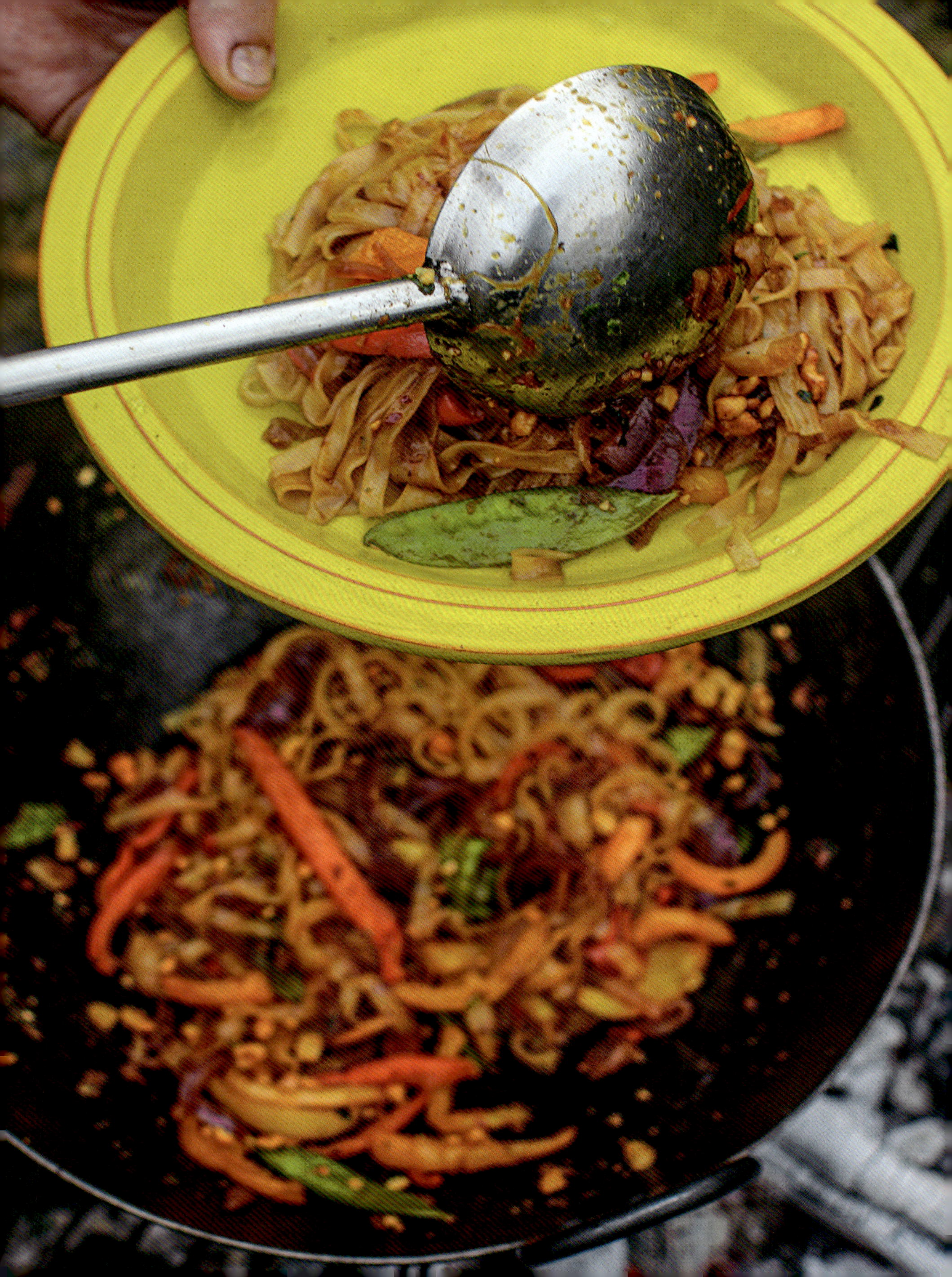

Simple & quick

Be inspired by these mouth-watering, simple and quick recipes, which are sure to spice up your mid-week meals or last-minute barbecues. Enjoy these clever concoctions that are big on flavour but little in time, prepared in under 30 minutes. Experiment with your cooking style and bring together delicious new dishes without any stress.

CAVEMAN TOMAHAWK

Tomahawk steaks are a thick cut of Ribeye still on the bone, ideal for dirty cooking on the hot embers of a fire. For succulent steaks that have a tender centre, skip the cooking accessories and just use natural naked flames.

Prep time: 10 minutes
Cooking time: 10 minutes
Recommended Heat: Medium

2 tbsp salted butter
1 garlic clove, finely chopped
2 tsp fresh parsley, chopped
1 Tomahawk steak (approx. 900g), cut about 4-5cm thick
Salt and freshly ground black pepper to taste

Serves 2

Put the butter in a small bowl with the garlic, parsley and a pinch of salt and pepper. Mash with a fork until well blended then set aside.

Season both sides of the steak generously with salt and pepper.

Using the Tongs, place the steak directly on the hot coals and cook for about 3 to 4 minutes on each side for medium-rare. Holding the bone, slowly roll the steak a few times to sear the edges.

Spoon the butter mix onto the top of the steak and leave to melt for a minute. Carefully remove the meat from the coals with the Tongs to a serving board or plate.

Allow to rest for 5 to 10 minutes before serving.

Equipment:

Tongs

TIP: This is delicious with dirty-cooked onions, garlic and tomatoes.

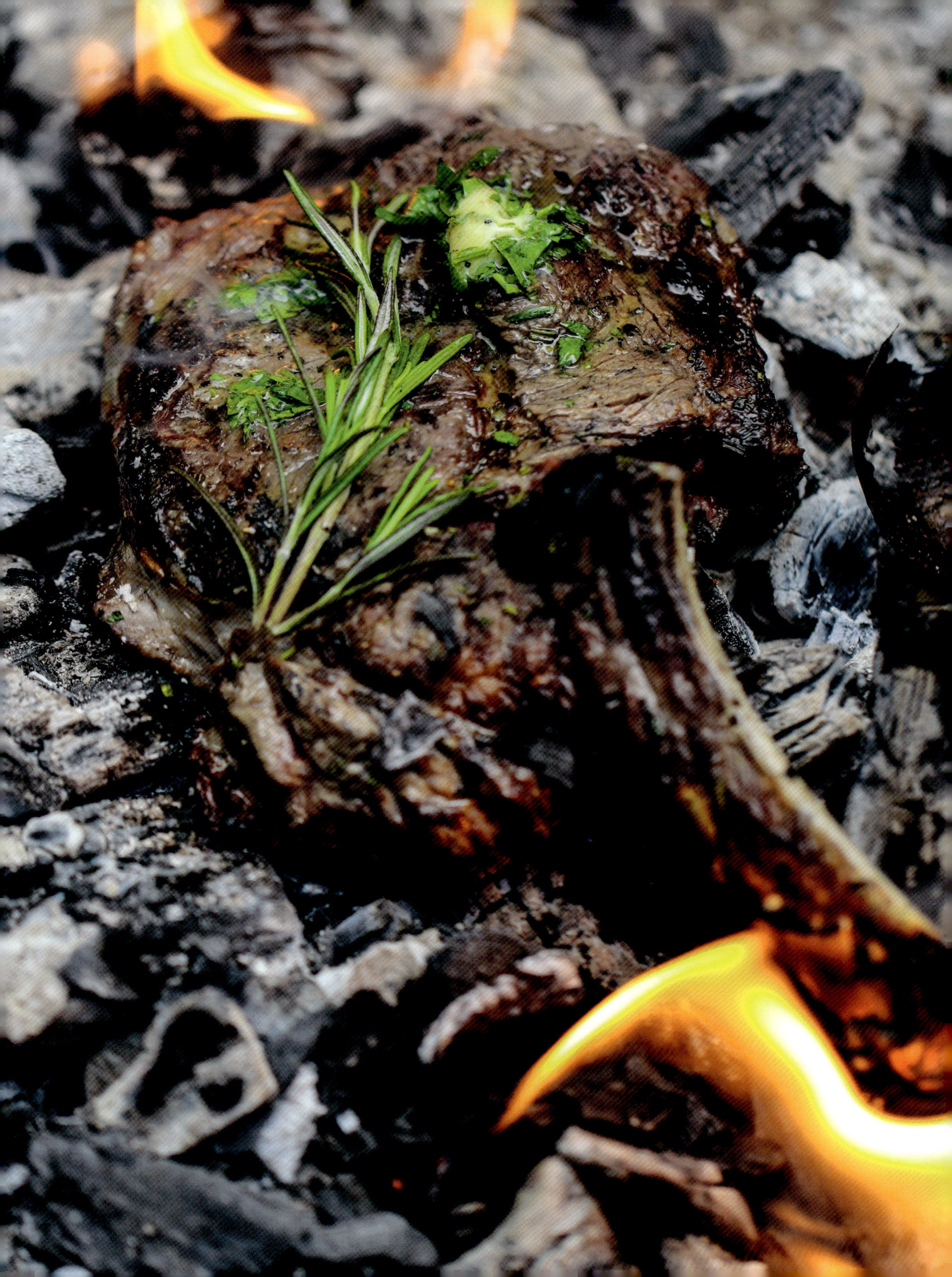

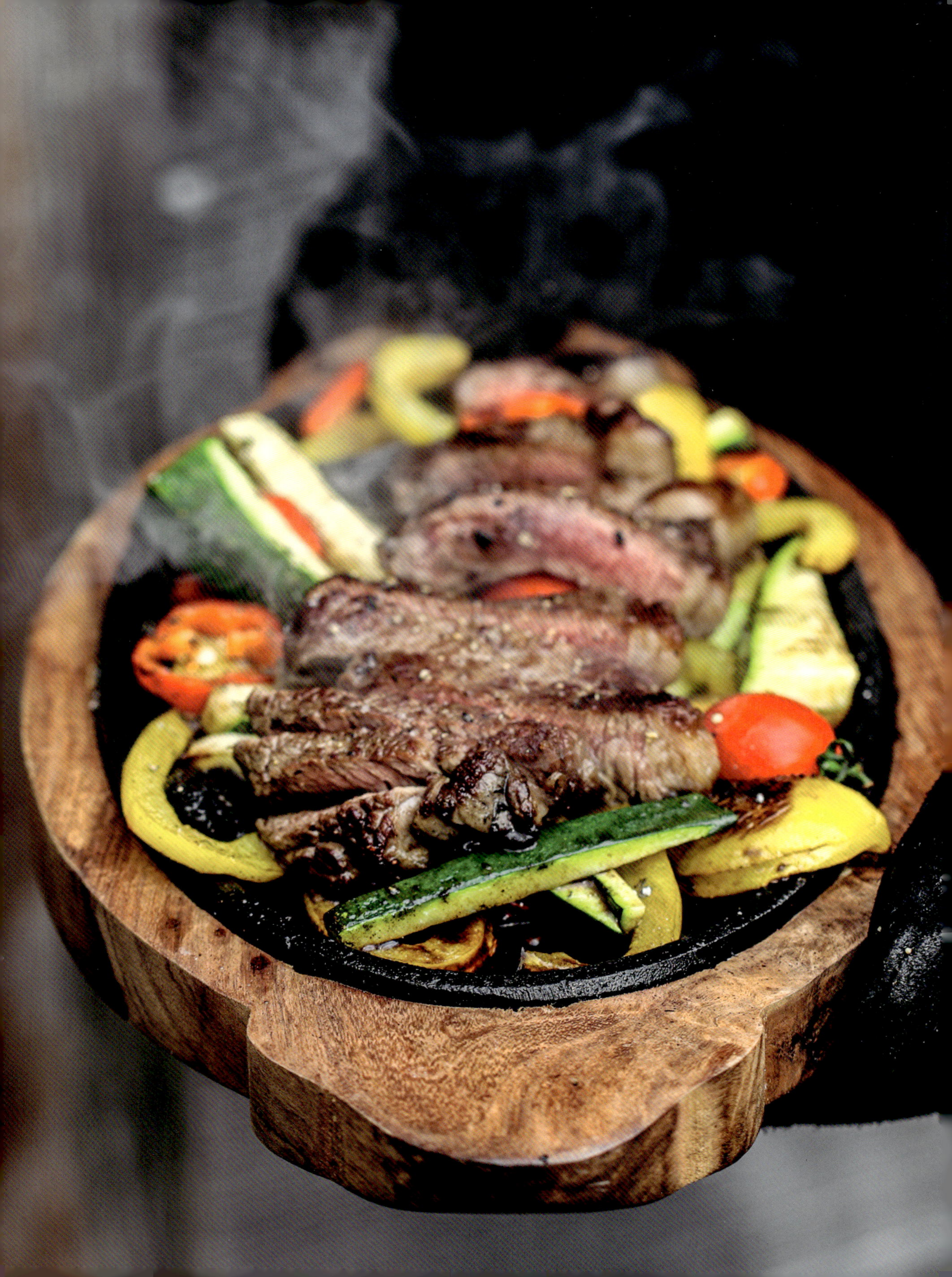

STEAK & VEGETABLE STIR-FRY SIZZLER

Sizzle, sizzle - this recipe is about all things hot and smoky. Sear mouth-watering and juicy steaks every time over burning hot coals with the Sizzling Plate. Impress your guests' sense of sight, smell and taste with this super-quick succulent sizzler recipe, dating back to a Japanese style of cooking.

Prep time: 10 minutes
Cooking time: 10 minutes
Recommended Heat: High

Drizzle of olive oil
2 rump steaks, cut 2-3cm thick
1 yellow pepper, halved, deseeded and sliced lengthways
1 red pepper, halved, deseeded and sliced lengthways
1 courgette, sliced lengthways
150g cherry tomatoes, halved
Salt and freshly ground black pepper to taste

Serves 2

Carefully using the Tongs, flatten out the hot charcoal in the Kadai.

Place the cast-iron part of the Sizzling Plate directly onto the charcoal embers using the heat-proof Gloves.

Once the Plate is hot, drizzle the oil and place the steaks in the middle of the dish. Cook the steaks to your preference. Lift them onto a Chopping Board and leave to rest for a few minutes.

Add the peppers, courgette and tomatoes to the hot Sizzling Plate. Cook for approximately 5 minutes, turning occasionally.

Season the steaks with salt and pepper and cut them across into slices.

Place the steak slices on top of the sizzling vegetables and, using the heat-proof Gloves, move the cast-iron Sizzling Plate onto the wooden serving tray.

Equipment:
Tongs, Sizzling Plate, Chopping Board

SEARED STEAK SALAD
with ROCKET & ITALIAN PESTO

Generously drizzle our fresh homemade pesto over some succulent sirloin steaks and crisp rocket for a simple yet impressive mid-week meal. With just a Kadai firebowl recreate this delicious salad for lunch or dinner.

Prep time: 5 minutes
Cooking time: 10 minutes
Recommended Heat: High

2 sirloin steaks, cut 2-3cm thick
80-100g rocket leaves
½ quantity pesto (see pg. 55)
1 tbsp finely grated parmesan
Drizzle of olive oil
Salt and freshly ground black pepper to taste

Serves 2

Season the steak on both sides and leave to rest at room temperature.

Once the Kadai is ready to cook on, add the steaks directly to the Grill using the Tongs and sear for 2 minutes each side, taking care not to overcook. For medium rare, grill for 4 minutes in total.

Transfer the steaks to a plate or Chopping Board and leave to rest for 5 minutes before slicing.

Add the rocket, sliced steak and generous portion of pesto sauce to each serving plate and scatter with parmesan. Season with a drizzle of olive oil and pinch of salt and pepper.

Equipment:
Tongs, Chopping Board

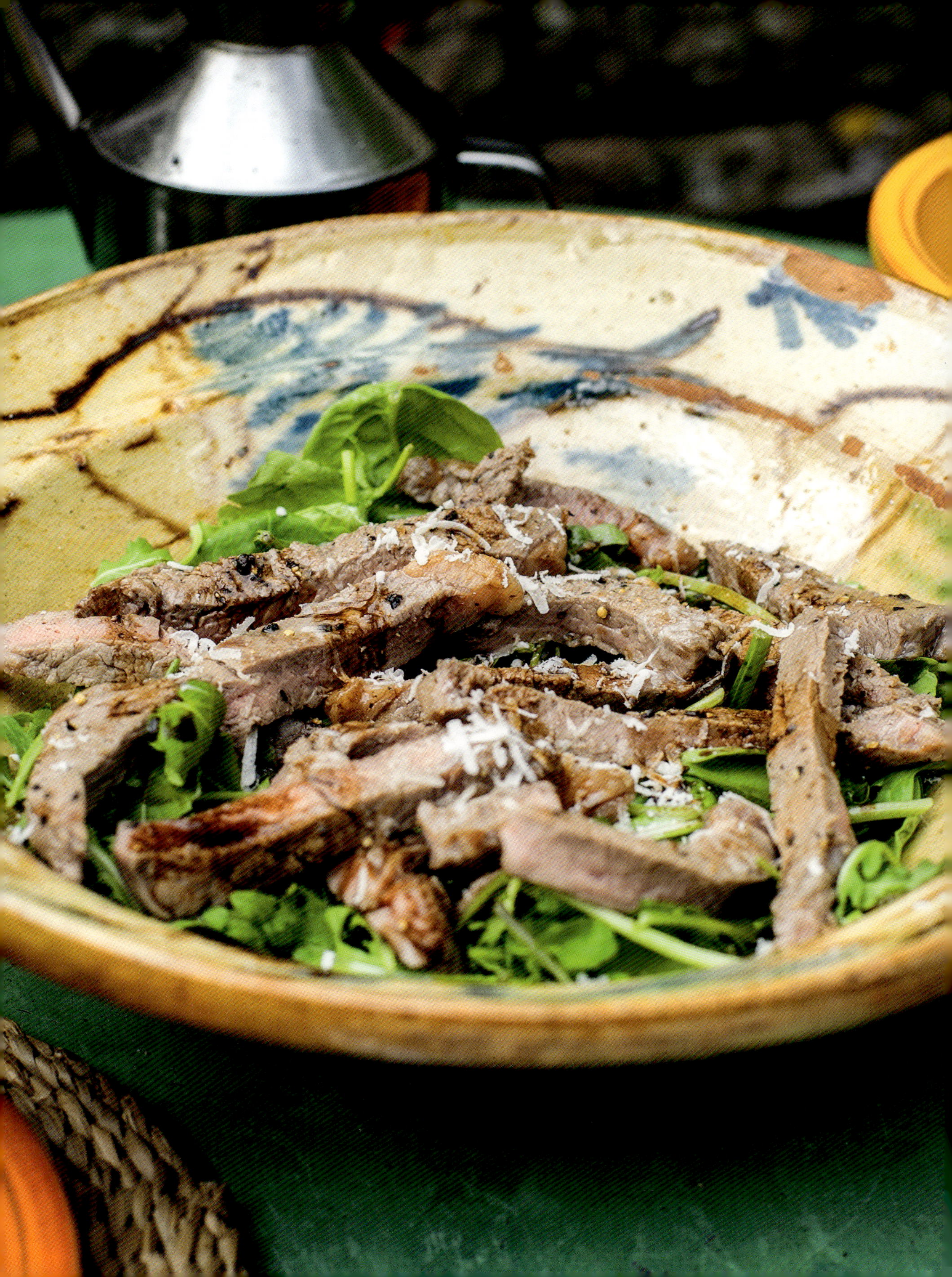

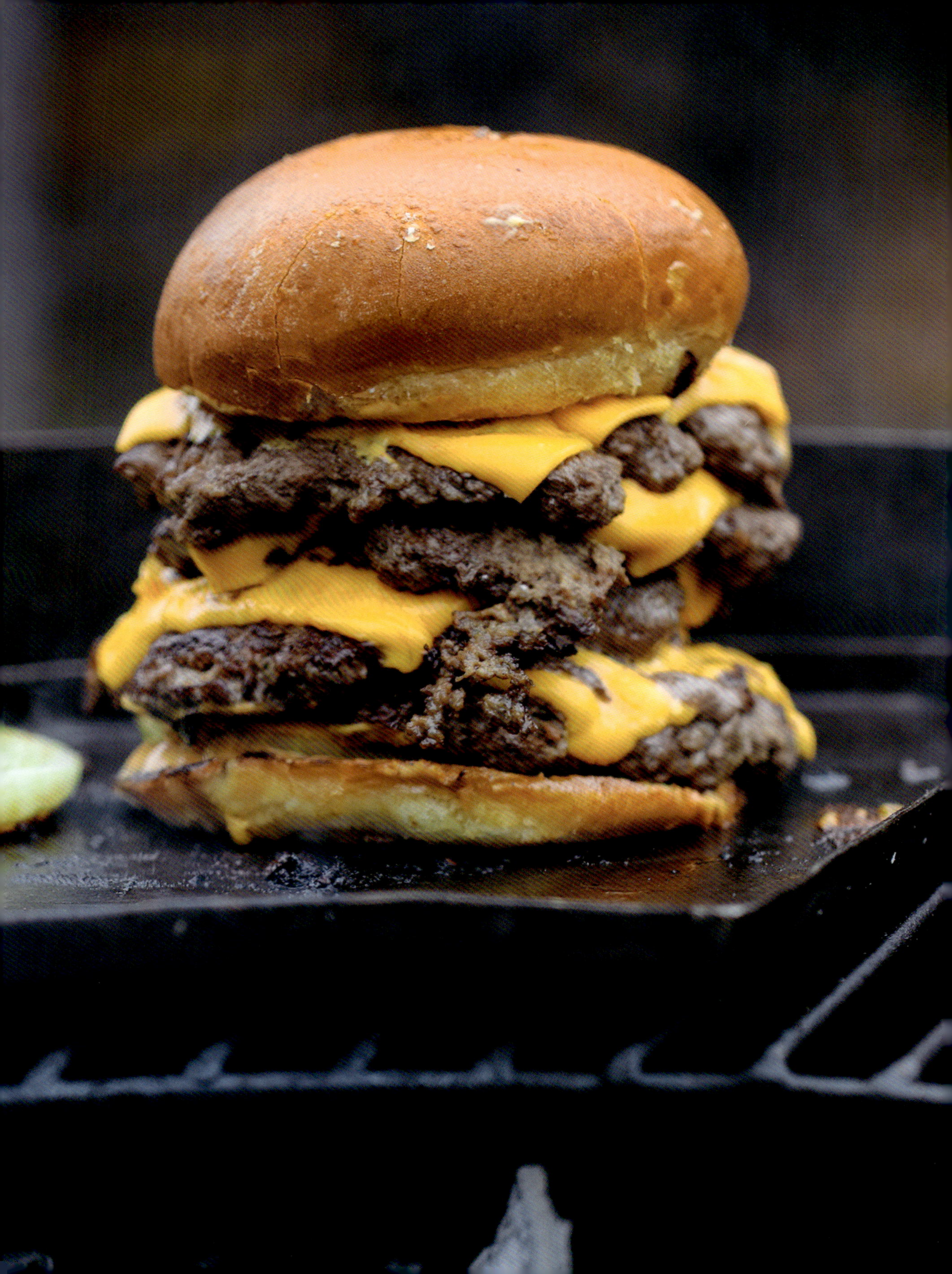

SMASHED PATTY STACK *with* HOMEMADE BURGER SAUCE

Beloved by all, these burgers are decadent and messy. The ultimate showstopper, this recipe stacks good-quality patties, homemade burger sauce, American cheese and crispy onions, all between a soft brioche bun.

Prep time: 10 minutes
Cooking time: 15 minutes
Recommended Heat: Medium/High

For the burger sauce:
1 tbsp tomato sauce
1 tbsp mayonnaise
1 tbsp American mustard
1 tbsp pickled gherkin juice
1 gherkin, finely chopped
Handful of fresh dill, chopped
½ tsp chilli flakes (optional)

For the burger:
350g minced beef or pork (20% fat content)
Drizzle of rapeseed oil
4 slices American-style cheese
1 large white onion, sliced
4 large brioche buns, halved
Sea salt and freshly ground black pepper to taste

Serves 4

Make the burger sauce by mixing all the ingredients together in a medium bowl and set aside.

Place the minced meat into a bowl and combine thoroughly with your hands. Season with salt and pepper. Using your hands, shape the mince mixture into 4 evenly sized balls.

Place the Hot Plate onto the Kadai, ensuring the hot coals are directly under the plate and lightly drizzle with oil.

Place the 'balls' of mince onto the Hot Plate. Let them start to sizzle and begin to turn brown. Now it's time to 'smash' them; using the Barbecue Tool press down on the 'balls' to create a flat burger shape. Leave the burger to char. Once the meat is charring on one side, use the Barbecue Tool to flip the burger over and char the other side. Add the cheese to the top of the burgers and leave to melt.

Add the onion to the Hot Plate and cook until soft. Slice the buns in half and place the bun tops, flat side down, onto the Hot Plate for a minute until they start to toast slightly.

Construct the burger. Put the burger sauce on the bottom bun and then stack the burger, onion and bun on top.

Equipment:
Hot Plate, Barbecue Tool

SALAMI SKEWERS COATED *in* HAWAIIAN PINEAPPLE SAUCE

If you are a fan of pork and pineapple, then you will love these tantalising skewers. Each piece of salami sausage, fruit and vegetable is smothered in a sweet and sticky barbecue sauce that caramelises over the open fire. Easily create this Hawaiian-inspired dish using just the Travel Kadai and Skewers.

Prep time: 10 minutes
Cooking time: 8-10 minutes
Recommended Heat: High

For the sauce:

230ml Kadai's barbecue sauce (see pg. 54)

115ml pineapple juice

1 tbsp garlic paste or crushed garlic

Salt and freshly ground black pepper to taste

For the skewers:

400g salami sausage, chopped into 2cm pieces (we used Shropshire Salumi - Hunter's)

400g fresh pineapple, chopped into 3cm chunks

2 red peppers, halved, deseeded and chopped into 4cm pieces

2 orange peppers, halved, deseeded and chopped into 4cm pieces

2 red onions, chopped into 4cm pieces

2 courgettes, chopped into 4cm pieces

400g chestnut mushrooms, chopped in half

Salt and freshly ground black pepper to taste

Serves 4

Whisk the barbecue sauce, pineapple juice, garlic, salt and pepper thoroughly in a medium bowl. Set half of the sauce to one side in a small bowl for serving.

Thread the salami pieces onto the Skewers alternating with pieces of pineapple, peppers, onion, courgette and mushroom.

Brush the Skewers with barbecue sauce before placing on the Grill to cook for 8 to 10 minutes or until the vegetables are tender and charred. Remember to turn the Skewers occasionally to ensure an even cook.

Place the Skewers on a serving dish and brush lightly with the remaining barbecue sauce.

Equipment:

Set of Skewers, Travel Kadai

TIP: If cooking on a bigger Kadai, we recommend using our set of 8 Skewers and Rack.

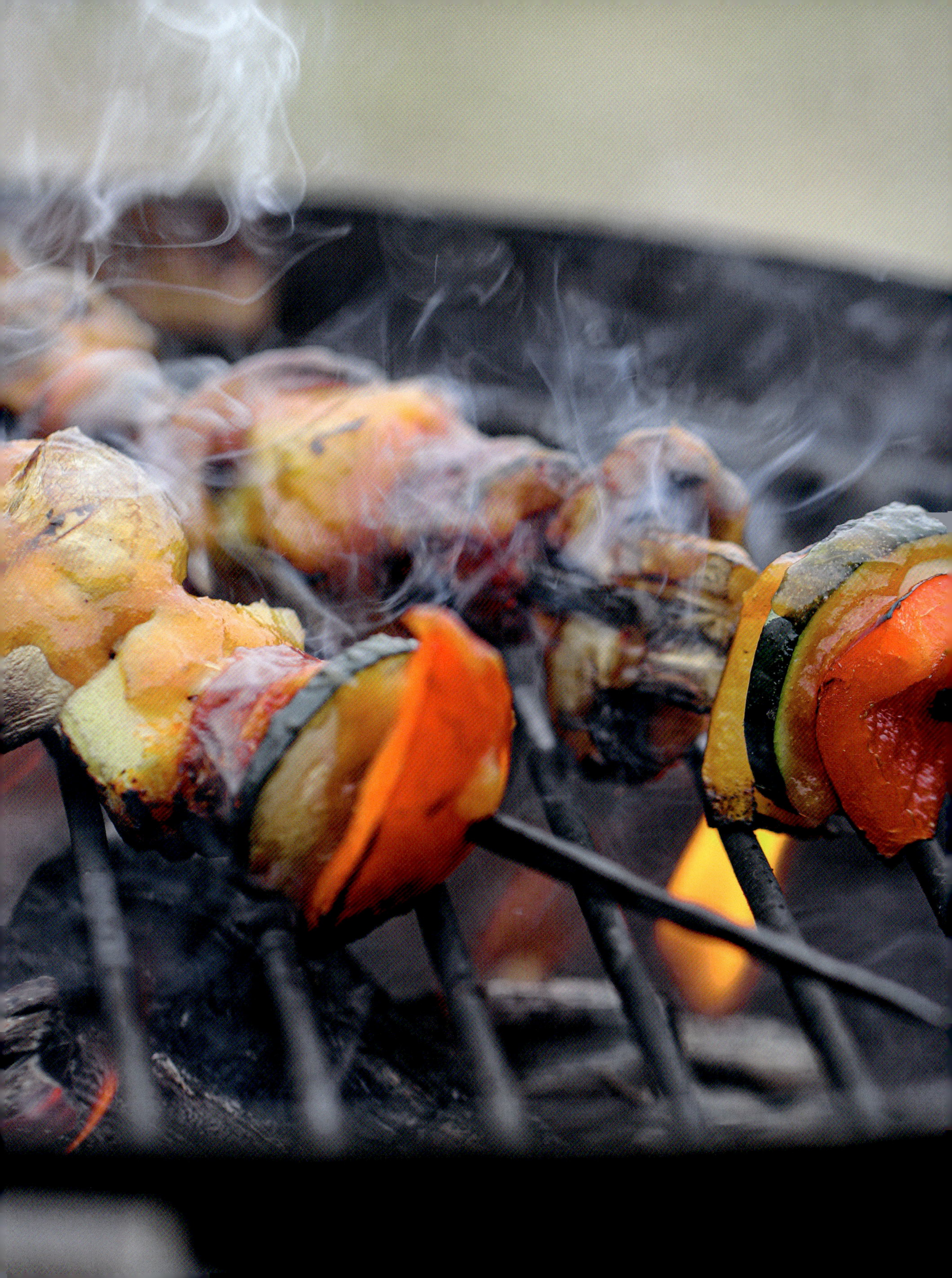

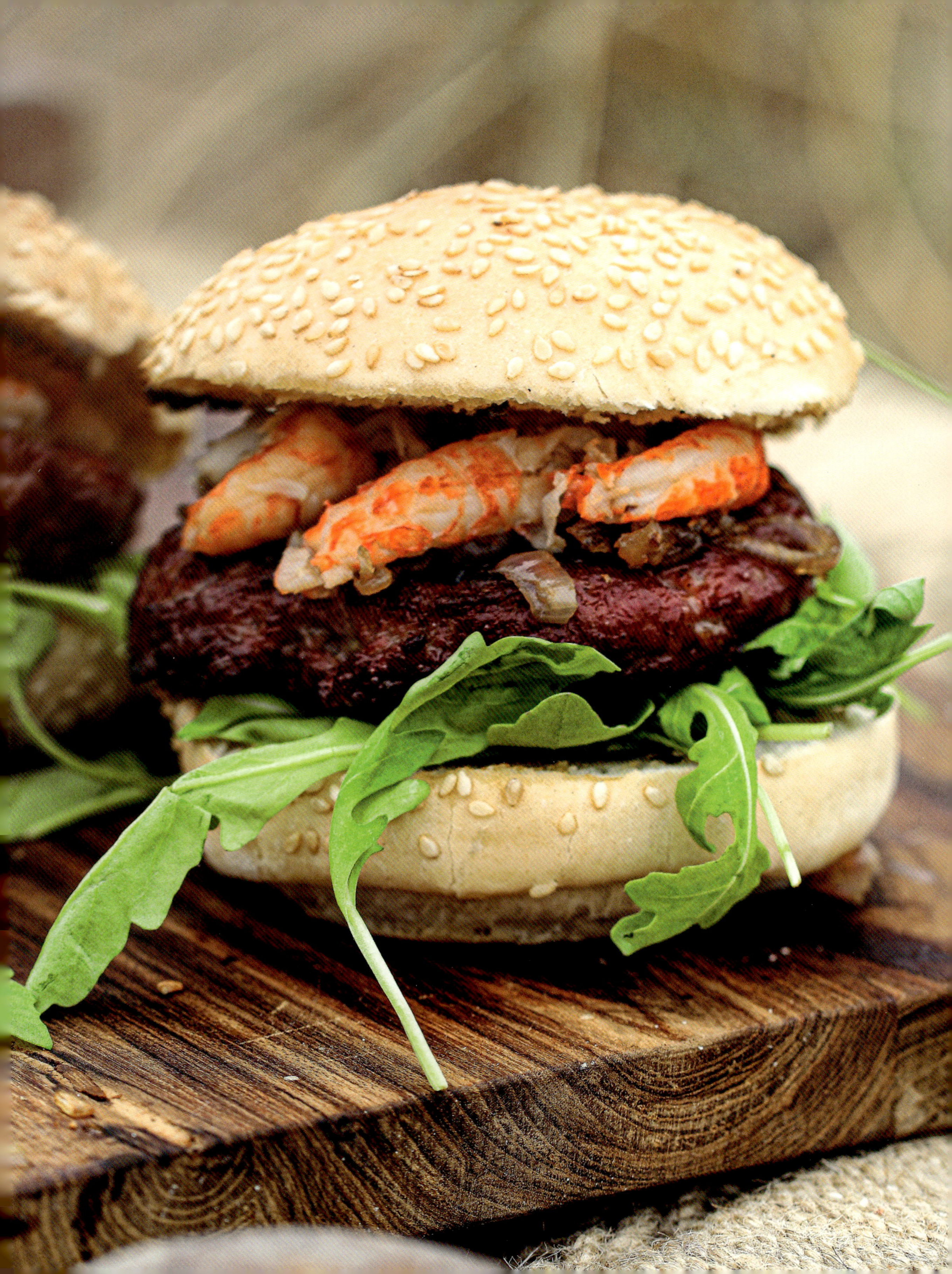

KADAI'S SURF & TURF *with* CRISPY SHALLOTS

Turn your garden into a gourmet restaurant with the exquisite combination of surf and turf. Enjoy fresh crayfish tails with a rich beef patty, bathed in a sweet shallot sauce in this land and sea burger, perfect after a long day at the beach.

Prep time: 5 minutes
Cooking time: 15 minutes
Recommended Heat: High

Drizzle of vegetable oil
4 banana shallots, finely chopped
4 beef burgers
4 seeded buns, halved
100g pot-cooked and peeled crayfish tails (from your local fishmonger)
Large handful of fresh rocket leaves
Salt and freshly ground black pepper to taste

Serves 4

Suspend the Travel Skillet on the Travel Hook and allow to heat. Add the oil to the Skillet, and then add the shallots. Cook, stirring occasionally, for about 3 minutes until softened.

Meanwhile, place the beef burgers directly on the Grill and leave to cook for 3 to 4 minutes on each side, turning occasionally.

When the burgers are almost cooked and the shallots have softened, add the crayfish tails to the Skillet and leave to cook for 2 minutes before removing the Skillet from the heat.

Place the burger buns cut face down on the bars of the Grill to lightly toast.

Remove the buns from the heat and top the bases with some rocket leaves, the cooked burgers, crayfish and shallots. Cover with the top half of the buns and serve.

Equipment:

Travel Kadai, Travel Hook, Travel Skillet /Cooking Tripod, Tripod Skillet

HONEY & MINT LAMB RACK
with a PISTACHIO CRUST

Bring a centrepiece dish to your table with this French trimmed lamb. Barbecued with a pistachio cumin and honey crumb, the lamb has a succulent centre and scrumptious crust, sure to impress your guests again and again.

Prep time: 5 minutes
Cooking time: 10-15 minutes
(plus resting time)
Recommended Heat: Medium

1 rack of lamb, French trimmed
100g shelled pistachios, crushed
1 tsp cumin seeds
2 tbsp honey
½ lemon, juiced
1 tsp sumac
50g fresh mint, finely chopped
Salt and freshly ground black pepper to taste

Serves 2

Bring the lamb rack up to room temperature before cooking and season generously with salt and pepper.

Place the whole lamb rack on the Grill, turning regularly to reduce flare-ups as the fat renders.

When the rack reaches an internal temperature of 50°C for medium, between 10 to 15 minutes, remove from the Grill to a Chopping Board and put to one side to rest.

Meanwhile, place a Skillet on the bars of the Grill and leave it to get hot. Add the pistachios and cumin seeds to the dry pan and toast until golden.

Add the honey, lemon juice, sumac, fresh mint and a pinch of salt to the pan, stir everything together and remove from the heat.

Spoon the pistachio mixture onto the fatty side of the lamb rack and pat down to form an even crust. Rest for another few minutes before slicing the lamb between the bones into cutlets. Serve immediately.

Equipment:
Chopping Board, Set of 3 Skillets

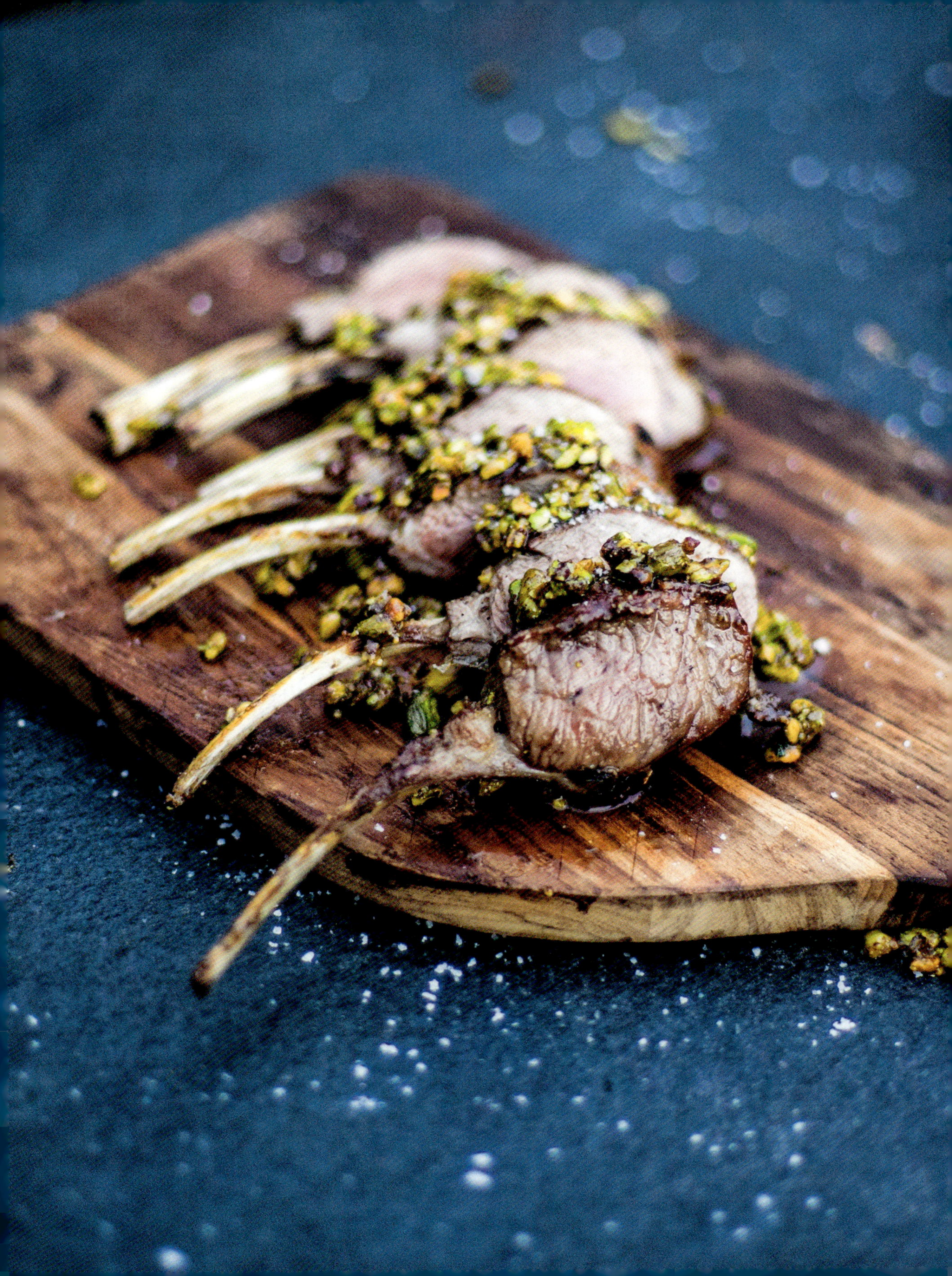

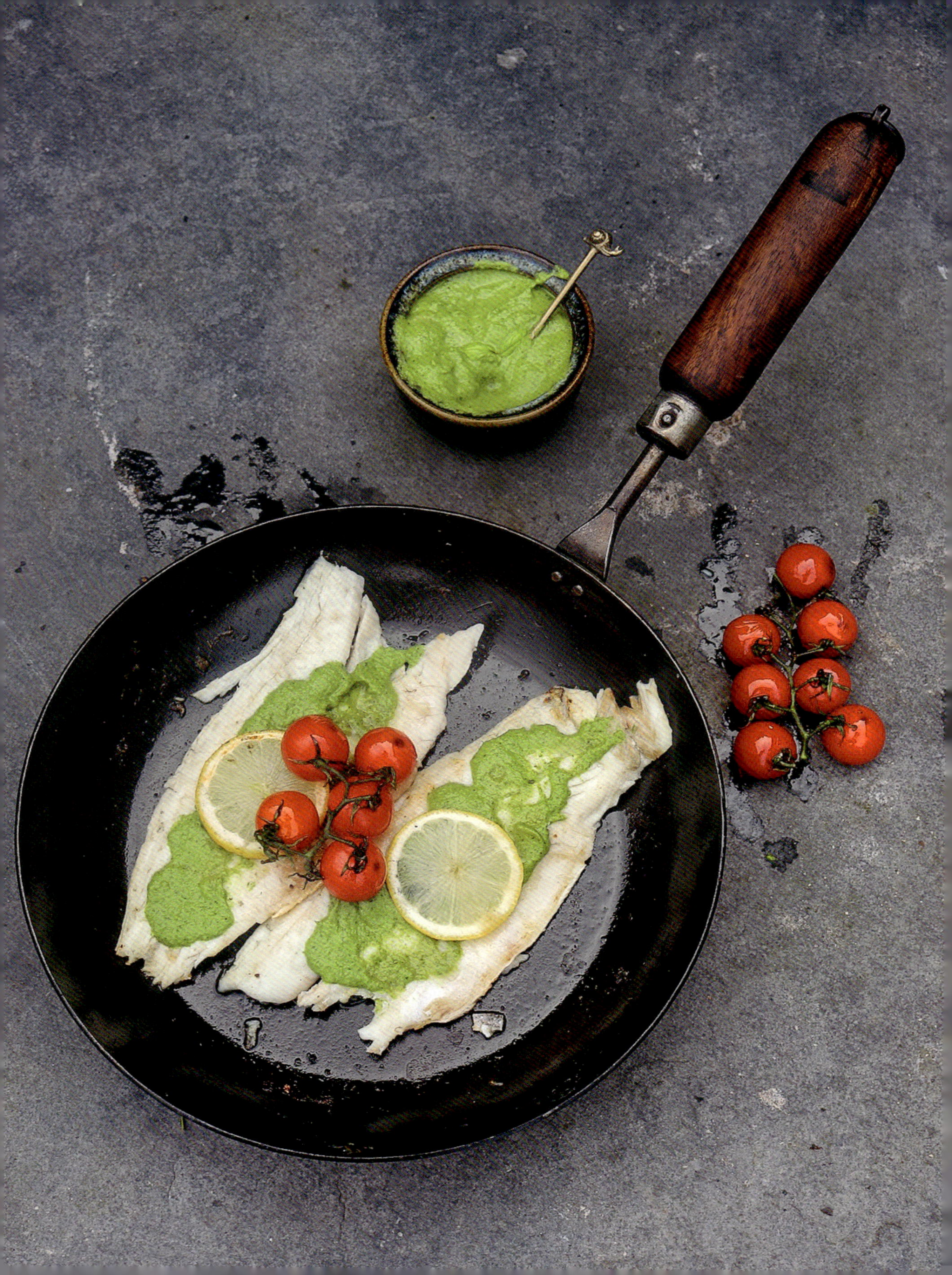

PAN-FRIED SEA BASS, VINE TOMATOES & SALSA VERDE

Enjoy our flavoursome Salsa Verde with some beautifully soft and delicate sea bass fillets. Lightly grilled in the Frying Pan to lock in the salty, fresh and zesty aromas, perfectly balanced by sweet cherry tomatoes.

Prep time: 5 minutes
Cooking time: 6 minutes
Recommended Heat: High

Drizzle of olive oil
2 sea bass fillets, each approx. 200g
½ quantity Salsa Verde (see pg. 57)
150g cherry tomatoes

Serves 2

Heat the Frying Pan for 1 minute on the Grill with a splash of olive oil.

Add the sea bass and cook skin side down for approximately 4 minutes.

Using the Barbecue Tool, flip the fish over and sear the top for approximately 1 minute until it is cooked through.
Move the fillets to a plate and spoon a couple of dollops of Salsa Verde sauce onto each piece.

Serve with vine tomatoes and roasted potatoes (see pg. 99).

Equipment:
Frying Pan, Barbecue Tool

MOULES MARINIÈRE *with* CREAM, GARLIC & PARSLEY

An all-time French favourite, this dish can be cooked perfectly on the barbecue for smoky, zesty and creamy bathed mussels. This mouth-watering and warming bowl of fresh seafood is best served with some crusty bread.

Prep time: 10 minutes
Cooking time: 15 minutes
Recommended Heat: Medium

2 tbsp olive oil
30g unsalted butter, cubed
1 white onion, finely chopped
4 garlic cloves, finely chopped
1kg fresh mussels (i.e., those with tightly closed shells, beards removed)
175ml dry white wine
100ml double cream
1 tbsp fresh parsley, finely chopped
½ lemon, juiced
Salt and freshly ground black pepper to taste

Serves 2

Heat the olive oil and half the butter in a Tripod Skillet on the Cooking Tripod (see pg. 34).

Sauté the onion and garlic for about 5 minutes or until softened.

Add the mussels to the Skillet with the wine, cream, the rest of the butter and parsley. Season well with salt and pepper to taste.

Mix well until the mussels are cooked through and opening. This should take about 10 minutes.

Serve the mussels along with the juices from the pan and a good squeeze of lemon juice. Discard any mussels that stay closed.

Equipment:
Cooking Tripod, Tripod Skillet

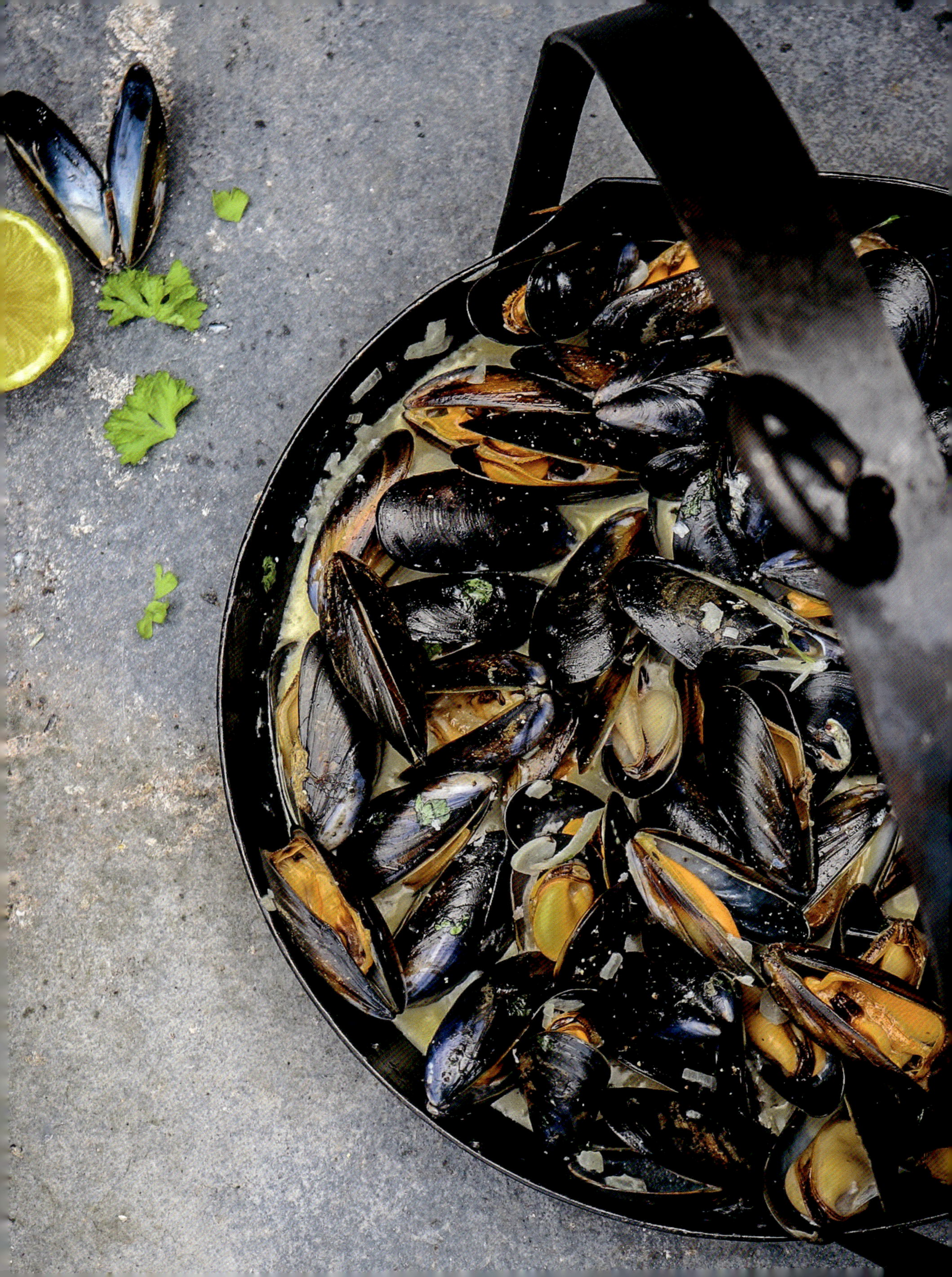

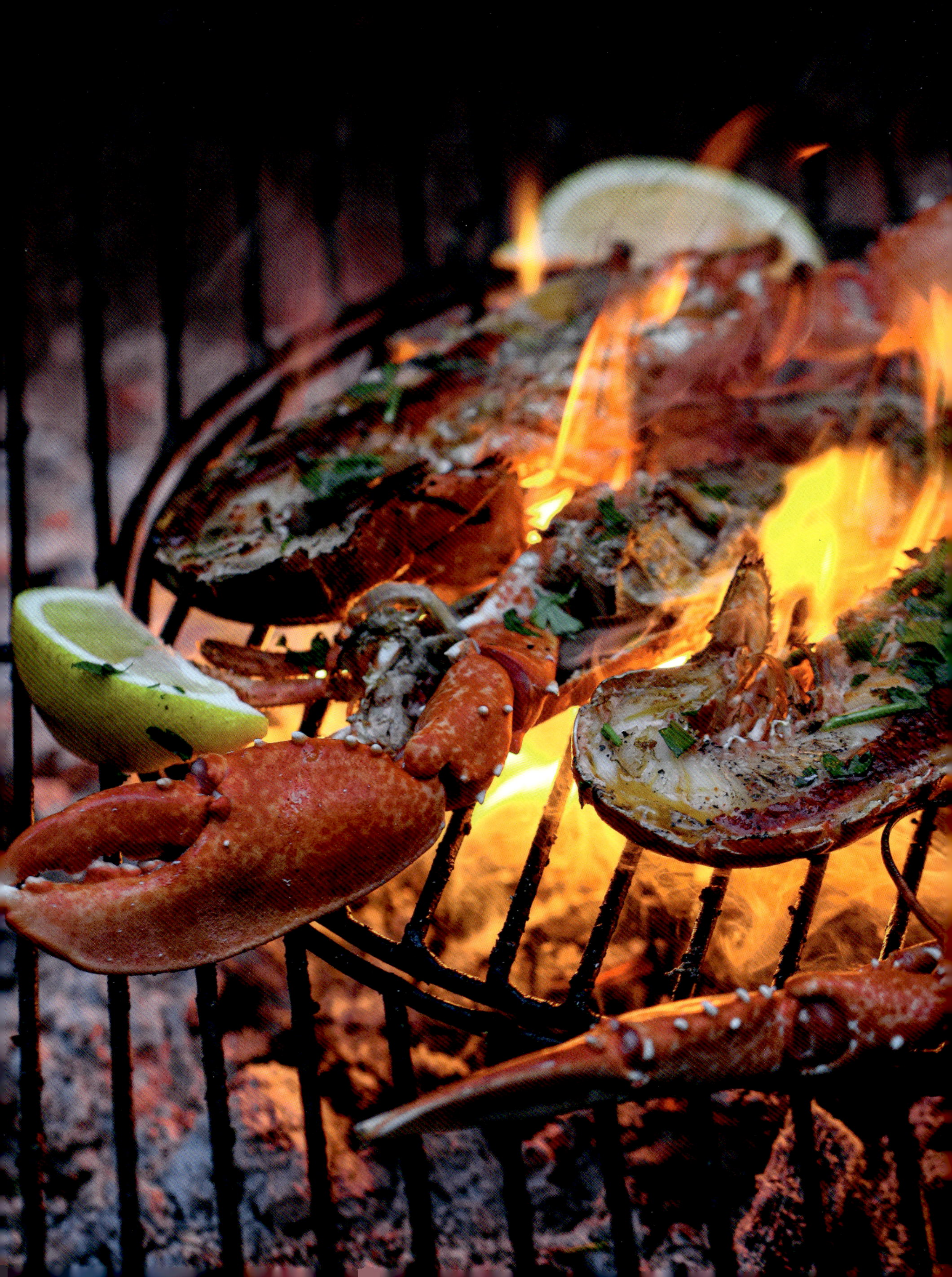

GRILLED LOBSTER

Ever wondered if you can grill lobster on your Kadai? Well, with just your Grill and Kadai Lid, you can easily make this exquisite and succulent recipe, finished with a creamy garlic butter.

Prep time: 10 minutes
Cooking time: 10 minutes
Recommended Heat: High

120g unsalted butter, softened
2 tbsp fresh parsley, finely chopped
4 garlic cloves, finely chopped
1 lemon, zested
1 fresh lobster, approx. 500-700g, halved (ask the fishmonger to prepare it for you)
30ml olive oil
Salt and freshly ground black pepper to taste
Lemon wedges, to serve

Serves 2

Mix the butter, parsley, garlic and lemon zest together in a small bowl. Season with salt and pepper and set aside. Cut the remaining lemon into wedges.

Remove the soft yellow-green mass (the tomalley) from each lobster half, before drizzling the lobster meat with olive oil and seasoning with salt and pepper.

Place the lobster halves on the Grill, meat side up. Cover with the Kadai Lid and grill for 6 to 8 minutes or until the meat is opaque, be careful not to overcook them.

Finish by turning the lobster halves over to char the meat for a minute or so.

Remove from the heat and dollop half the butter mix over each grilled lobster.

Serve with a wedge of lemon.

Equipment:
Kadai Lid

TIP: A Cookware Lid works just as well as a Kadai Lid.

HERB-ROASTED RAINBOW TROUT

Trout is a delicate fish that cooks perfectly in the Roasting Oven, resulting in soft, flaky fish that melts in the mouth. The vegetable bed protects the fish from any hot spots, as well as making this a very simple all-in-one dish to prepare and cook.

Prep time: 5 minutes
Cooking time: 20 minutes
Recommended Heat: Low/Medium

400g baby new potatoes,
200g cherry tomatoes
1 aubergine, sliced
2 whole rainbow trout, gutted
1 lemon, thinly sliced
2 large sprigs of fresh parsley or dill
1 tbsp olive oil
Salt and freshly ground black pepper to taste

Serves 2

Put the potatoes, tomatoes and aubergine in an even layer over the bottom of the Roasting Oven to make a vegetable bed.

Stuff the trout with the lemon slices and parsley or dill and lay them on top of the vegetables.

Drizzle the fish and vegetables with the oil and season well with salt.

Close the lid of the Roasting Oven and place it directly on the coals. Bake for approximately 20 minutes, or until the fish is cooked through.

Equipment:
Roasting Oven

TIP: Drizzle over a little white wine as well as the oil before cooking, but make sure you line the Roasting Oven with tin foil first to lock in all the juices.

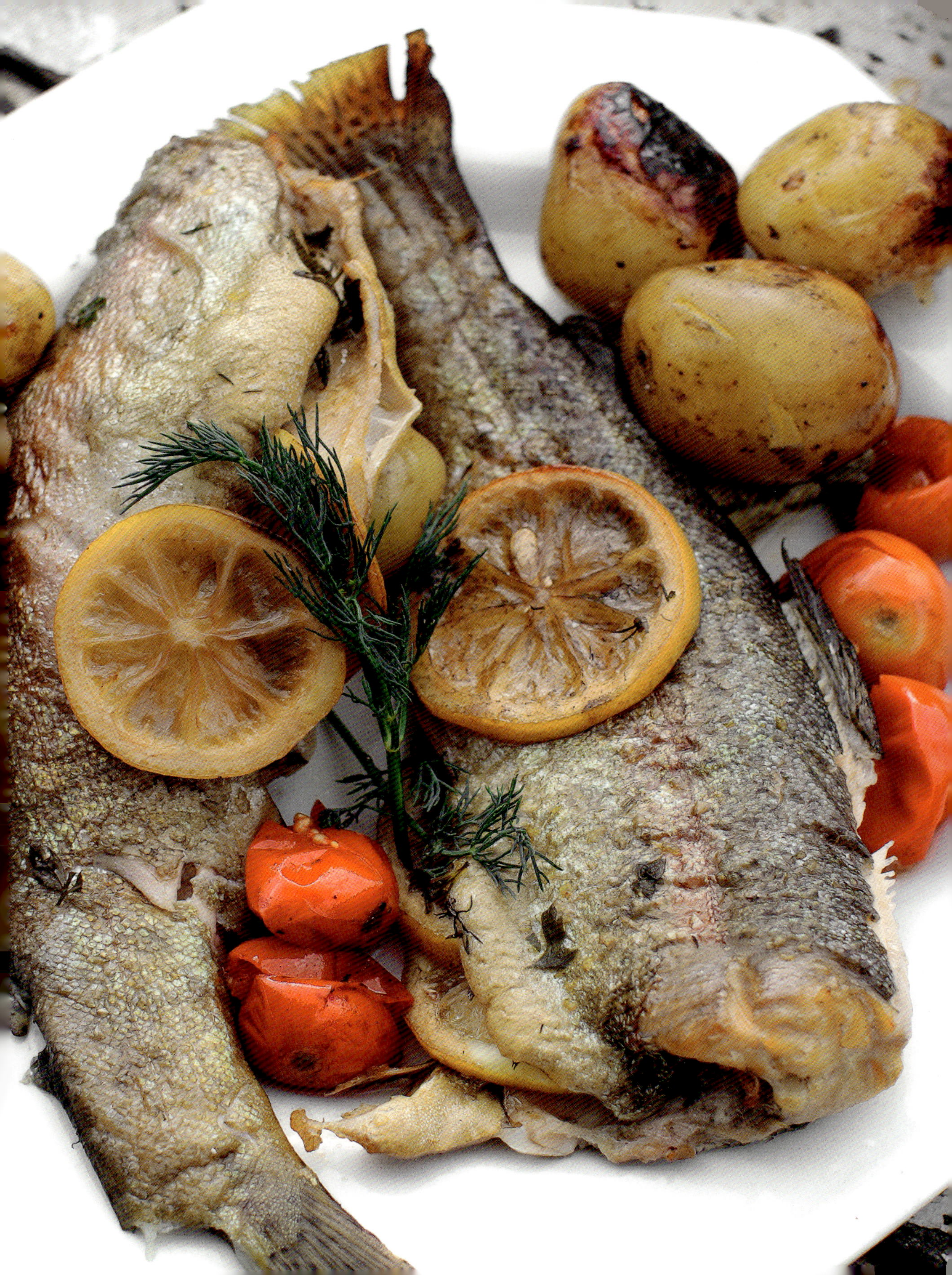

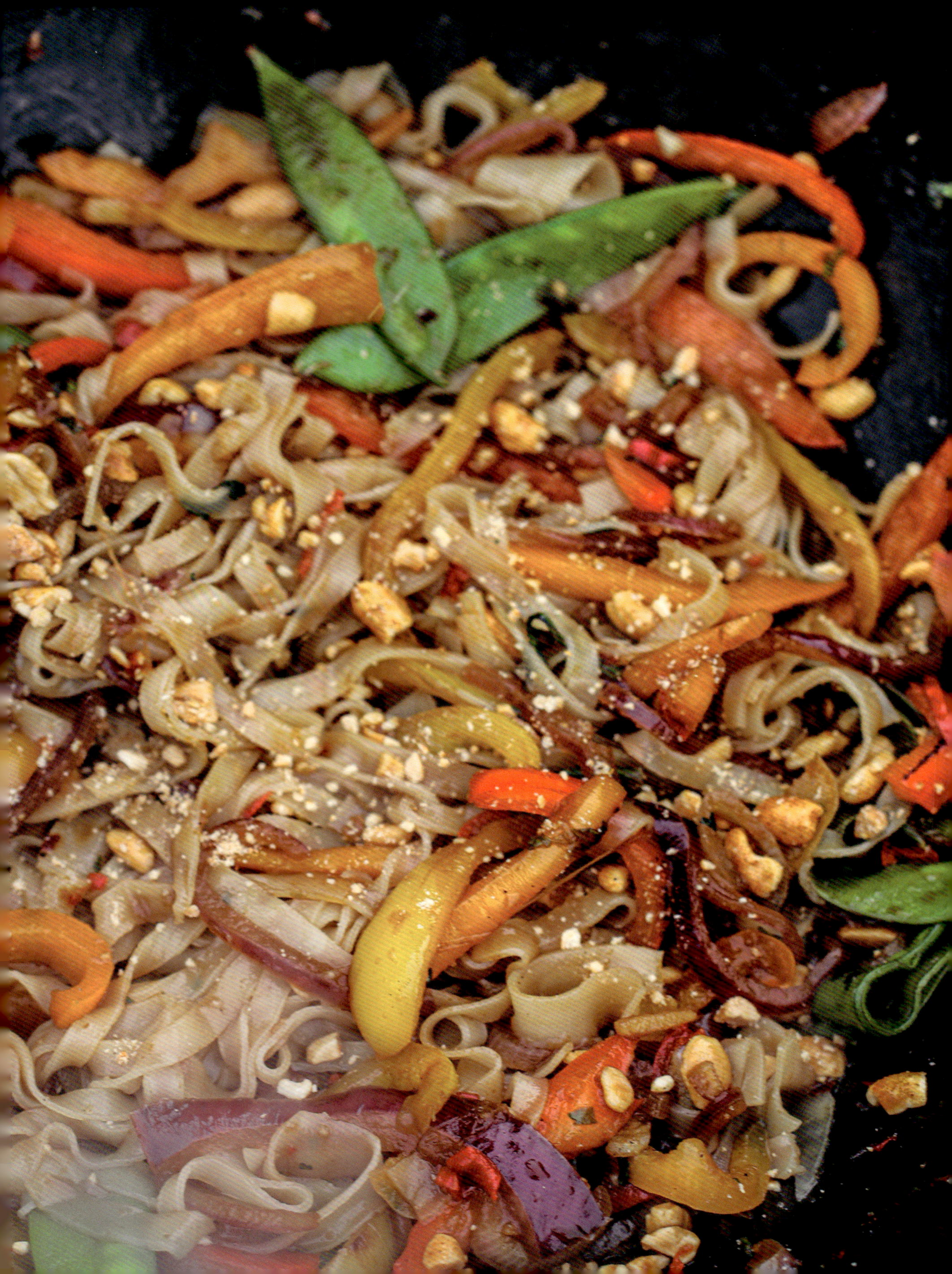

PAD THAI

Transform the Cooking Bowl into a wok to recreate this traditional noodle dish, an everyday staple on the bustling streets of Thailand.

Prep time: 10 minutes
Cooking time: 10 minutes
Recommended Heat: High

For the sauce:

50ml soy sauce

1 lime, juiced

1 tsp chilli flakes

3 tbsp brown sugar

2-3cm piece peeled fresh ginger, finely grated

For the pad thai:

Generous drizzle of sesame seed oil

2 garlic cloves, finely chopped

1 red chilli, deseeded and chopped (optional)

2 red peppers, deseeded and chopped

2 white onions, chopped

150g mangetout

Handful of fresh coriander, chopped

3 nests Pad Thai noodles

2 medium free-range eggs

100g roasted peanuts

1 lime, juiced

Serves 4

To make the sauce, add the soy sauce, lime juice, chilli flakes, brown sugar and ginger to a small bowl and mix well.

Remove the centre from the Holi Grill and place the Cooking Bowl in the middle, over a high heat. Pour in the sesame seed oil.

Add the garlic, chilli, peppers, onions and mangetout, and stir well with the Spatula.

Add the coriander and the pre-prepared sauce mix and stir. Allow to simmer gently over the heat.

Steep the noodles in a pan of boiling water to one side of the Kadai and simmer for 3 minutes. Drain the water from the pan.

Add the noodles to the Cooking Bowl, then push to the side. Crack 2 eggs directly into the centre of the pan, mix them together and allow them to 'scramble'. Once the eggs are scrambled, mix with the noodles until combined.

Crush the roasted peanuts using a pestle and mortar. Dish out the noodles, and top with the crushed peanuts and a drizzle of lime juice.

Equipment:
Cooking Bowl, Set of 3 Utensils

TIP: Add tofu or chicken to this dish for something a little different.

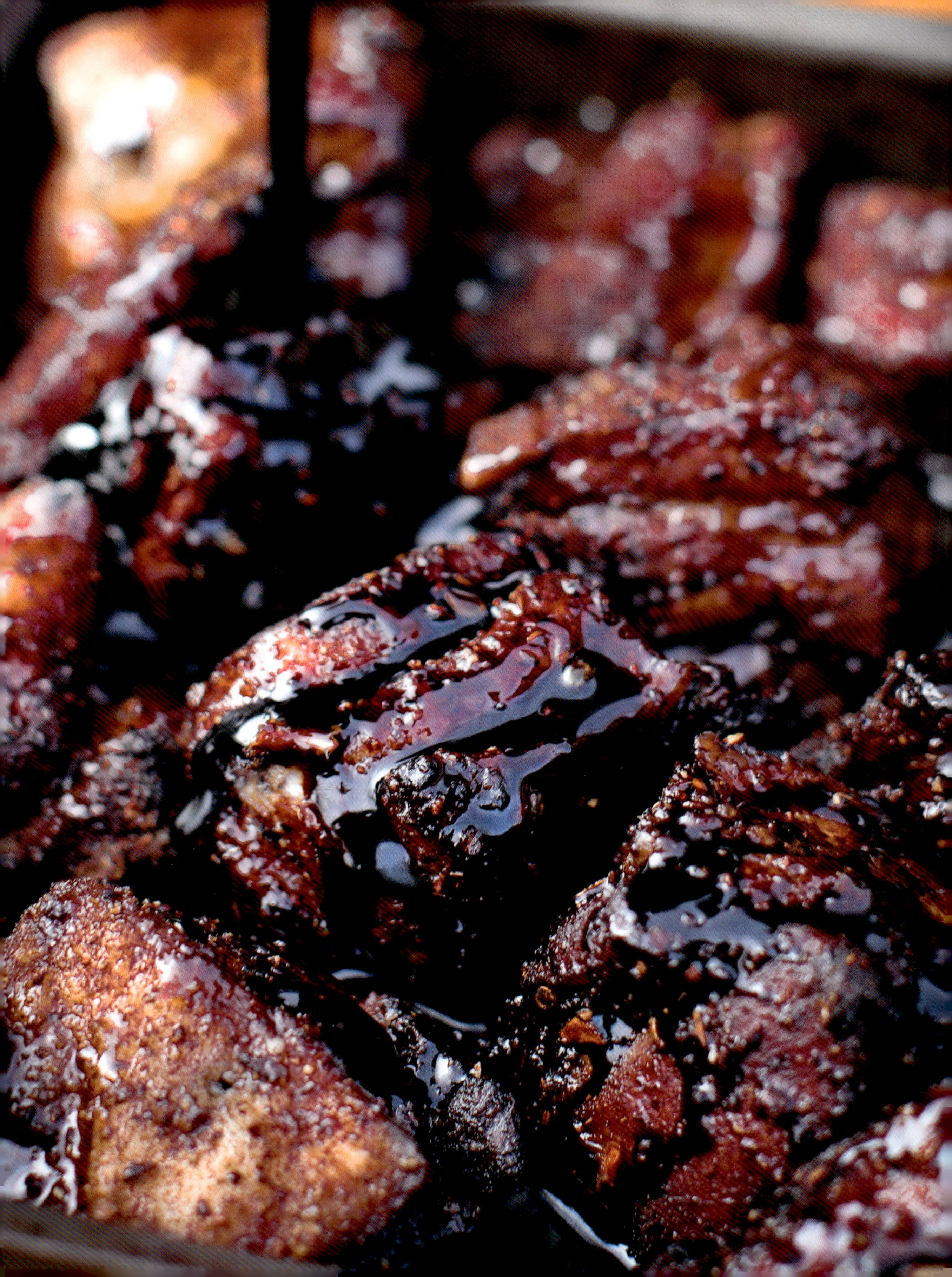

If you have time...

Slow-barbecue cooking takes time, where patience is key. Our focus here is on the notion of 'low and slow' barbecuing, from classic, succulent, burnt pork ends to a whole brisket, slow roasted. Master the art of barbecuing with time and discover a whole new style of cooking. Here you will find recipe inspirations to make incredible meals, which are only possible on a versatile barbecue such as a Kadai.

LOW 'N' SLOW BEEF BRISKET *with* KADAI'S BARBECUE SAUCE

In our beginners guide to a slow-cooked favourite, this beef brisket is prepared so it melts in your mouth. It is one of the best cuts of meat to experiment with, when learning about low and slow cooking, as its tough nature allows gentle tenderisation on the Kadai.

Prep time: 20 minutes
Cooking time: Approx. 6 hours
Recommended Heat: Medium/ High

½ full beef brisket, approx. 5-7kg
1 litre beef stock (homemade or a stockpot)
4 servings of Kadai barbecue sauce (see pg. 54)

For the 'slaw':
½ red cabbage, finely sliced
3 red onions, finely sliced
3 carrots, grated
12 tbsp mayonnaise
1½ tsp garlic powder
1½ tsp paprika
Handful of fresh parsley, chopped

Serves 8

Put the brisket into a roasting tin and fill with the beef stock, place the pan onto the Grill and cover with the Kadai Lid.

Cook for approximately 4 hours (turning halfway through) or until the meat is tender and can easily be pulled apart. At least 90°C internal temperature.

Whilst the brisket is cooking, prepare the homemade slaw.

To make the slaw, add the cabbage, onions and carrot to a bowl and combine. Add the remaining ingredients and mix well together.

Once the brisket is cooked, remove from the roasting tin and place on the Grill over an indirect heat for 1 hour on each side.

Use a basting brush to coat each side of the brisket with the Kadai barbecue sauce, 20 minutes before it is ready so the sugars will not burn.

Once the brisket is cooked through and tender, shred it and serve with the homemade 'slaw.'

Equipment:
Kadai Lid

TIP: If you have any left-over brisket, why not try our nacho sharer bowl recipe? (see pg. 132)

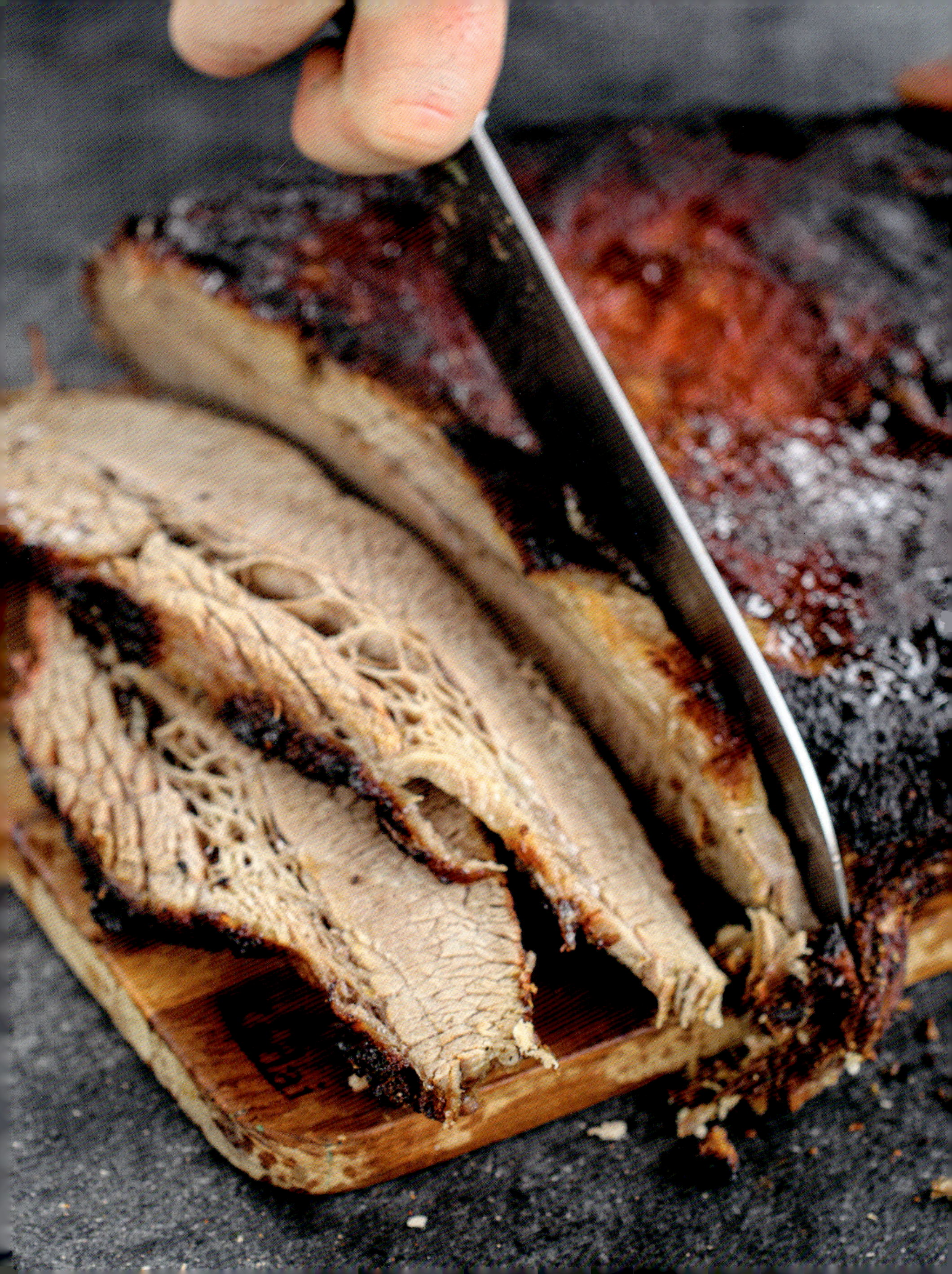

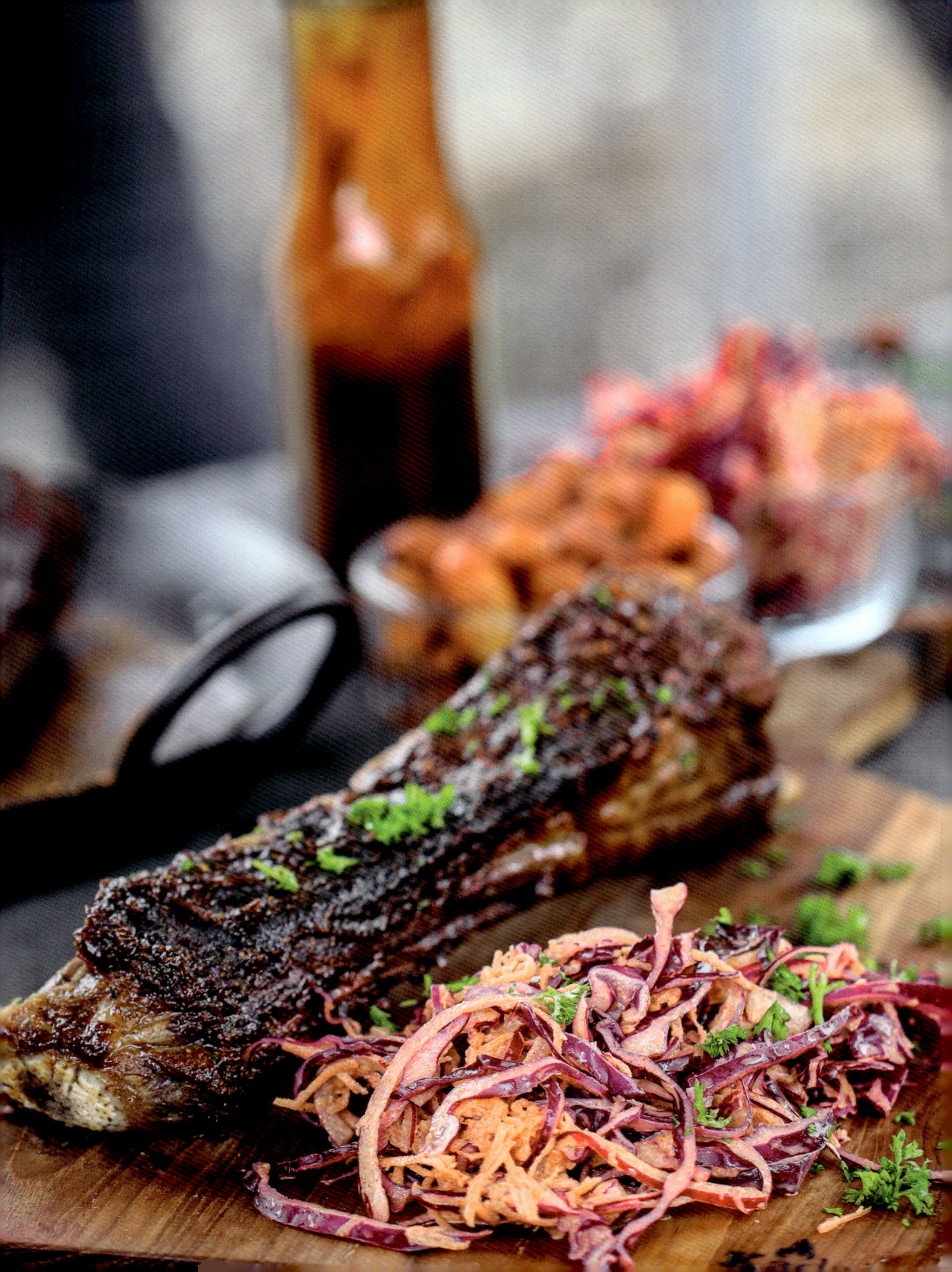

BEEF RIBS, SMOKY BEANS & HOMEMADE 'SLAW'

In love with the deep smoky flavour of a barbecue? Then this recipe is for you. Slowly cooked and marinated in the Kadai Lid, these beef ribs are mouth-watering. Complete with smoky beans and a barbecue slaw, this inviting dish is just waiting to be enjoyed around a roaring fire.

Prep time: 30 minutes
Cooking time: Approx. 1 hour 30 minutes
Recommended Heat: Medium/High

For the smoky barbecue seasoning:

2 tbsp smoked paprika

110g brown sugar

2 tbsp mesquite flavouring

2 tbsp garlic powder

2 tbsp dry mustard powder

2 tbsp celery salt

20g fresh coriander, chopped

½ tbsp salt and freshly ground black pepper

For the ribs:

1.5kg beef ribs

Drizzle of rapeseed oil

3 tbsp Kadai's barbecue sauce (see pg. 54)

For the smoky beans:

400g borlotti beans, drained and rinsed

400g butter beans, drained and rinsed

150g passata

3 tbsp Kadai's barbecue sauce (see pg. 54)

For the 'slaw' (see pg. 128)

Serves 4

To make the smoky barbecue seasoning, combine all the ingredients in a small bowl and mix well.

Place the ribs in a roasting tin and coat them with rapeseed oil. Cover the ribs in a generous coating of barbecue rub. Once coated, wrap the ribs tightly in tinfoil to create a parcel.

Place the wrapped ribs directly on the Grill over a medium heat and cover with the Kadai Lid; grill for approximately 1 hour 30 minutes.

While the ribs are cooking, mix the ingredients for the smoky beans in a medium Skillet. Place the Skillet directly on the Grill over a medium heat. Leave to simmer for 10 minutes until warmed through.

Once the beef ribs are cooked through, remove from the Grill, unwrap, and coat the top with more barbecue seasoning, then smother the ribs all over in barbecue sauce. Place the ribs directly on the Grill for 10 minutes, turning once, to ensure the barbecue sauce thickens and creates a sticky crust over the meat.

Then, make the slaw (see pg. 128)

Once the ribs have reached an internal temperature of at least 56 to 60°c (for medium), remove the ribs and beans from the heat and serve with the barbecue slaw.

Equipment: Kadai Lid, Set of 3 Skillets

NACHO SHARER BOWL *with* PULLED BEEF BRISKET

Who said leftovers can't be as delicious second time around? These Pulled Brisket Nachos are a brilliant way to use up all your slow-cooked beef brisket. Get everyone involved dipping some crispy nachos into a steaming bowl of spicy tomato brisket.

Prep time: 10 minutes
Cooking time: 30 minutes
Recommended Heat: Medium

Drizzle of rapeseed oil
1 large white onion, chopped
400g (approx.) leftover beef brisket, (see pg. 128) pulled into coarse shreds
1 red pepper, deseeded and sliced
1 tsp paprika
1 tsp ground cumin
2 garlic cloves, finely chopped
400g tin chopped tomatoes
1 beef stock cube, crumbled
400g tin red kidney beans, drained and rinsed
2 tbsp tomato purée
1 tsp hot chilli powder
2 red chillies, deseeded and finely chopped (optional)
2 bags of nachos (400g)

Serves 4

Place the Cooking Tripod on a lit Kadai and suspend the Cooking Bowl (see pg. 34). Once the bowl is hot, add a drizzle of oil and the onions, leaving to sweat for 5 minutes.

Stir in the leftover brisket and peppers. Then add the paprika, cumin and garlic, fry for a further 3 minutes. Stir constantly to ensure the spices do not burn.

Pour in the chopped tomatoes, mixing thoroughly.

Then add the stock cube, red kidney beans, tomato purée, chilli powder and chillies. Simmer for 10 minutes, stirring occasionally.

Transfer the Cooking Bowl onto its stand using the heat-proof Gloves, then serve with the dipping nachos.

Equipment:
Cooking Tripod, Cooking Bowl

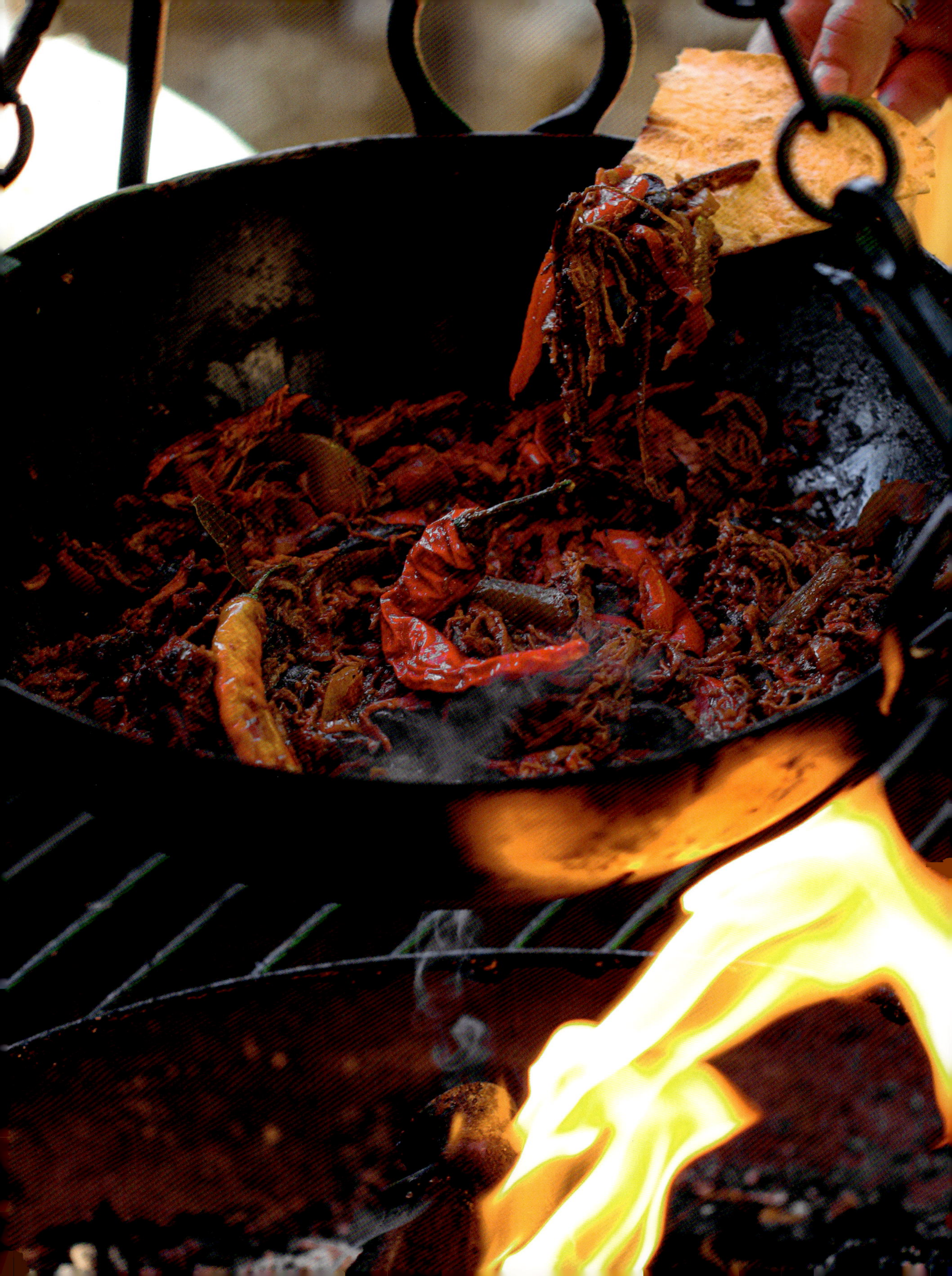

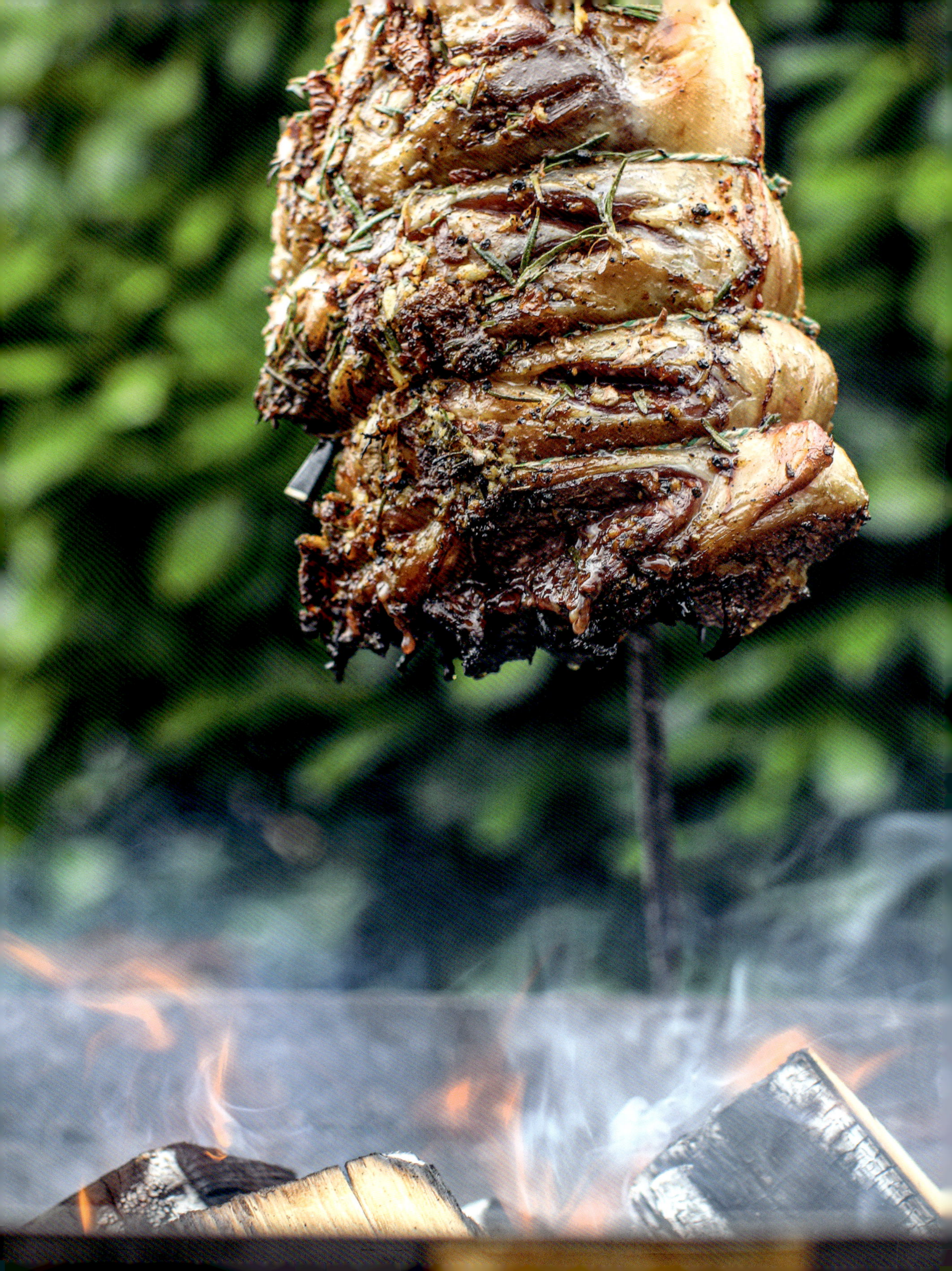

MEDITERRANEAN FIRE ROASTED LEG OF LAMB

This succulent leg of lamb has a delicious Mediterranean twist that complements the flame-grilled flavour of the barbecue. Enjoy as a traditional roast as the cold evenings draw in or as the perfect pairing for a salad on a warmer day.

Prep time: 15 minutes
(plus minimum 30 minutes marinating time)
Cooking time: Approx. 5 hours
Recommended Heat: Medium

10 garlic cloves
1 small bunch of fresh rosemary
1 tbsp black peppercorns
1 tbsp salt
150g sun-dried tomatoes in a jar with oil
1 whole leg of lamb, approx. 2.5kg

Serves 6

Put the garlic, rosemary, peppercorns and salt into a mortar and grind to a paste with the pestle. Add the sun-dried tomatoes along with 50ml of their oil and grind everything together to a roughly textured marinade.

To prepare the leg of lamb for cooking, score all over the joint in a diamond formation using a sharp knife to allow the fat to render. Rub the marinade deep into the scores on the fat and all over the meat. Leave to rest for at least 30 minutes. You can also prepare the meat the day before.

Hang the lamb over the fire using the Cooking Tripod and chain (see pg. 34). Leave to cook slowly for about 5 hours. A medium-cooked joint should have an internal temperature of 60°C but cook for a little longer if you prefer it well done.

Equipment:
Cooking Tripod

WILD BOAR STEAKS *with* BRAISED CARROTS, FENNEL & A CHARCOAL CREAM SAUCE

A wonderful, lean and flavoursome alternative to pork, wild boar is one of the UK's finest game meats. Served with beer-soaked carrots and our speciality charcoal cream, these pan-fried steaks are truly irresistible.

Prep time: 15 minutes
Cooking time: 30 minutes
Recommended Heat: Medium

For the steaks:
4 wild boar steaks
Drizzle of rapeseed oil
1 tbsp salt
3 tbsp dry meat rub (see pg. 46)

For the rest:
100ml double cream
4 carrots, cut in half lengthways
2 fennel bulbs, cut in half lengthways
50g unsalted butter
350ml golden real ale
Handful fresh parsley, chopped

Serves 4

Allow the steaks to reach room temperature then drizzle with the oil and rub them all over with salt.

Put the cream into a glass jar with a loosely fitting lid. Use the Tongs and take a thumb-sized piece of lit charcoal and drop it into the cream. Put the lid on, not securing too tightly so the charcoal smoke can infuse into the cream. Leave for 20 minutes then strain the cream through a sieve.

Take the carrots and fennel and place them flat side down in a large Skillet, add the butter and place on the Grill over a medium fire. Once the butter starts to turn a golden-brown colour, pour the ale into the Skillet and leave the vegetables to simmer in the sauce.

Grill the steaks over the coals until the internal temperature is around 60°C, then move to a board to rest. Season the steaks with the rub. Once the liquid in the Skillet has reduced by approximately 100ml, remove the vegetables and char them directly on the Grill.

Move the Skillet with the remaining liquid to an indirect heat and add the charcoal cream. Stir the cream into the buttery beer sauce and add the chopped parsley. Slice up the steaks and plate up the vegetables. Pour the charcoal cream sauce over the top and serve.

Equipment:
Tongs, Set of 3 Skillets

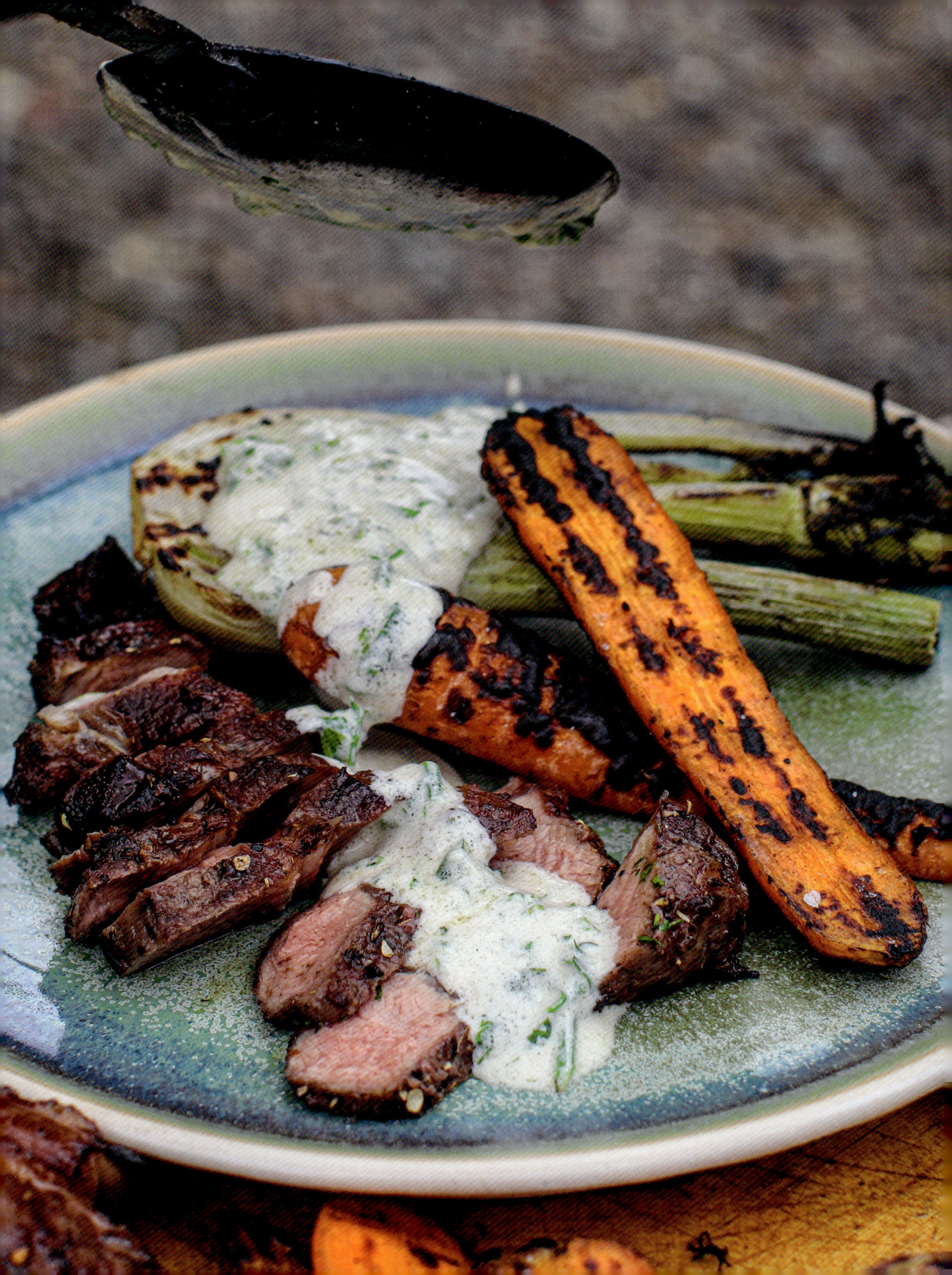

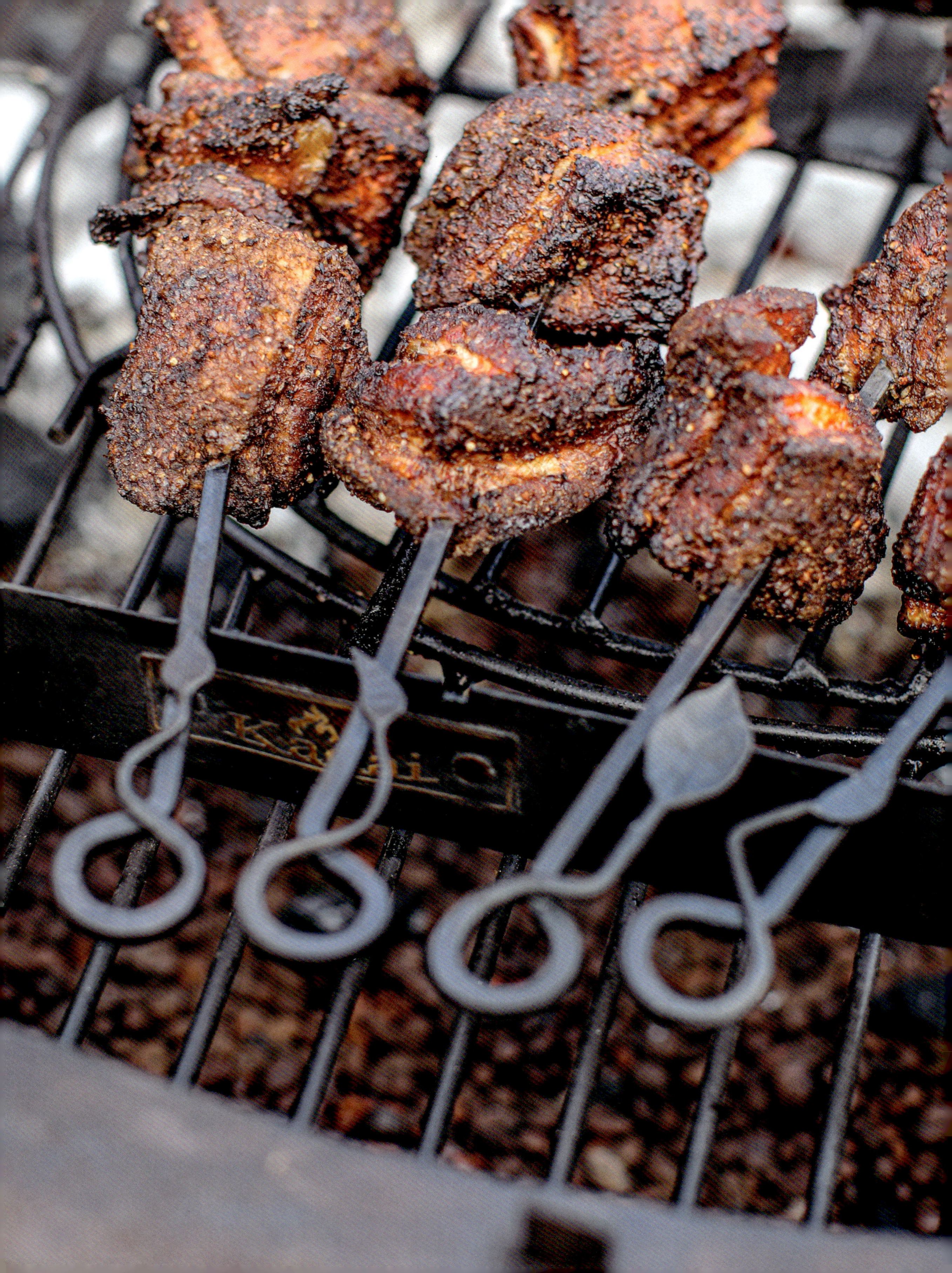

PORK BELLY ENDS

Sticky, smoky and covered in sauce - that is how we like our pork belly. Excellent as a sharing plate, this slower cooked recipe is packed with spices and fragrance. Get the family involved and try the great combination of the Set of 3 Skillets, Skewers and Kadai Lid.

Prep time: 10 minutes
Cooking time: Approx. 2 hours 30 minutes
Recommended Heat: Medium

For the spice rub:

2 whole star anise

1 small cinnamon stick

4 whole cloves

2 tsp fennel seeds

2 tsp black peppercorns

2 tsp sea salt

Pork belly ends:

1.5kg pork belly, de-boned and the rind taken off

Drizzle of rapeseed oil

For the braise:

100ml light soy sauce

100ml rice wine

100ml honey

150g unsalted butter, cubed

For serving:

1 red chilli, deseeded and finely chopped (optional)

1 spring onion, finely chopped

1 tbsp sesame seeds

Serves 6

Gently heat the small Skillet on the Grill. Add the star anise, cinnamon, cloves and fennel seeds and lightly toast. Add the spices into a mortar with the peppercorns and salt and grind to a paste with the pestle to make a 5-spice.

Cut the pork belly into 6cm squares, drizzle with oil and rub with the 5-spice mix. Thread about 3 to 4 pork cubes onto each Skewer, leaving a gap for the smoke to move freely.

Generate smoke by adding a few pieces of wood to the fire. Place the Skewer Rack on the Grill over an indirect heat and cover with the Kadai Lid. Cook for approximately 1 hour, turning the Skewers occasionally. Once the pork has reached 70°C, transfer the Skewers to the large Skillet. Add the soy sauce, rice wine, honey and butter. Cover the Skillet with foil and return to an indirect heat.

After 30 minutes, turn the Skewers in the braising liquid and re-cover with foil. Leave to cook for a further 20 to 30 minutes.

Remove the Skillet from the heat and leave to rest for 5 minutes. Plate up the pork belly ends and scatter with chilli, spring onion and sesame seeds.

Equipment:
Set of 3 Skillets, Set of 8 Skewers, Kadai Lid

KADAI'S STICKY RIBS

Exceptionally easy, these barbecue ribs demand little effort yet look spectacular. Pork ribs are slowly cooked on the Asado Cross using an Argentinian cooking method. Perfect for entertaining guests, this dish delivers a truly memorable flavour.

Prep time: 10 minutes
Cooking time: Approx 4 hours
Recommended Heat: Medium/Low

For the smoky barbecue seasoning:
3 tbsp smoked paprika
170g brown sugar
3tbsp mesquite
3tbsp garlic powder
3tbsp dry mustard powder
3tbsp celery salt
30g fresh coriander, chopped
1tbsp salt and freshly ground black pepper

For the rest:
2kg pork ribs
2 servings of Kadai's barbecue sauce (see pg. 54)

Serves 3

To make the seasoning, combine all the ingredients in a small bowl and mix well.

Rub the pork ribs with the barbecue seasoning, making sure to coat both sides of the meat well.

Build a fire with a charcoal core and logs on top, then push to one side. Once the fire is ready, attach the ribs to the Asado Cross (see pg. 34) by threading food-safe wire through all four corners and tying them to the T bar. Slot the Pole into the base and cook on the third slot.

Slowly cook the ribs for approximately 4 hours, occasionally building up the fire with more wood or charcoal.

About 30 minutes before the ribs are removed from the heat, brush the Kadai barbecue sauce evenly on the meat.

Once the ribs have reached an internal temperature of 80°C to 85°C, they are ready.

Remove from the heat and enjoy.

Equipment:

Asado Cross, Tongs

TIP: Alternatively, you can cook this recipe on an Oak Plank (see page 30).

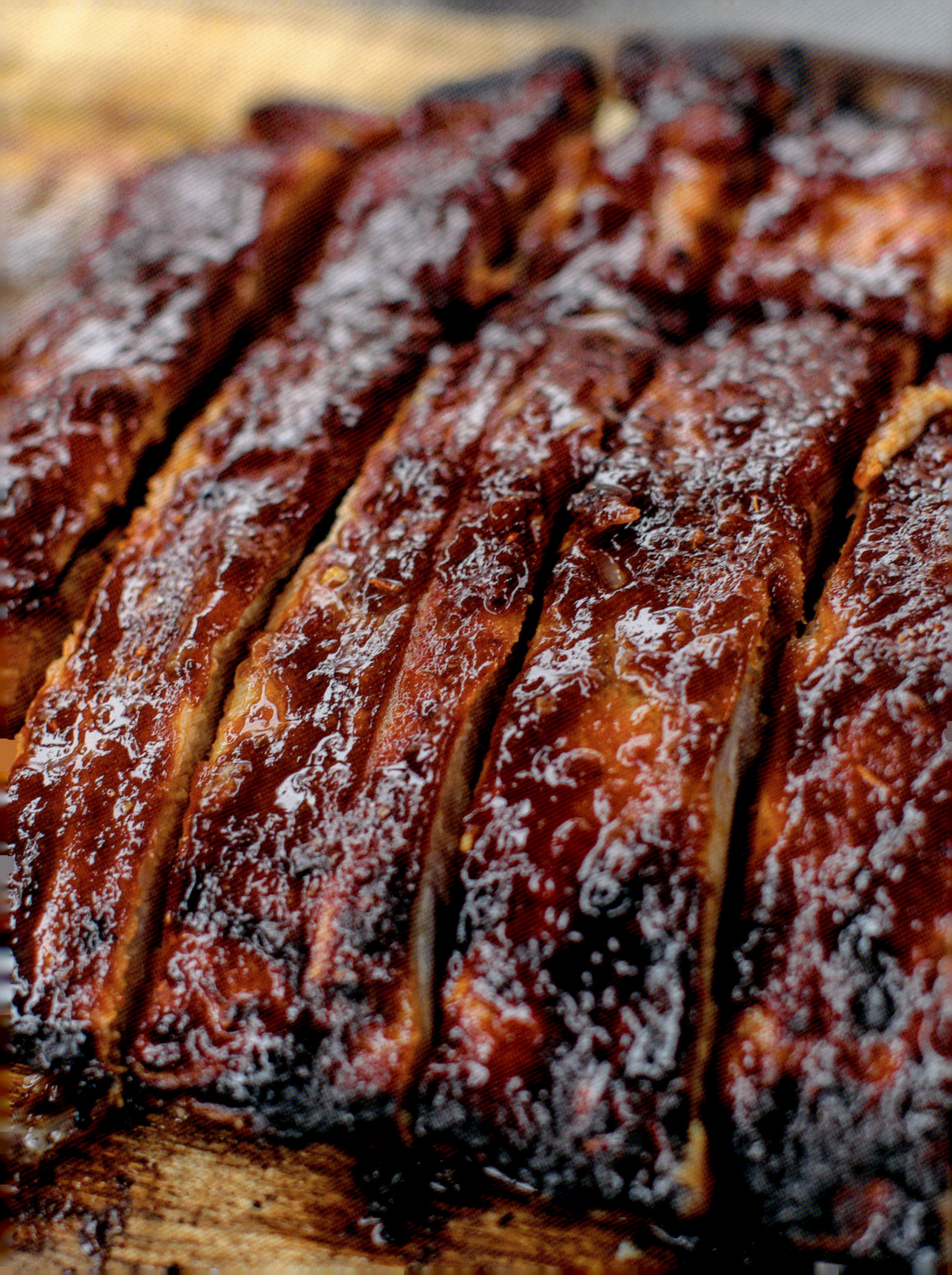

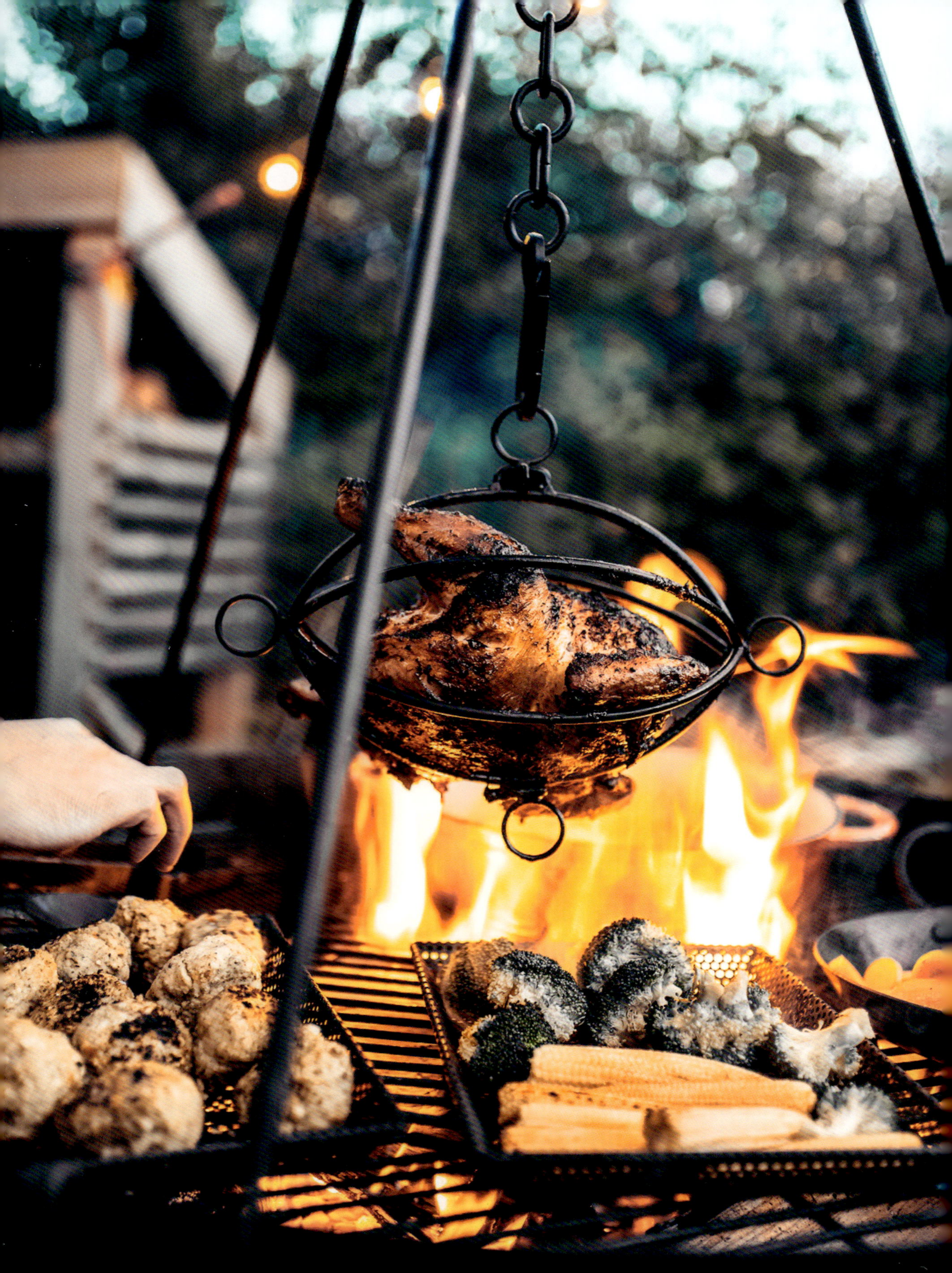

WHOLE ROASTED CHICKEN *in a* GARLIC & LEMON MARINADE

A delicious and simply prepared roast chicken marinated with a homemade seasoning; great served with some fresh, seasonal greens or roasted vegetables.

Prep time: 15 minutes
(plus minimum 60 minutes marinating time)
Cooking time: Approx. 2 hours
Recommended Heat: Medium

For the marinade:

2 tbsp black peppercorns

4 garlic cloves

Handful of fresh wild garlic, chopped

Small bunch of fresh tarragon, chopped

Handful of fresh sage leaves, chopped

Small bunch of fresh chives, chopped

1 lemon, juiced and zested

2 tbsp rapeseed oil

For the rest:

1 large whole chicken

Salt and freshly ground black pepper to taste

Serves 4

For the marinade, place the peppercorns, garlic and a pinch of salt into a mortar and grind them to a paste with the pestle. Add the wild garlic and grind further, making sure it is broken down into a paste before adding the tarragon, sage and chives.

Add the lemon zest, lemon juice and oil. The marinade is finished once the herbs have turned dark green in colour.

Using a sharp knife, score the flesh of the chicken on the thickest parts – two incisions on each breast and one across each drumstick and thigh. Place the chicken in a bowl, pour over the marinade, and work it well into the meat. Cover and leave to marinate for at least 1 hour or overnight in the fridge (make sure the chicken is back up to room temperature 1 hour before cooking).

Secure the chicken in the Tripod Roaster and hang on the Cooking Tripod (see pg. 34) over a prepared Kadai. Cook the chicken for approximately 2 hours, turning the Tripod Roaster every 15 minutes, so that it cooks evenly. The chicken is ready once it reaches an internal temperature of 75°C and the juices run clear when pierced with a skewer.

Take the chicken off the heat to a Chopping Board and let it rest for 15 minutes before serving.

Equipment:
Cooking Tripod, Tripod Roaster, Chopping Board

WILD MUNTJAC

A muntjac is a small deer commonly found in the English countryside. Caught in the wild, this sustainable meat is flavoursome and the perfect size to be mounted whole on the Kadai Asado Cross and slowly roasted. Hopefully, this recipe will encourage you to try this tasty venison that is sure to turn heads at your next barbecue.

Prep time: 10-15 minutes
Cooking time: Minimum of 2 hours
Recommended Heat: Medium

1 prepared whole muntjac deer (5-6kg)
Drizzle of rapeseed oil
Salt and freshly ground black pepper to taste
250g unsalted butter

Serves 6-8

Butterfly the deer open to maximise its surface area on the cross. Prepare the front end of the deer by applying a little pressure to the ribs, pressing outwards, and cracking them open by hand along the chest cavity. Use a knife to cut down between the back legs, so the meat lies flat. Your butcher may prepare this for you.

Mount the muntjac on the Asado Cross (see pg. 34) with the shoulder end starting closest to the fire, as it needs more heat to cook. Leave enough space between the end of the long bar and the animal to ensure the Asado can fit into the bracket on the bowl. Put the T bar between the muntjac's legs and shoulders, only tighten once the bars have been lined up. Secure the muntjac to the bar with uncoated wire. Bind the carcass in all 4 corners by each leg and once in the middle of the loin.

Score the skin in a diamond shape across the legs and shoulders before rubbing with oil and seasoning. Set the cross into the bracket on the bowl, bone side of the carcass down, to conduct the heat into the meat. Build up the fire with large pieces of wood.

Fill the Flambadou with good quality unsalted butter, place over a direct heat until it begins to melt.

Cook the muntjac over the fire, turning and basting with the Flambadou every 30 minutes. Check the meat after 2 hours with a meat thermometer. Serve the muntjac medium cooked to an internal temperature of 65°C to 70°C. Remove from the Asado Cross and enjoy as a large feast.

Equipment:

Asado Cross, Flambadou

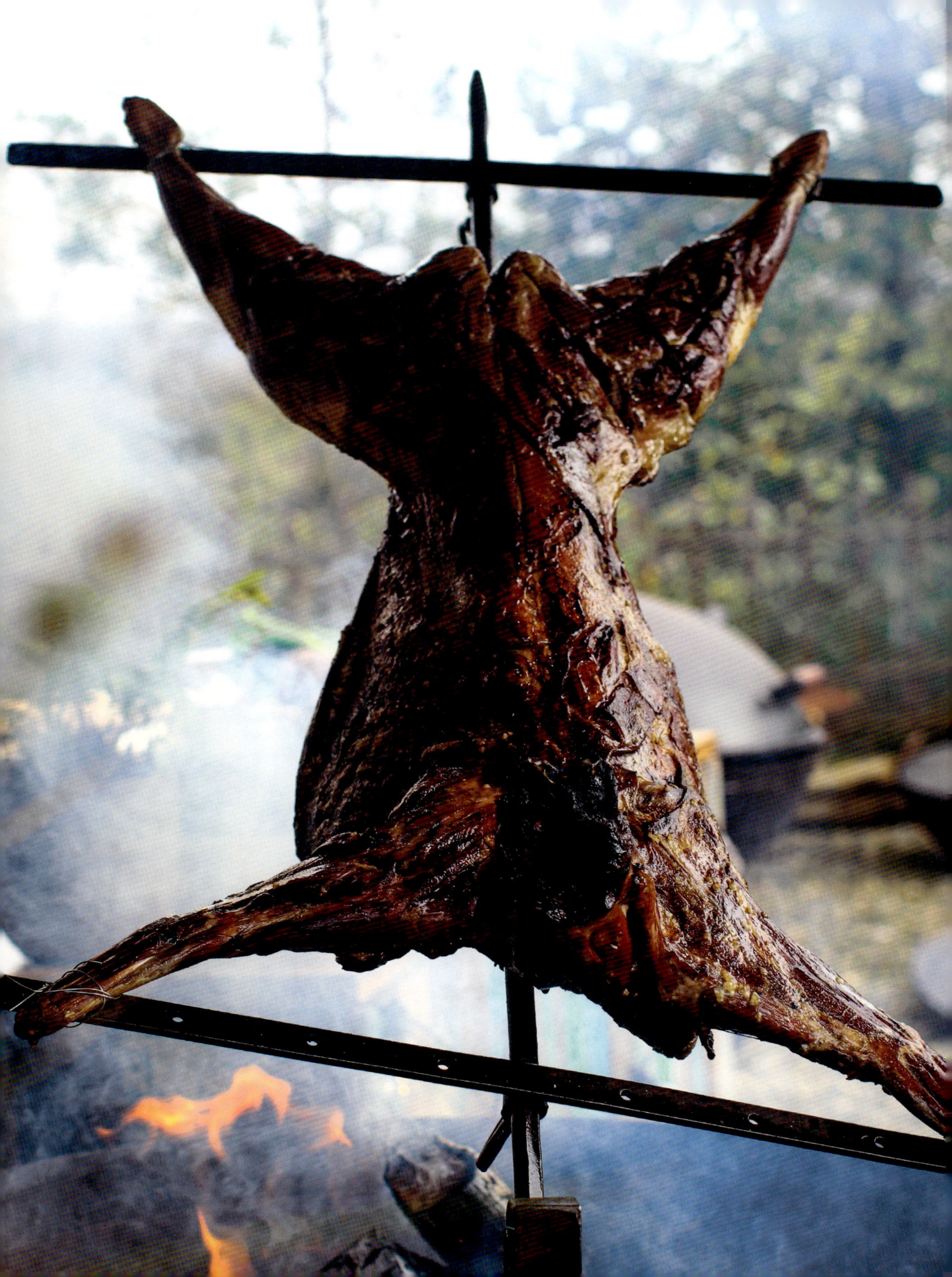

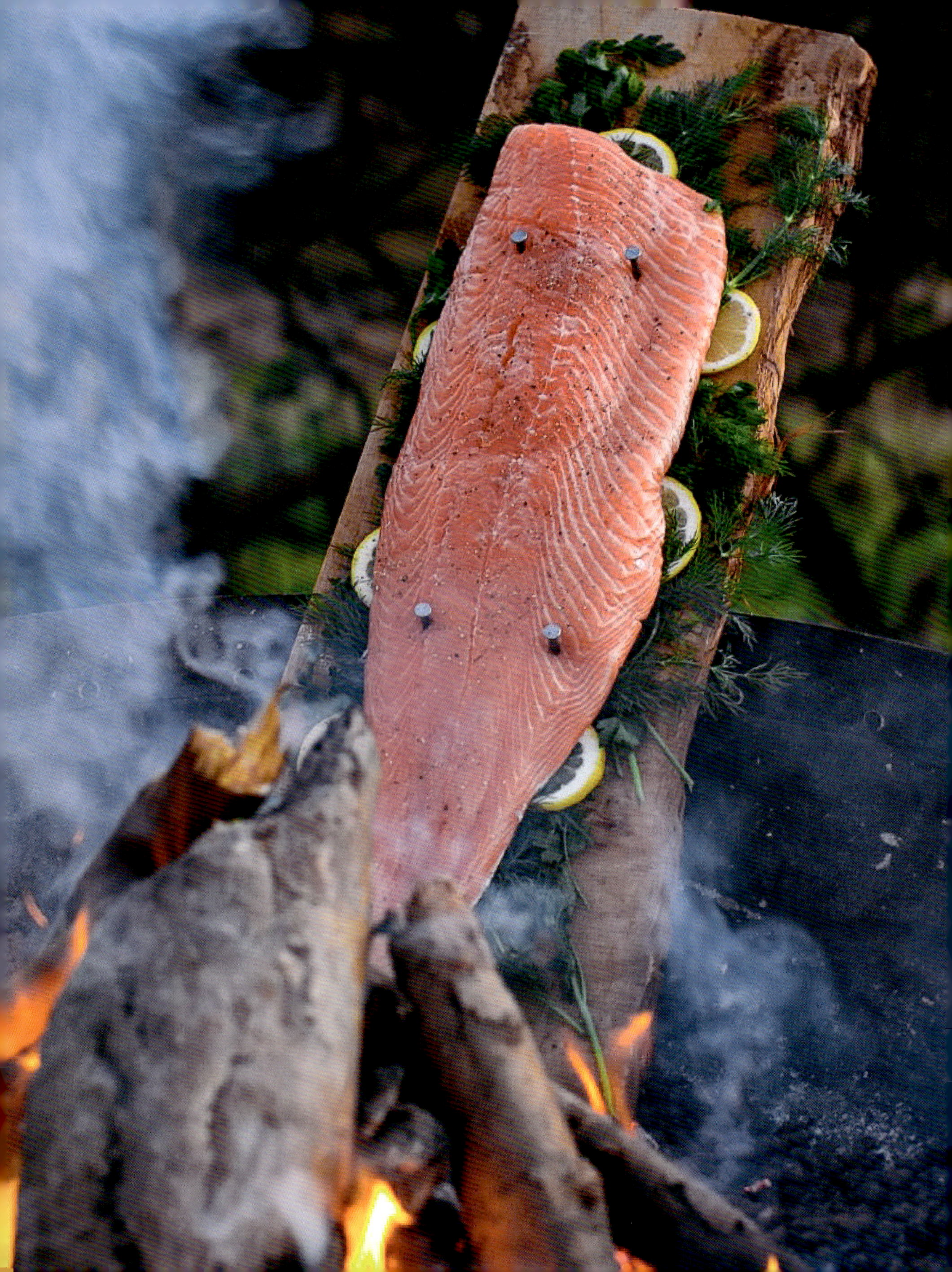

PLANK-SMOKED SALMON *with* LEMON, DILL & PARSLEY

Oak is the preferred wood for smoking fish as it releases flavourful compounds when heated and withstands the heat from a gradual cook. Barbecue a salmon fillet that is rich and deep in flavour every time with this Oak Cooking Plank recipe.

Prep time: 15 minutes
(plus oak plank soaking 8 hours)
Cooking time: Approx. 40-80 minutes
(depending on fillet size)
Recommended Heat: Medium

Handful of fresh dill sprigs
Handful of fresh parsley sprigs
1 lemon, sliced
1 unskinned side of salmon (about 800g) pin bones removed
Salt to taste
Lemon wedges, to serve

Serves 4

Build a fire using well-seasoned wood to one side of the bowl and set up the Oak Cooking Plank Frame on the opposite side (see pg. 30).

Spread the fresh dill and parsley sprigs evenly over the Oak Cooking Plank and top with the lemon slices.

Lay the salmon on top, skin-side down, season with salt and secure the fish with nails. Rest the fish against the Oak Cooking Plank Frame vertically inside the Kadai, fish facing the fire.

Leave to cook for 60 to 80 minutes, flipping the plank regularly to ensure even cooking.

The fish is ready when the meat flakes away from the skin easily and you can see moisture coming to the surface. The internal temperature should be 60°C. Serve with wedges of lemon for squeezing.

Equipment:
Oak Cooking Plank, Oak Cooking Plank Frame

DIRTY ONION & WILD GARLIC RISOTTO with CHIMICHURRI

This warming, seasonal dish is perfect to keep out the chill on a cool, spring day. We recommend making the stock a day or two in advance to develop its flavour and allow for an easier cook on the day.

Prep time: 15 minutes
(plus 4 hours stock cooking time)
Cooking time: 1 hour
Recommended Heat: Medium

For the stock:

5kg white onions

3 bulbs garlic

Drizzle of rapeseed oil

1 bottle red wine

4 litres water

For the risotto:

1kg red onions, whole and unpeeled

Drizzle of rapeseed oil

500g arborio risotto rice

Large bunch of fresh wild garlic, chopped

100g parmesan, finely grated

Salt and freshly ground black pepper to taste

3 servings of chimichurri sauce (see pg. 55)

Serves 10-12

To prepare the stock pre-heat the oven to 200°C. Cut onions and garlic in half, keeping the skins on. Lay them over a roasting tray and drizzle with oil.

Leave them in the oven for 1 hour, until they caramelise. Add the red wine, stirring the contents all together and return to the oven for 45 minutes. Transfer the content of the tray to a large pan and add the water. Simmer uncovered for 2 hours or until the liquid has reduced by half. Strain the content through a sieve and once cool store in the fridge until needed.

Dirty-cook (see pg. 33) the onions by placing them whole and unpeeled directly into the hot coals. Leave to cook for 10 minutes, until they are soft. Remove the onions from the coals and once cool, peel and slice them into chunks.

Place the Paella Pan onto the Grill. Add the oil followed by the dirty onions and fry them for 2 to 3 minutes. Add the rice to the Paella Pan and stir well to ensure all the grains are coated in oil. Add the stock, a ladleful at a time, stirring constantly. Bring the stock to a simmer and keep adding more as the rice cooks. This should take 30 to 40 minutes. Whilst the stock simmers, create the chimichurri sauce (see pg. 55).

When the rice is almost cooked, add the wild garlic to the Paella Pan with a further ladle of stock. Stir through until the garlic wilts. Add plenty of salt and pepper to taste and the parmesan. Serve with a dressing of the chimichurri sauce.

Equipment:

Paella Pan, Ladle

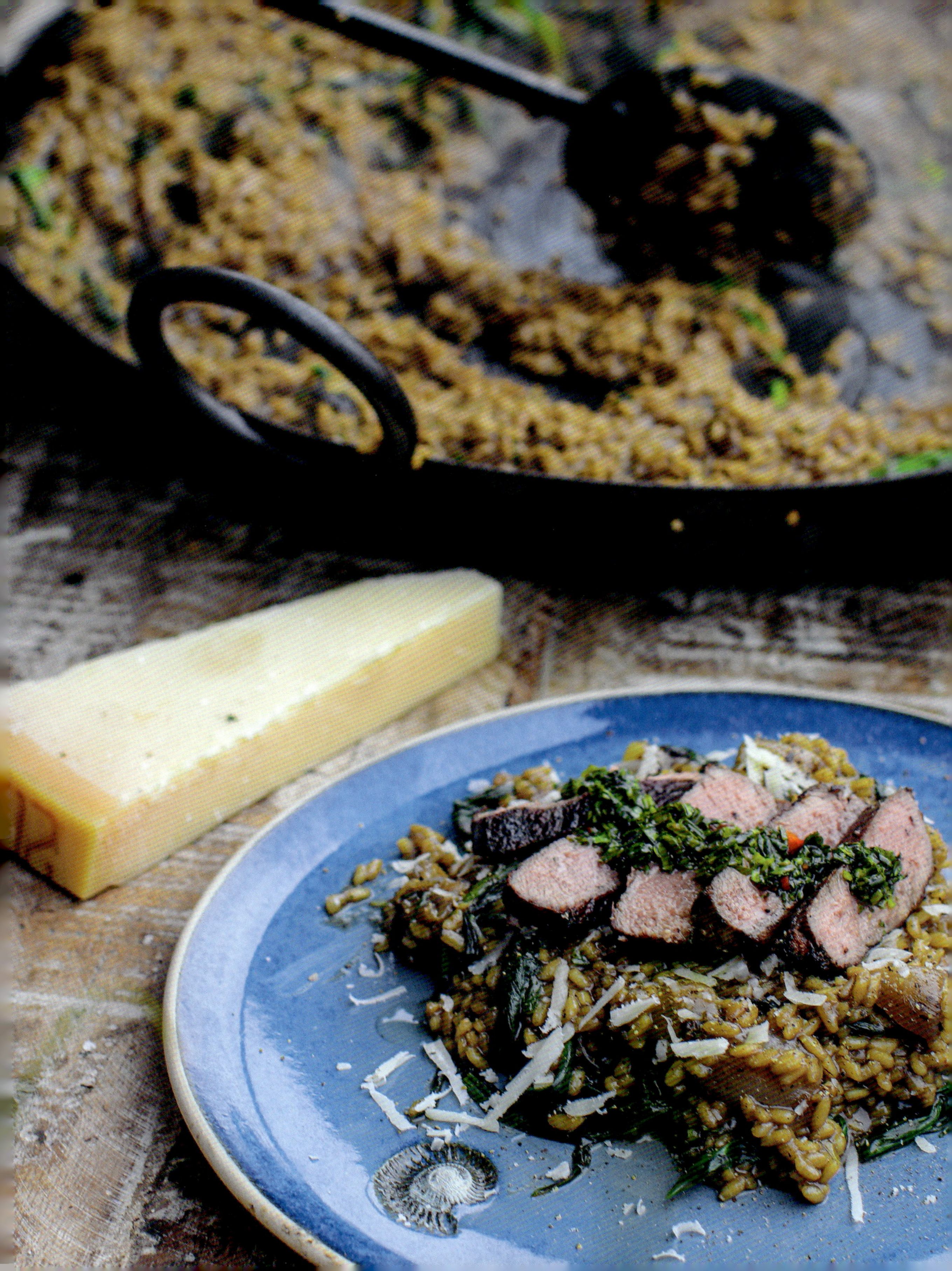

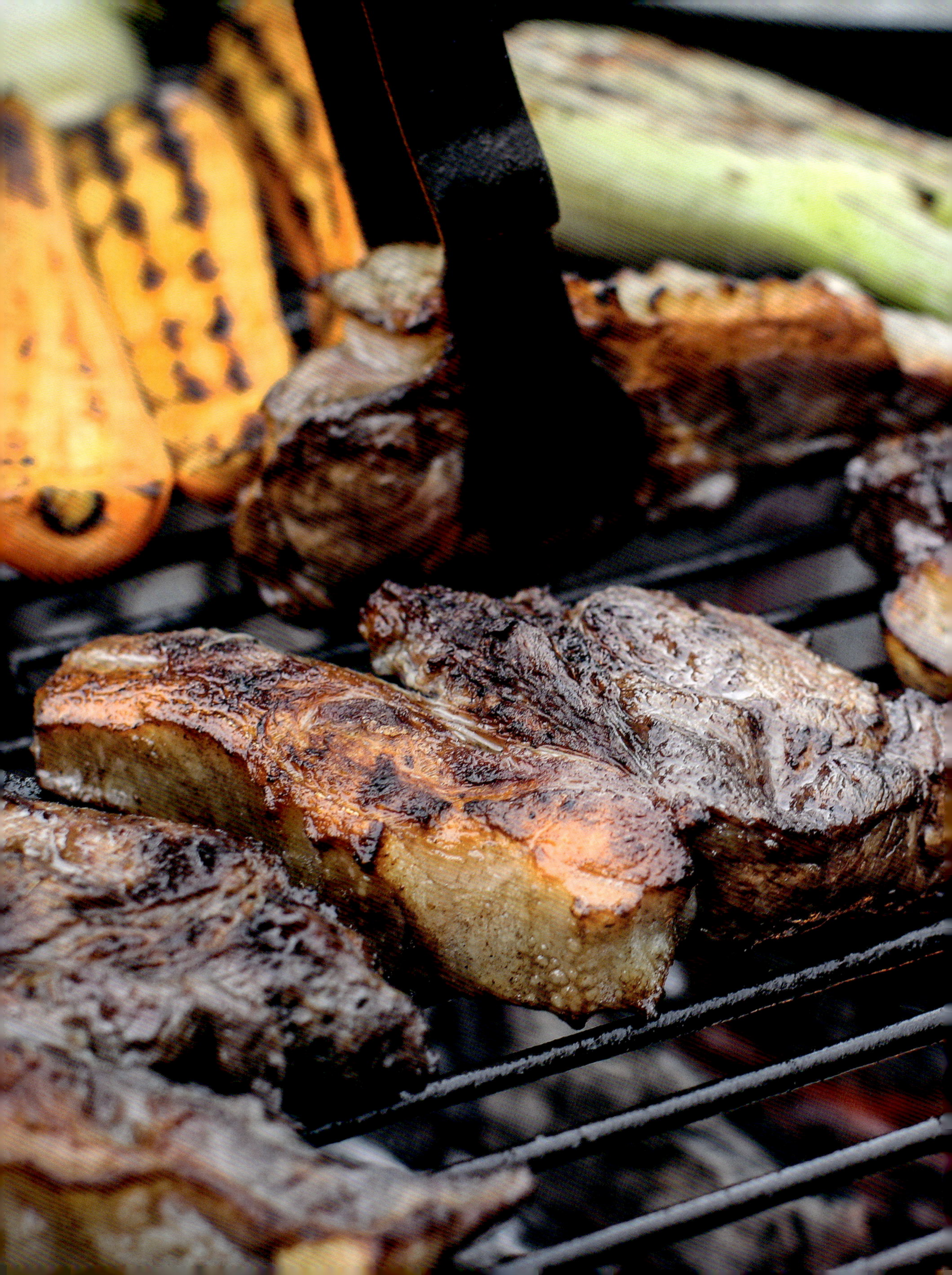

Feeding family & friends

Barbecuing for us is all about sharing, entertaining and experiencing the great outdoors with both friends and family. Try these inspirational recipes to create memorable moments as you cook something truly special. From a traditional Sunday roast to a more adventurous curry, cooking on a Kadai together is what it's all about.

TRADITIONAL SUNDAY ROAST BEEF

Cooking a whole Sunday roast on a Kadai is easier than you may think. Moving your roast and all the trimmings to the barbecue, makes this family feast far more sociable and relaxed. During sunny afternoons, revel in the garden creating this hearty classic.

Prep time: 15 minutes
(plus 30 minutes resting before cooking)
Cooking time: 2-2 hours 30 minutes
Recommended Heat: Medium

1.5kg beef rump cap

For all the trimmings:

Drizzle of vegetable oil

Sprig of fresh rosemary

200g Chantenay carrots, par-boiled for 7 minutes

200g Maris Piper potatoes, peeled, cut into large chunks and par-boiled for 10 minutes

300g tenderstem broccoli

Salt and freshly ground black pepper to taste

Serves 4

Trim the fat on the rump cap so there is a ½ cm thick even layer. Reserve the trimming for later.
Score diamonds on the remaining rump fat and generously season with salt and pepper. Leave the rump to sit at room temperature for 30 minutes and prepare the Kadai. Place the rump on the Grill on an indirect heat, fat side up and cover with the Kadai Lid. Turn the rump occasionally whilst it cooks. Once the beef has reached an optimum temperature of 60°C, remove from the Grill and transfer to a chopping board.

Put the large Skillet on the Grill and leave to heat up. Add a splash of vegetable oil and trimmed beef fat. Render the fat down and add a sprig of rosemary, the par-boiled carrots, and potatoes. Cover with the Kadai Lid and leave to cook for approximately 30 minutes, turning the vegetables occasionally.

When the food is almost ready to serve, cover the broccoli in oil, season and lay on the Grill Trays, leave to char for 5 minutes.

Put the beef back on the Grill, fat-side down for a few minutes to heat through. Carve the beef and serve with the barbecued vegetables.

Equipment:

Kadai Lid, Chopping Board, Cooking Bowl, Set of 3 Skillets, Set of 3 Grill Trays

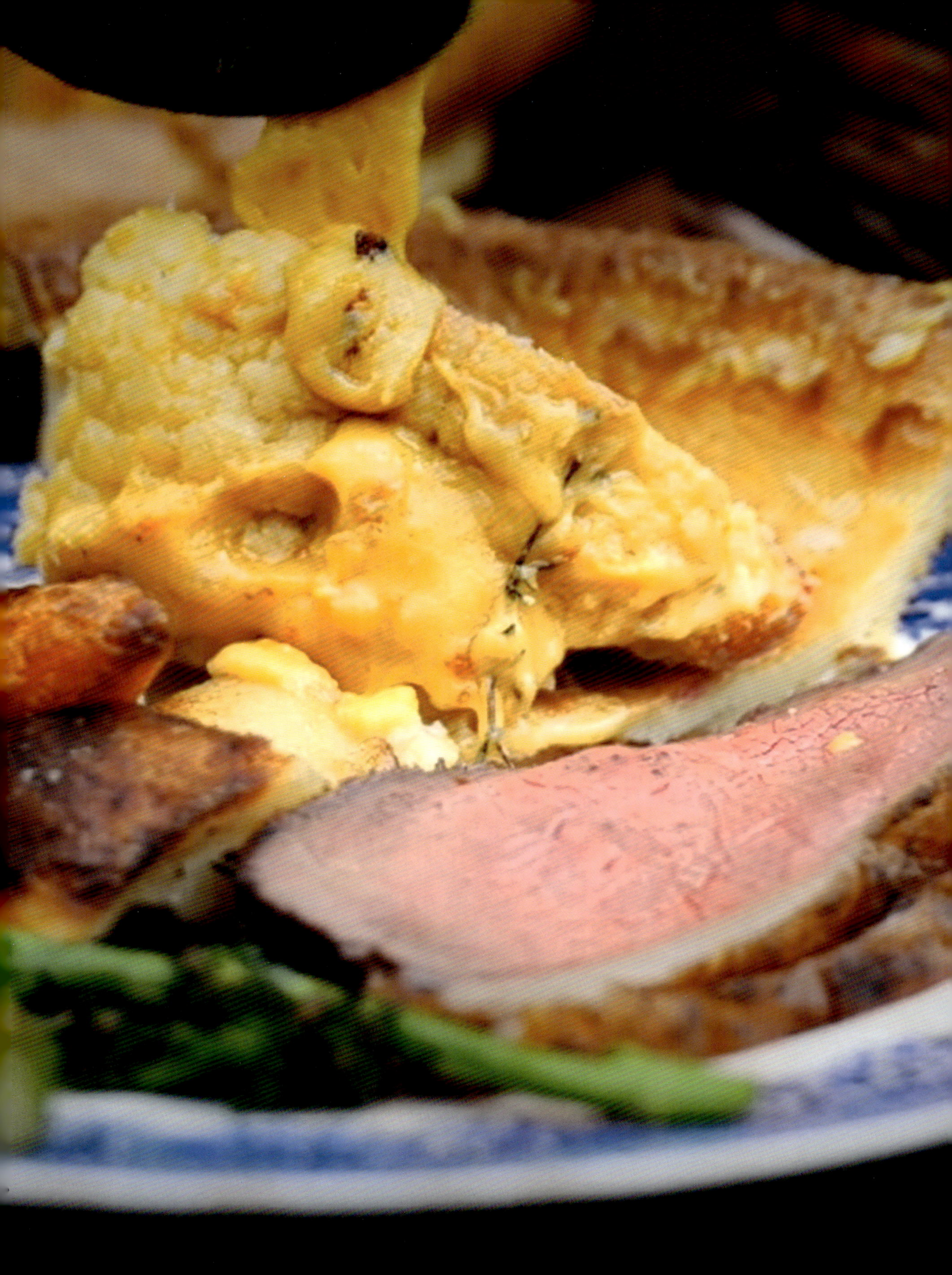

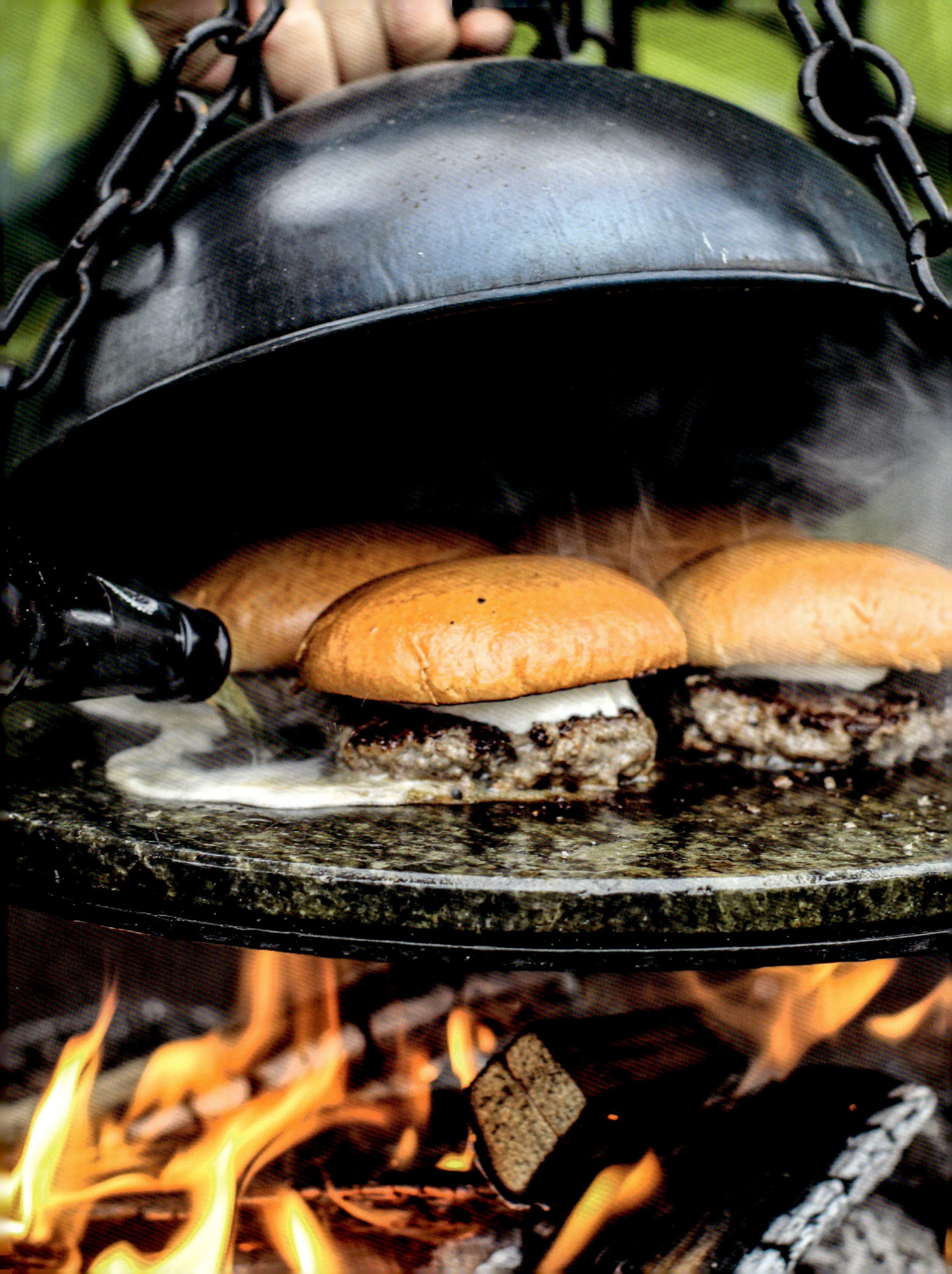

BOAR-SOME BURGERS *with* DIRTY APPLE SAUCE

Ideal for sizzling on the Stone Griddle Plate, these smashed boar-mince burgers are infused with a smoky beer aroma. Accompanied by a sweet and tangy 'dirty-cooked' apple sauce, your taste buds will be tingling with the distinctive flavour of this sensational combination.

Prep time: 10 minutes
Cooking time: Approx. 40 minutes
Recommended Heat: High

For the sauce:

8 Bramley apples
75g brown sugar
50ml apple cider vinegar
A handful of fresh sage leaves

For the burgers:

4 brioche buns, halved
500g wild boar mince (at least 20% fat)
100g mozzarella, sliced
A splash of beer (or water)
Sea salt and freshly ground black pepper to taste

Serves 4

To make the sauce, place the apples around the edges of a prepared Kadai. Leave them to bake slowly in the residual heat for 15 minutes until soft and gooey. Using heat-proof Gloves, carefully remove the apples and leave to cool before squeezing the flesh into a Skillet. Add the sugar, vinegar and sage leaves.

Put the Grill over the fire, place the Skillet on the bars, and bring everything up to a slow simmer.

Cook for 10 minutes stirring occasionally, then set aside. Heat the Stone Griddle on the Cooking Tripod (see pg. 34). Divide the mince into 4 equal balls. Once the Stone Griddle is hot, add the balls of mince, quickly season, and use the back of the Barbecue Tool to firmly 'smash' the balls down into patties.

Leave the patties to cook for approximately 2 minutes as a crust builds up, then flip. Toast off the buns by placing them directly on the Grill.

Load each patty with mozzarella slices and place half the bun on top. Splash the Stone Griddle with beer and cover with the Cookware Lid; leave to cook. Whilst the buns steam and the cheese melts, 'load' the bottom half of the buns with apple sauce.

Once the burgers are ready, stack all the parts together and serve immediately.

Equipment:

Set of 3 Skillets, Cooking Tripod, Stone Griddle Plate, Barbecue Tool, Cookware Lid

GOAT CURRY

A taste sensation, this firecracker curry is the perfect dish to try on your Kadai. For generations Kadais have been used as huge cooking pots for large celebrations and festivals. Going back to our roots, this Indian-inspired curry is one of our favourite recipes delivering big on flavour and aroma.

Prep time: 40 minutes
Cooking time: 1 hour 40 minutes
Recommended Heat: Medium

For the curry:
Drizzle of vegetable oil
4 large white onions, finely sliced
2 tbsp garlic paste
2 tbsp ginger paste
400g tin chopped tomatoes
2 large tomatoes, chopped
600g diced goat
1 tbsp chilli powder
2 scotch bonnet chillies, deseeded and finely chopped
2 tbsp cumin seeds
2 tbsp garam masala
2 tbsp coriander powder
2 tbsp curry paste
300ml lamb stock

For the rice:
500g long grain rice
2 tsp turmeric
2 tsp cumin seeds
4 cardamom pods

TIP: For a complete authentic experience, try serving on a banana leaf plate with naan bread.

Serves 4

Heat the vegetable oil in the Cooking Bowl on the Cooking Tripod (see pg. 34).

Add the onions and allow them to brown and soften. Remove from the heat and add to a blender with the garlic and ginger paste. Blitz into a smooth purée and put in a bowl to one side.

Add the tin of chopped tomatoes to the blender and make a smooth passata and put in a bowl to one side. Add the 2 tomatoes to the blender and blitz into a fine salsa. Place the Cooking Bowl back onto the heat and add more vegetable oil. Add in the goat, chilli and all the spices and fry until browned.

Add in the onion purée and curry paste to the goat, mixing well. Pour in the tomato passata and salsa, followed by the stock.

Stir the mixture well and allow to cook over a high heat for about 90 minutes until the meat is tender, the sauce has thickened and the stock is absorbed.

To make the rice, wash it under the tap to remove excess starch. Add the rice, turmeric, cardamom pods and cumin seeds to the Roasting Tin. Cover with water to the top of the rice and mix everything together.

Place next to the hot coals in your Kadai and cook for 15 to 20 minutes, checking regularly that the rice has enough liquid to continue cooking without burning.

Serve the curry over the rice and enjoy a traditional taste of India.

Equipment:
Cooking Tripod, Cooking Bowl, and Roasting Tin

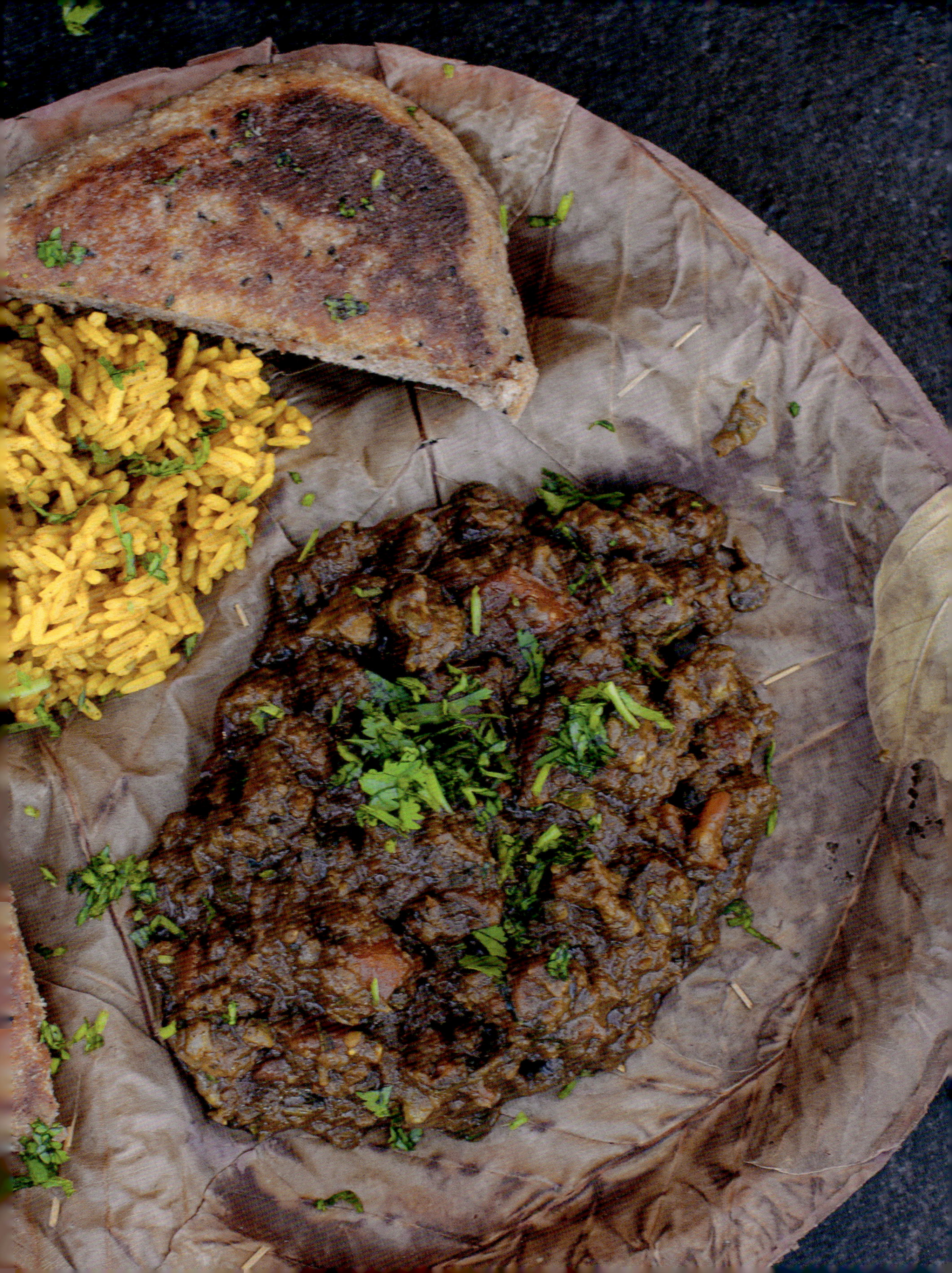

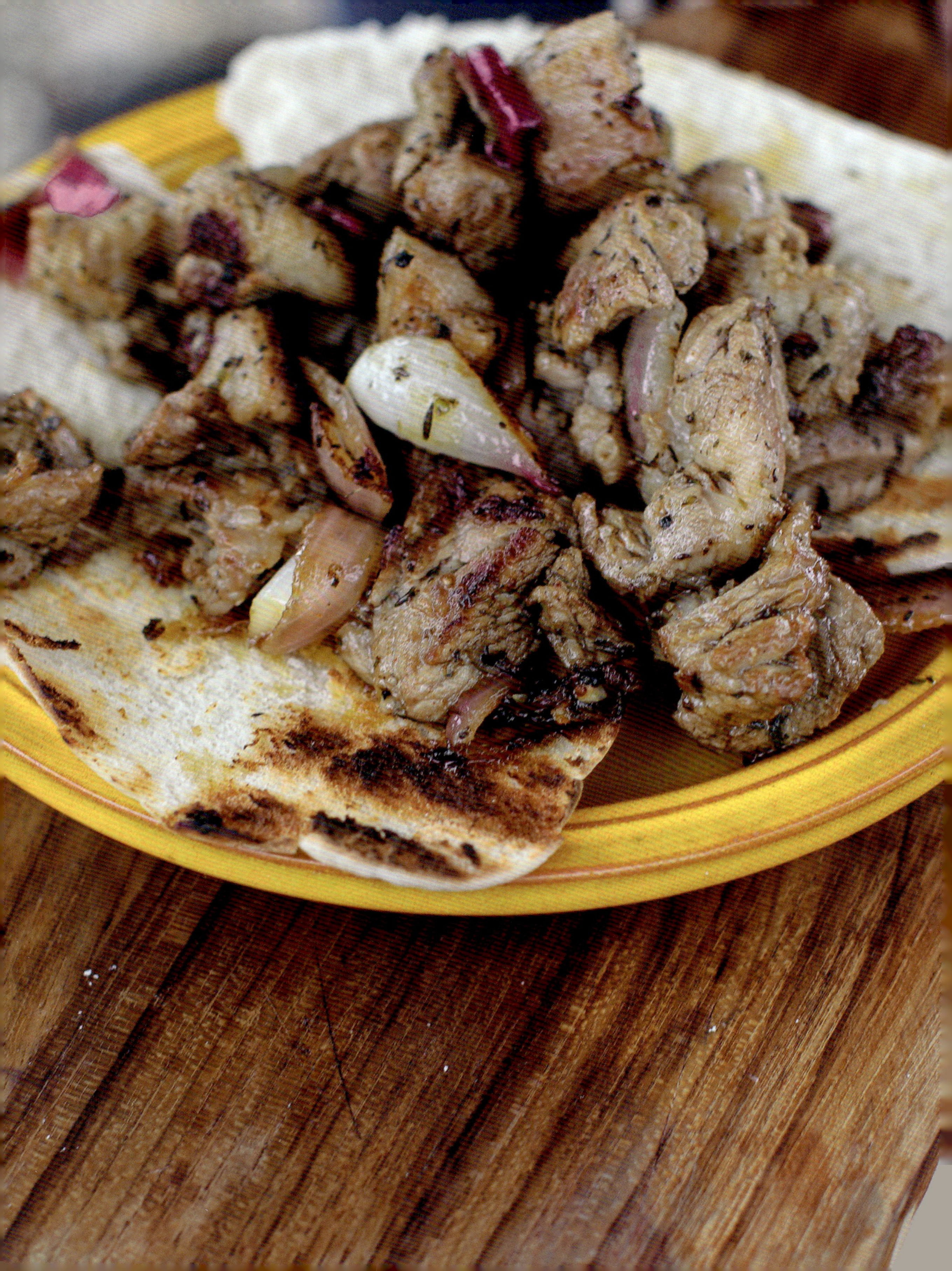

LAMB SOUVLAKI

Lamb Souvlaki is a traditional Greek dish, which comes on Skewers. Either prepare the night before and serve with a fresh Greek salad for lunch or have as part of a sharing platter for dinner. Bring the classic pairing of lamb, tzatziki and pitta to your barbecue with this recipe.

Prep time: 15 minutes (plus minimum 4 hours marinating time)
Cooking time: 30 minutes
Recommended Heat: Medium

5-6 tbsp olive oil

2 garlic cloves, crushed

1 lemon, juiced

1 tsp dried oregano

Small handful of fresh thyme leaves, chopped

½ tsp sweet paprika

1kg boneless lamb (leg or shoulder), cut into 3cm chunks

2 red onions, cut into 3cm pieces

Freshly ground black pepper to taste

For the tzatziki:

500g Greek natural yoghurt

2 tbsp olive oil

2 garlic cloves, crushed

1 cucumber

1-2 tbsp red wine vinegar, to taste

Salt and freshly ground black pepper to taste

For serving:

6 pitta breads

Drizzle of olive oil

1 tsp dried oregano

Serves 4-6

For the marinade, put the olive oil, garlic, lemon juice, herbs and spices in a small bowl. Whisk all the ingredients to combine. Add the meat and chopped onions and mix well to coat. Cover the bowl, chill and marinate for at least 4 hours. It's best to leave the lamb souvlaki marinating overnight.

Prepare the tzatziki by adding the yoghurt, olive oil and garlic, into a mixing bowl and combining. Remove the seeds and skin of the cucumber and grate the flesh into kitchen roll and squeeze out the excess water. Season with salt and pepper and leave aside for 10 minutes. Wrap the grated cucumber in a tea towel and squeeze well to remove any further excess water. Stir the cucumber into the yoghurt, with red wine vinegar and salt to taste.

Take 8 to 12 Skewers. Lift the marinated lamb and onion out of the bowl and thread onto the Skewers, alternating regularly. Place the Skewers on the rack and cook over the hot Grill for 10 to 15 minutes, turning occasionally. Add the pitta breads to the Grill and toast for a few minutes or until they have browned.

Remove the lamb skewers from the Grill, sprinkle with a small amount of dried oregano, and serve in the toasted pitta breads with a good helping of tzatziki.

This recipe pairs perfectly with our halloumi grilled salad (see pg. 83).

Equipment:
Set of Skewers

CHORIZO STEW

We bring to you a deliciously warming and hearty Spanish stew with bacon, chorizo and butter beans. The trick is to add orange juice and zest, for a subtle, citrus touch that will get everyone wanting to know what the secret ingredient is.

Prep time: 15 minutes
Cooking time: 25 minutes
Recommended Heat: Medium

2 oranges
3 tbsp olive oil
1 large Spanish onion, finely sliced
100g thick-cut fatty bacon, cut into lardons
225g cooking chorizo, skinned and sliced
2 garlic cloves, finely chopped
2 bay leaves
1 tbsp sweet paprika
200g tinned chopped tomatoes
150ml chicken stock or water
400g butter beans, drained and rinsed
100ml double cream

Serves 4

Peel the zest from the oranges in strips using a potato peeler and then cut them lengthways into julienne (long very thin strips). Squeeze the juice from the oranges and discard the pithy white shells.

Heat the olive oil in the Paella Pan, add the finely sliced onion and the bacon, and cook until they are a lovely golden colour.

Add the chorizo, garlic, bay leaves and paprika. Sauté for a few minutes before adding the tomatoes, stock, orange juice and slivers of peel.

Simmer for 5 minutes, then add the beans and cream. Simmer for a further 3 minutes before serving, (remembering to remove the bay leaves before eating).

Equipment:
Paella Pan

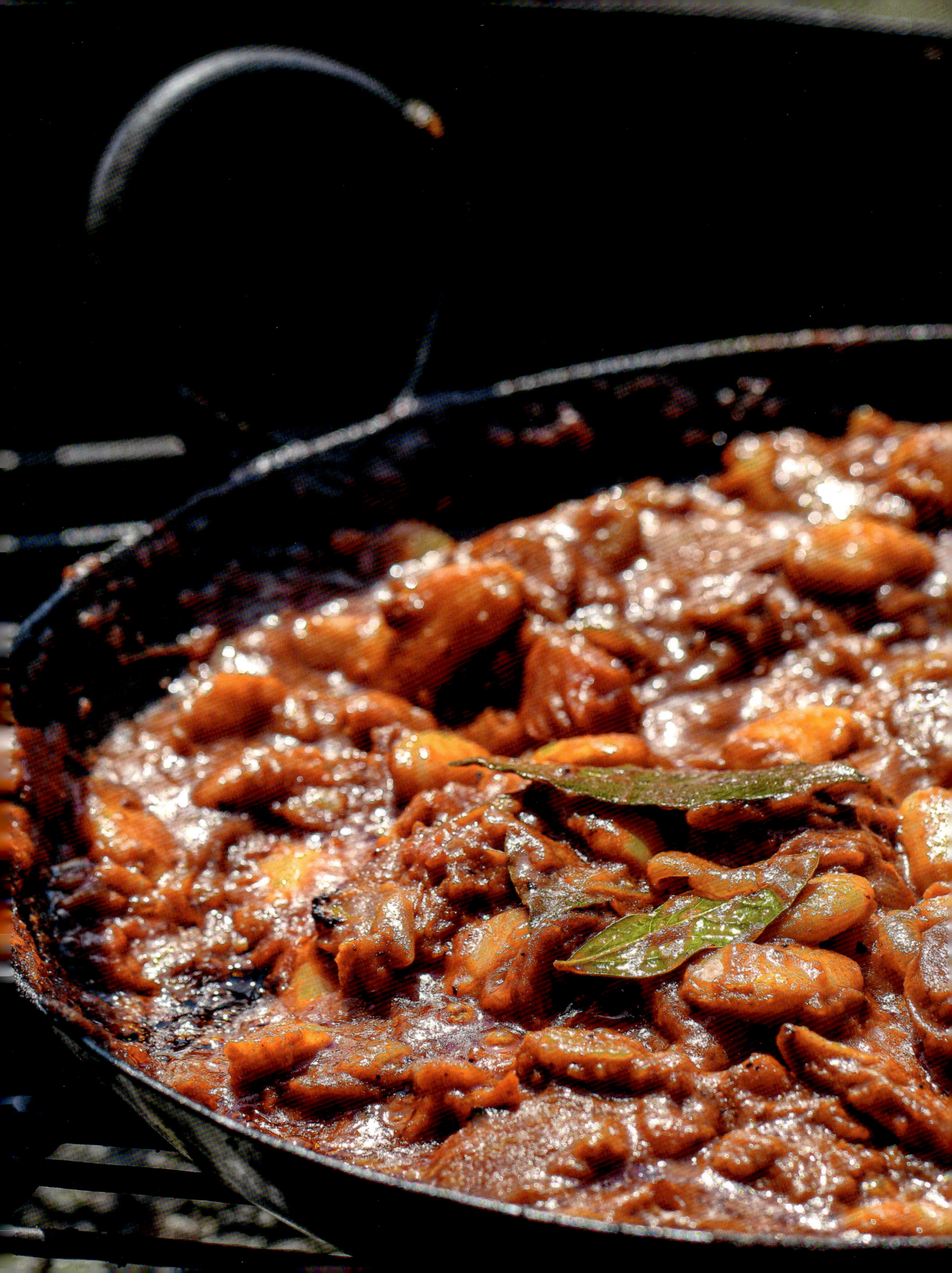

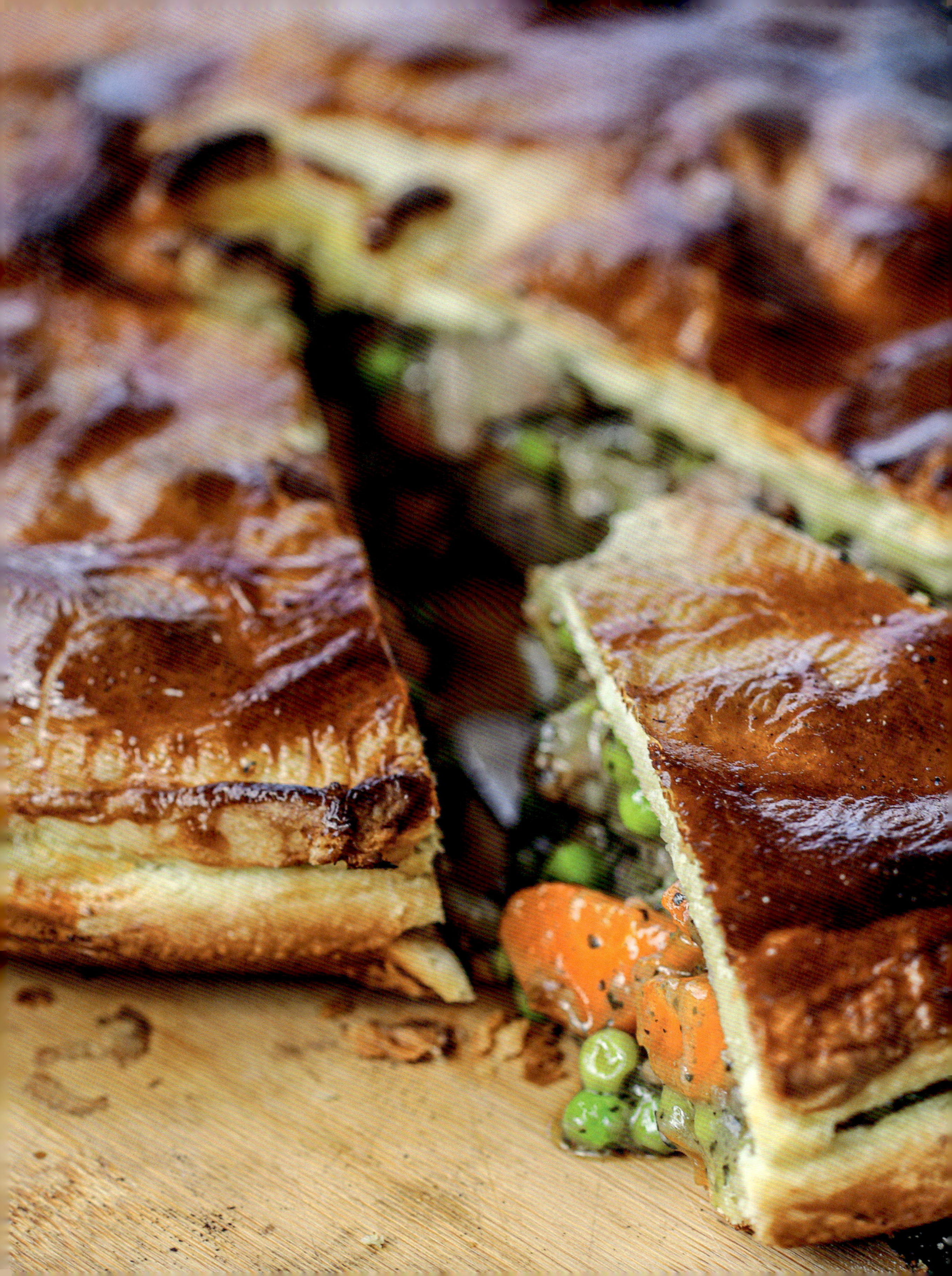

LAMB & MINT PIE

The smoky, wood flavour from the Wood Fired Oven works incredibly well with the rich and refreshing lamb, pea and mint filling of this pie. Relish in cold days outdoors, whilst you tuck into this wholesome and warming dish - comfort food at its finest.

Prep time: 20 minutes
Cooking time: 1 hour 20 minutes
Recommended Heat: Medium/High

Drizzle of olive oil
1 white onion, chopped
1kg boneless lamb (leg or shoulder), diced
2 carrots, chopped
1 courgette, chopped
200g peas
3½ tbsp mint sauce
750ml lamb stock
1 knob of butter
700g short crust pastry, ready-made
1 medium free-range egg

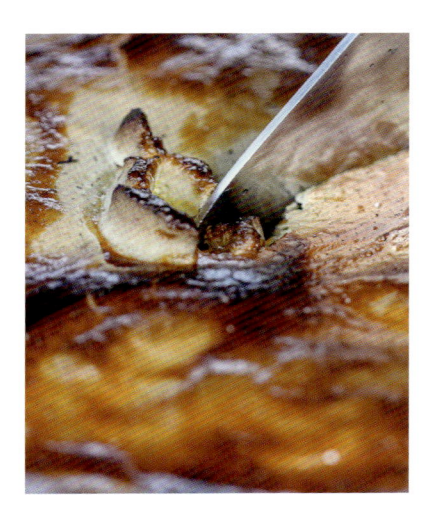

Serves 4

Drizzle the oil into the Frying Pan over a medium heat. Add the onion and lamb to the Frying Pan and allow them to brown. Add the carrots, courgette, peas and mint sauce. Stir well to combine all the ingredients.

Pour the lamb stock into the Frying Pan, making sure to cover all contents in the pan. Allow the mixture to simmer over a medium heat for 20 to 30 minutes, or until the lamb is cooked through and the vegetables have softened. Remove from the heat and decant the pie filling into a heat-proof bowl to set aside.

Wash and dry the Frying Pan to use in the next step. Grease the inside of the Frying Pan with butter and roll out the pastry. Line the bottom and sides of the Frying Pan with the rolled-out pastry, and pour in the pie filling, spreading evenly. Add the pastry top by stretching more pastry over the top of the Frying Pan and pinch it together with the pastry base to 'close' the pie. Score the edges with a fork.

Whisk the egg in a cup and brush the egg-wash over the top and sides of the pie.

Get the Wood Fired Oven up to a high temperature, about 200°C (see pg. 37). Place the Frying Pan into the Wood Fired Oven, handle out, and bake the pie for approximately 1 hour. Keep checking the oven temperature and regularly top up the fire with wood. Remove from the Wood Fired Oven once the pastry has turned golden brown.

Serve with some creamy mashed potatoes and a rich gravy for the perfect winter warmer.

Equipment:
Frying Pan, Wood Fired Oven

CHICKEN & WILD GARLIC PIE with a CHEDDAR & HAZELNUT CRUMBLE TOPPING

An elegant spring pie made with wild garlic, chicken, and buttermilk, which is finished with a cheddar cheese crumble topping and baked to perfection in the Wood Fired Oven.

Prep time: 15 minutes
Cooking time: 1 hour 40 minutes
Recommended Heat: High

For the filling:
Drizzle of rapeseed oil
12 boneless chicken fillets
50g unsalted butter
4 leeks, thinly sliced
30g plain flour
175ml dry white wine
500ml chicken stock
250ml buttermilk
1 bunch of fresh wild garlic and 50ml water, blitzed into a purée
Pinch freshly grated nutmeg
Sea salt and freshly ground black pepper to taste

For the crumble:
100g plain flour
100g salted butter, cubed
60g mature cheddar cheese, grated
30g parmesan, grated
35g hazelnuts, chopped
1 tbsp thyme leaves, finely chopped

Serves 4

Pour the oil into the Cooking Bowl and attach to the Cooking Tripod over a lit Kadai (see pg. 34). Add the chicken thigh fillets and fry to a deep golden colour. This may need to be done in 2 batches. Remove from the dish and season.

Melt the butter in the Cooking Bowl and add the leeks. Cook them until soft but not coloured. Stir in the flour and cook for a couple of minutes, then gradually stir in the wine, and cook for 2 more minutes. Return the chicken to the Cooking Bowl with the chicken stock and simmer for 30 minutes until the liquid has reduced. Add the buttermilk and simmer for another 20 minutes until the meat is falling apart and the sauce has thickened. Add the wild garlic purée, a grating of nutmeg and plenty of seasoning to taste.

Transfer the filling to a medium Skillet and leave to cool. To make the crumble topping, rub the flour and butter together in a bowl. Add the rest of the ingredients and mix well. Spread the crumble evenly over the top of the pie and set to one side. Heat the Wood Fired Oven to approximately 190°C using well-seasoned wood (see pg. 37). Slide the pie into the oven and bake for 30 to 40 minutes until the top is golden brown and the filling is cooked all the way through.

Equipment:

Cooking Bowl, Cooking Tripod, Set of 3 Skillets, Wood Fired Oven

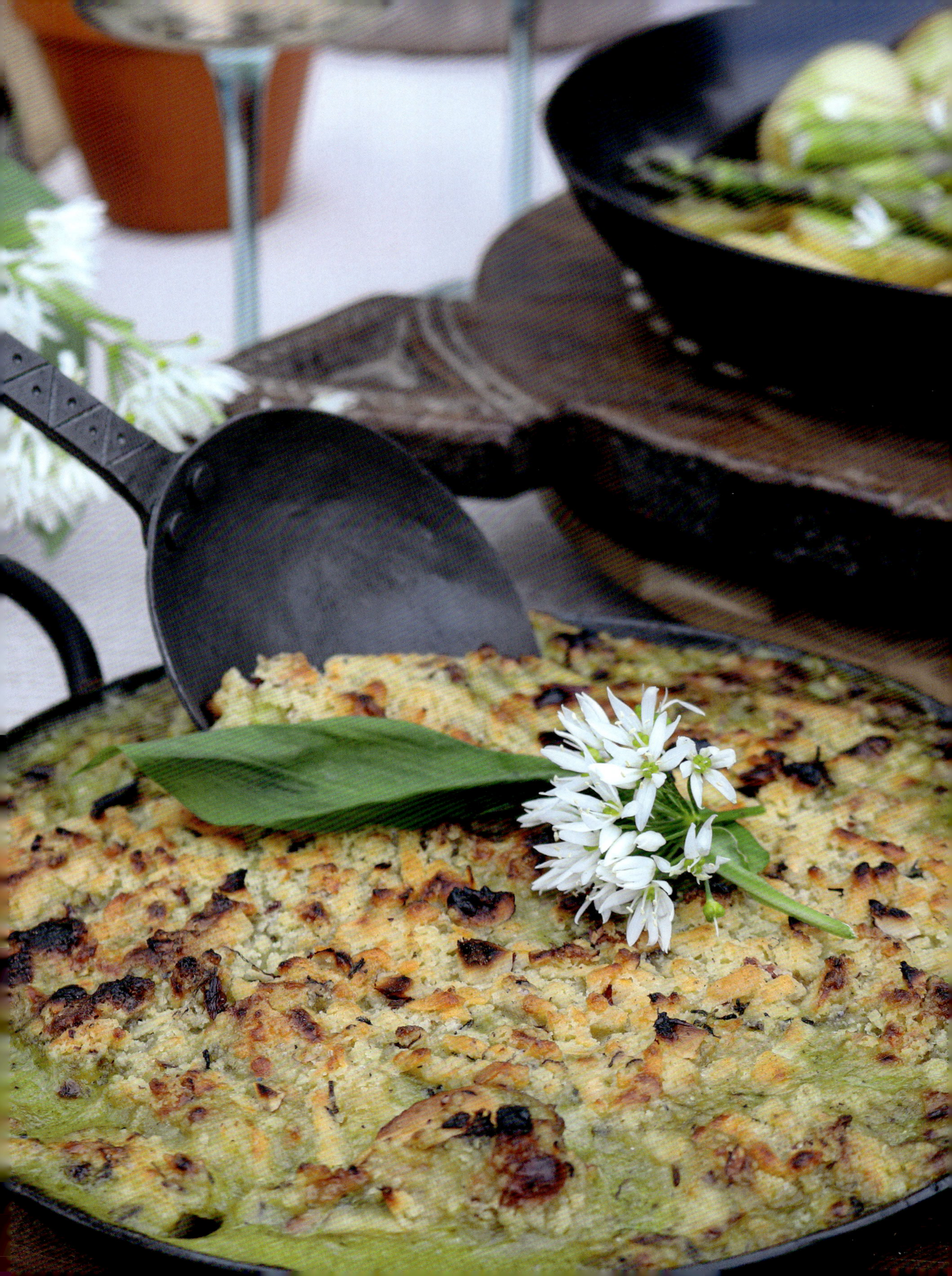

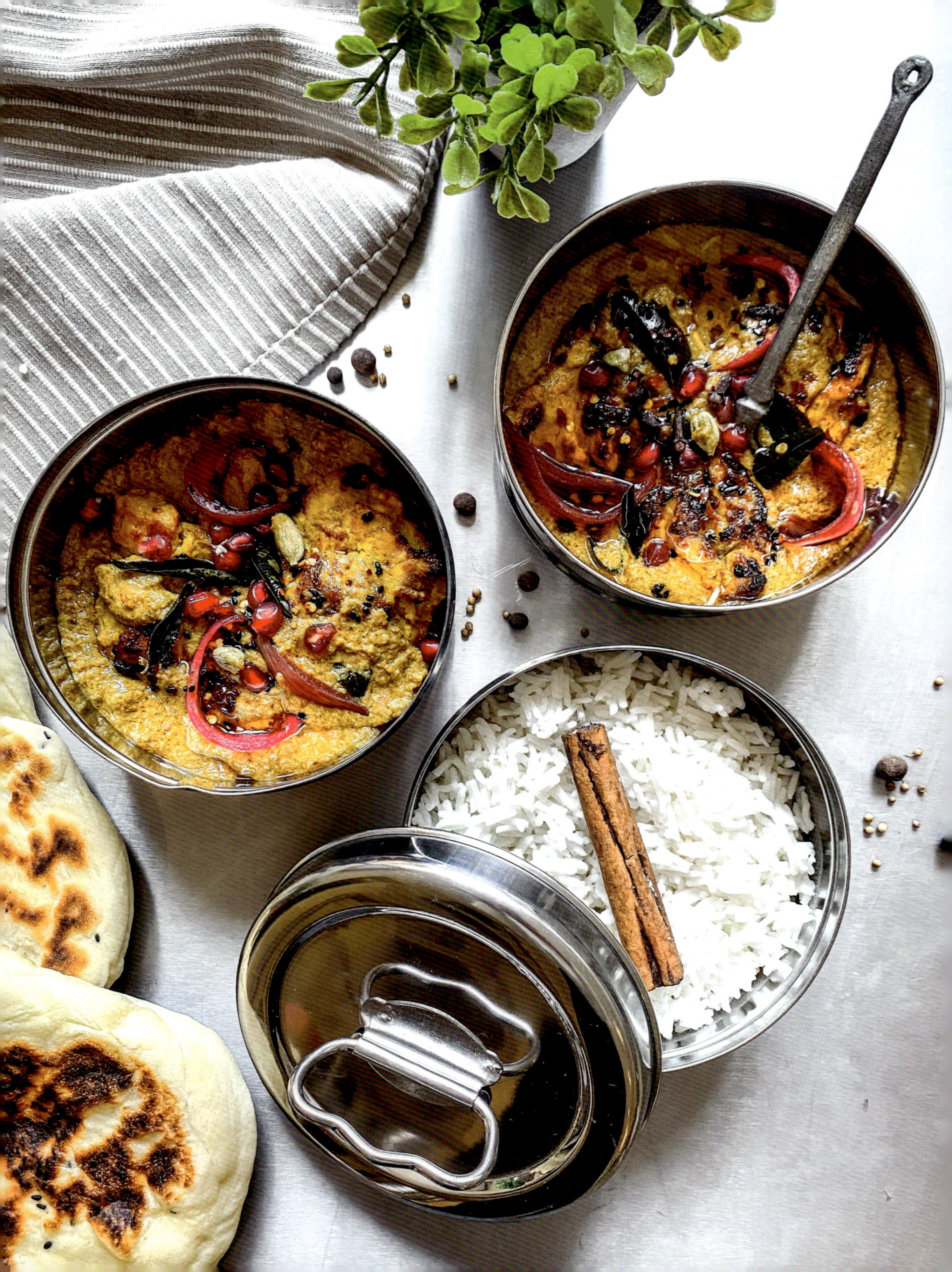

SRI LANKAN CURRY

This classic curry is creamy, aromatic and bursting with spice, which will transport you to the sunny beaches of Sri Lanka.

Prep time: 10 minutes
(plus overnight marinating time)
Cooking time: 35 minutes
Recommended Heat: High

For the chicken marinade:

8 large boneless chicken thigh fillets
2 tbsp natural full-fat yoghurt
2-3cm piece fresh ginger, finely grated
2 garlic cloves, crushed
1 tsp turmeric
1 tsp ground cumin
2 tsp ground coriander
½ tsp ground cloves
1 tsp freshly grated nutmeg
½ tsp chilli powder
1 lemon, juiced

For the Sri Lankan spice mix:

2 tsp coriander seeds
1 tsp cumin seeds
1 tsp fennel seeds
1 small cinnamon stick
½ tsp fenugreek seeds
½ tsp seeds from green cardamom pods
½ tsp yellow mustard seeds
½ tsp black peppercorns
2 dried red Kashmiri chillies

For the curry base:

1 tbsp coconut oil
10 curry leaves
1 medium white onion, chopped
2-3cm piece fresh ginger, finely grated
3 garlic cloves, finely chopped
1 tbsp Sri Lankan spice mix
2 tsp garam masala
1 tsp turmeric
500ml water
400ml coconut milk

Serves 4

Slice the chicken thigh fillets into medium-sized chunks. For the marinade, blend the yoghurt, ginger, garlic, spices and lemon juice in a bowl; add the chicken and mix well. Cover, refrigerate, and leave to marinate for at least 2 hours (overnight is best).

For the Sri Lankan spice mix, add all the spices to a mortar; grind with the pestle. Store in an airtight jar. Thread the chicken pieces onto the Skewers and place on the rack over the fire, turning regularly to ensure even cooking. Remove the chicken from the heat once cooked, about 20 to 25 minutes.

Heat the coconut oil in the Cooking Bowl on the Cooking Tripod (see pg. 34) until melted. Add the curry leaves and cook for 1 minute before adding the onion, stirring occasionally.

Once the onion is soft and a deep caramel colour, add the ginger and garlic and cook for a further 3 minutes. Add the spice mix, garam masala and turmeric.

Remove the chicken from the Skewers, straight into the Cooking Bowl with the onion and spices. Stir to coat the chicken in the spices and simmer for about 5 minutes. Add the water and coconut milk and leave to simmer for 30 minutes. Then serve.

Equipment:
Set of Skewers, Cooking Tripod, Cooking Bowl.

CHICKEN WINGS *with* BLUE CHEESE DIP

Calling all cheese lovers: try something new with these blue cheese chicken wings, the perfect addition to any barbecue sharing platter. Dip these hot and crispy wings into a cool and tangy cheese dip as an unusual and indulgent treat.

Prep time: 10 minutes
Cooking time: 30 minutes
Recommended Heat: Medium

For the dip:
25g blue cheese
½ lemon, juiced
Handful of fresh chives, finely chopped
5 tbsp sour cream

For the wings:
1kg chicken wings
1 tbsp rapeseed oil
Salt to taste
1 garlic clove, finely chopped
1 tsp paprika
1 tbsp cider vinegar
2 good shakes of hot sauce (we like Tabasco)
25g salted butter, melted

Serves 4

Put the blue cheese, lemon juice, chives and sour cream into a food processor and blend until smooth.

Season the chicken wings well with oil and salt.

In the Cooking Bowl, combine the garlic, paprika, cider vinegar, hot sauce and melted butter. Then add the wings and toss to coat.

Add the wings to the hot Grill Trays, turning occasionally until cooked through, with no pink showing. This should take about 15 to 20 minutes.

Serve the wings with the blue cheese dip on the side.

Equipment:
Cooking Bowl, Set of 3 Grill Trays

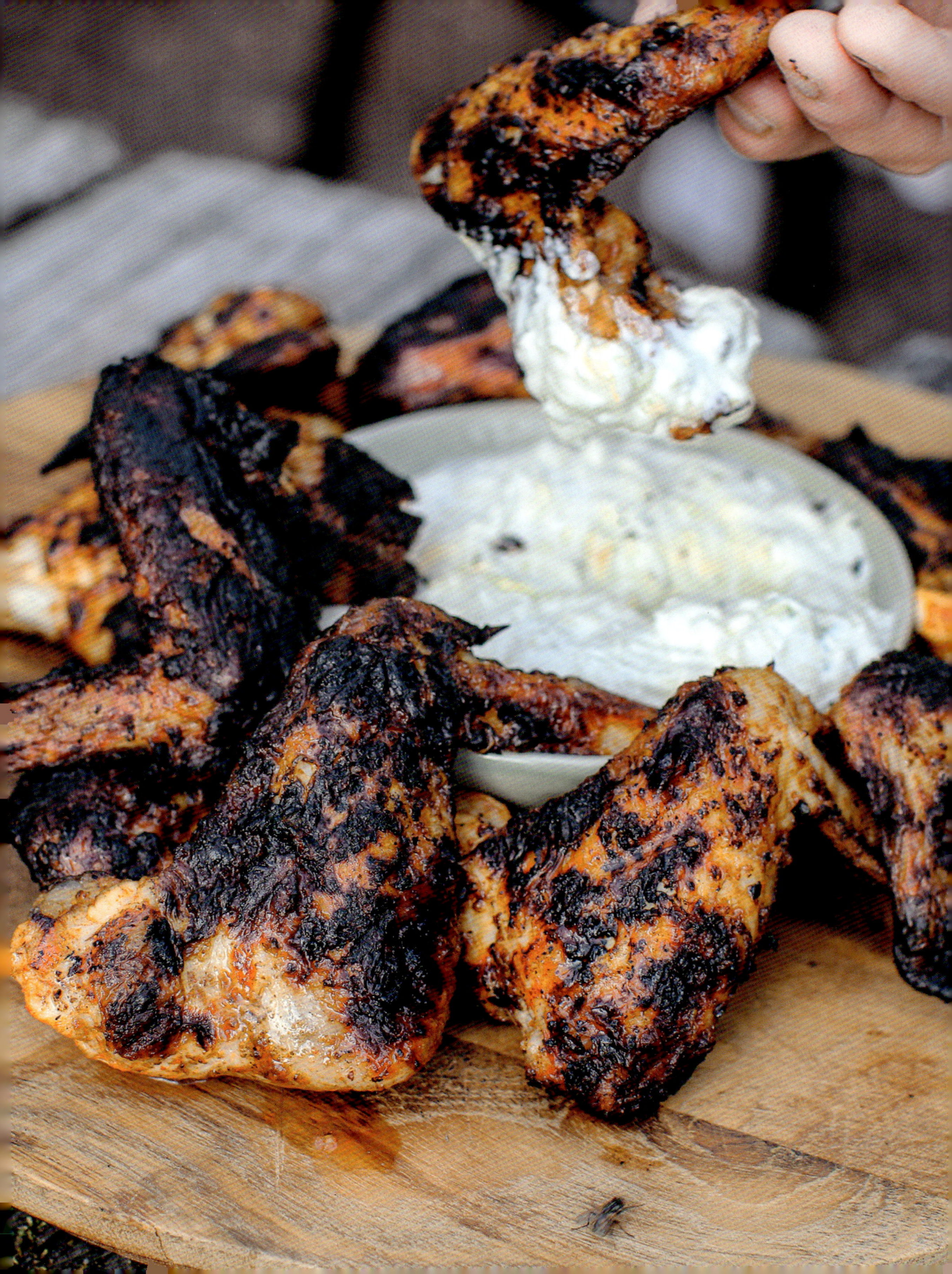

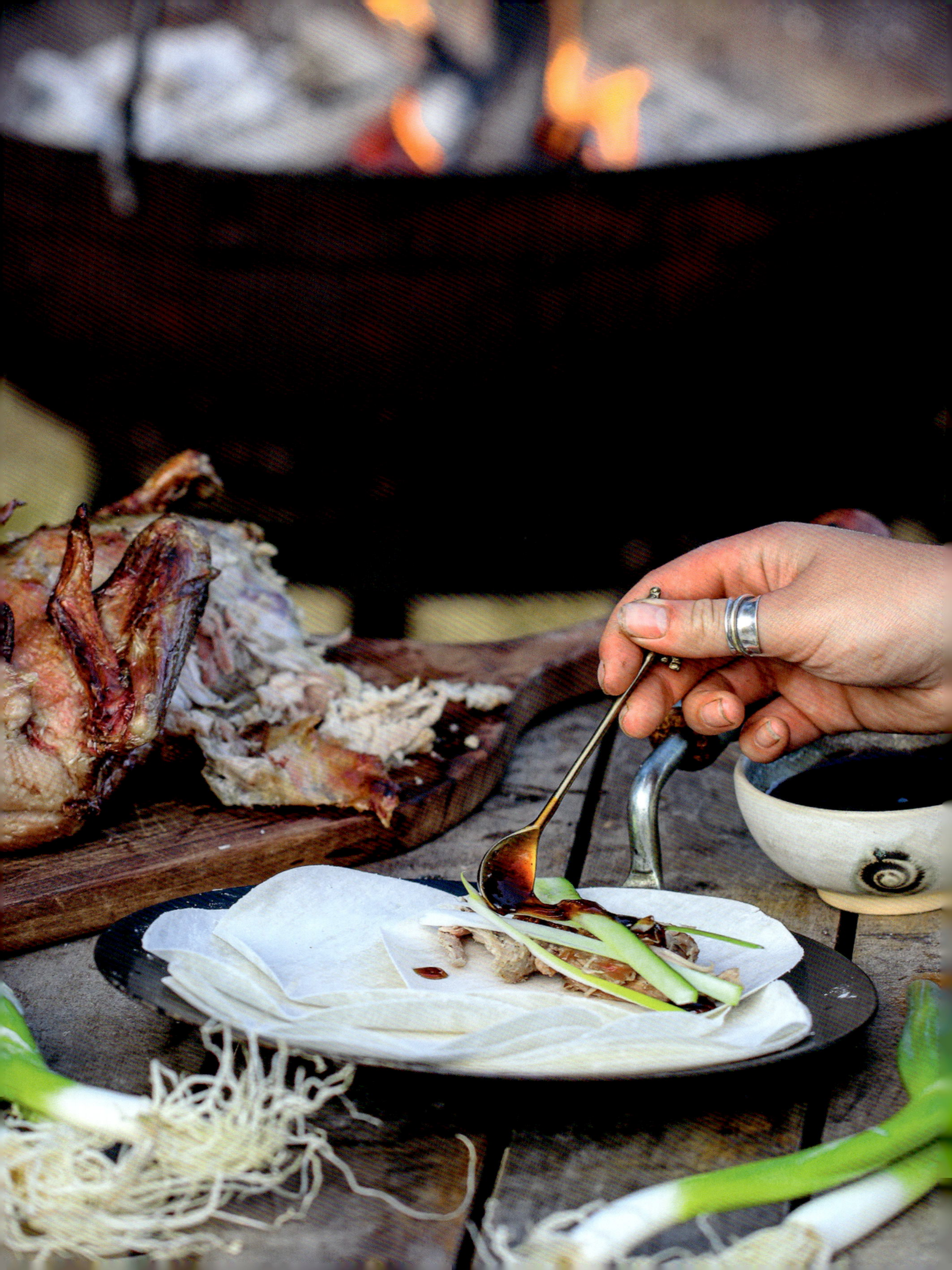

PEKING DUCK PANCAKES *with* HOISIN SAUCE

Once you have mastered roasting meats on your Kadai, there are no limits to the delicious dishes you will be able to cook over an open fire. We love our version of crispy duck with pancakes, recreating a takeaway classic at home.

Prep time: 20 minutes
Cooking time: 4 hours
Recommended Heat: High, allowing to cool to Medium/Low to warm the pancakes

1 medium-sized duck (weighing about 1.8kg)
Salt to taste
3 tsp Chinese five-spice powder (shop bought or make your own) (see pg. 44)
2 cucumbers, trimmed and sliced lengthways
1 bunch spring onions, trimmed and sliced lengthways
12 ready-bought Chinese pancakes
Hoisin sauce, to serve

Serves 2

Season the duck well with salt, both inside and outside, before sprinkling all over with the five-spice.

Place the bird in the Tripod Roaster and attach it to the Cooking Tripod (see pg. 34) directly over the heat. Leave to cook over the fire, turning occasionally to ensure even cooking, for approximately 3 hours or until cooked through.

Once cooked through, remove the duck from the Tripod using a heat-proof Glove and place on a suitable board to rest for 15 minutes before shredding.

When you are ready to eat, separate the pancakes and lay them out on the Chapati Pan a few at a time (not too many as they may stick together). Gently warm over the embers for a couple of minutes.

Once warmed, fill each pancake with some shredded duck, cucumber and spring onion before drizzling with a little hoisin sauce and rolling up.

Equipment:
Cooking Tripod, Tripod Roaster, Chapati Pan

PRAWN & COCONUT PENANG CURRY

Rich and tasty, this dish brings the wonders of pan-Asian cuisine to your Kadai. Infuse these delicious flavours in the Cooking Bowl, for a curry that is not only fragrant but looks amazing and is ready to serve in just 30 minutes.

Prep time: 15 minutes
Cooking time: 15 minutes
Recommended Heat: High

1½ tbsp coconut oil

1 red onion, chopped

30g Penang-style curry paste

1 tsp ground coriander

700ml coconut milk

1-2 whole birds eye chillies (optional)

128g fresh green beans, trimmed

100g baby sweetcorn

600g large raw prawns (shell-on), thawed if frozen

2 tbsp Thai fish sauce

20g fresh coriander, chopped

Salt and freshly ground black pepper to taste

Serves 4

Suspend the Cooking Bowl on the Cooking Tripod over the Grill (see pg. 34) and leave to get hot for about 2 minutes.

Add the oil to the Cooking Bowl and when hot, add the red onion, curry paste and ground coriander and cook, stirring for 5 minutes until fragrant.

Add the coconut milk and birds eye chillies to the Cooking Bowl and bring to the boil. Cook for a couple of minutes to allow it to thicken.

Add the green beans and baby corn to the Cooking Bowl and leave to cook for a couple of minutes before adding the prawns. Once the prawns start to turn opaque, add the remaining ingredients and leave to cook for approximately 5 minutes.

Season with salt and pepper to taste, and sprinkle over the fresh coriander to serve.

Equipment:
Cooking Tripod, Cooking Bowl

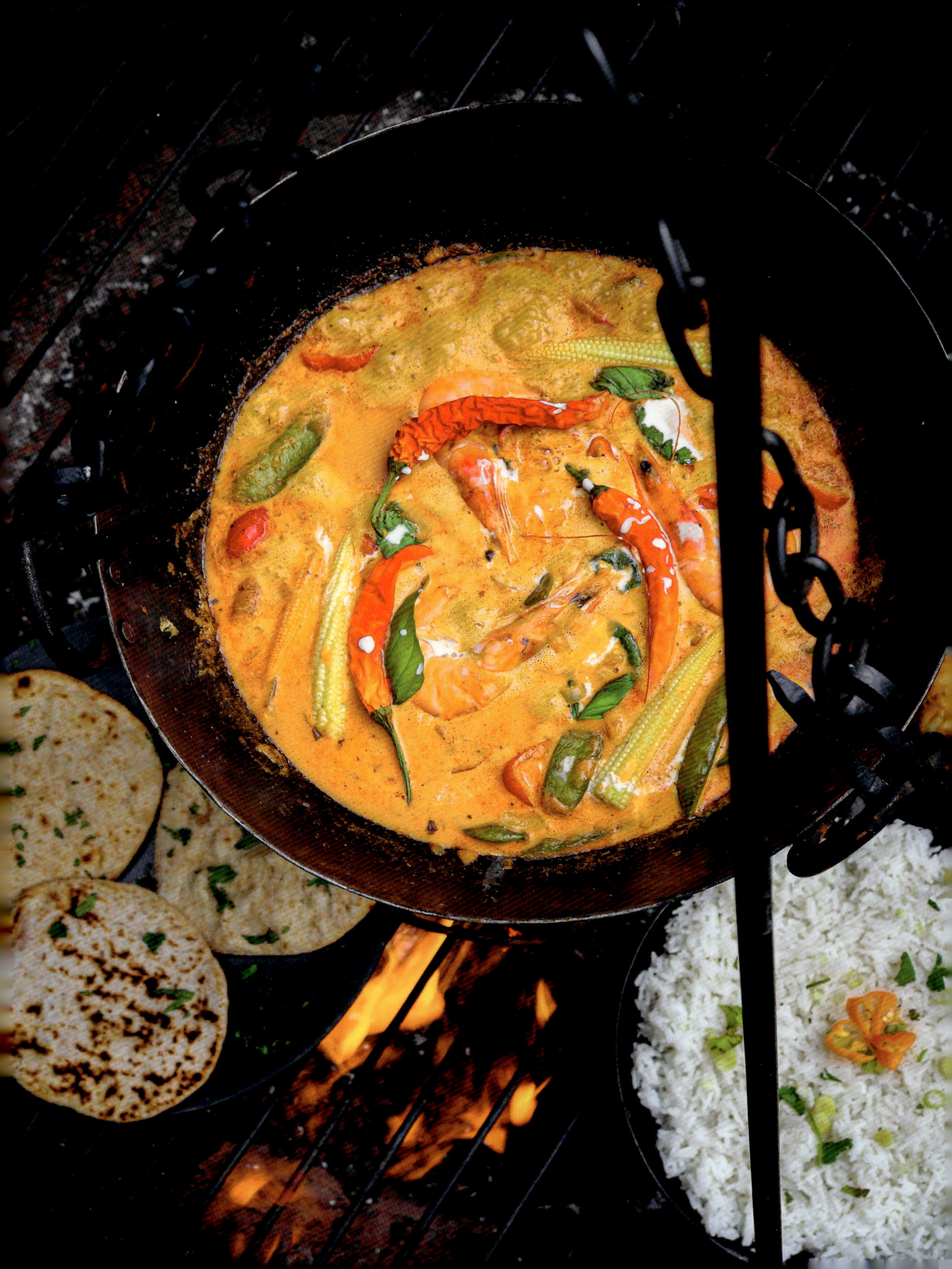

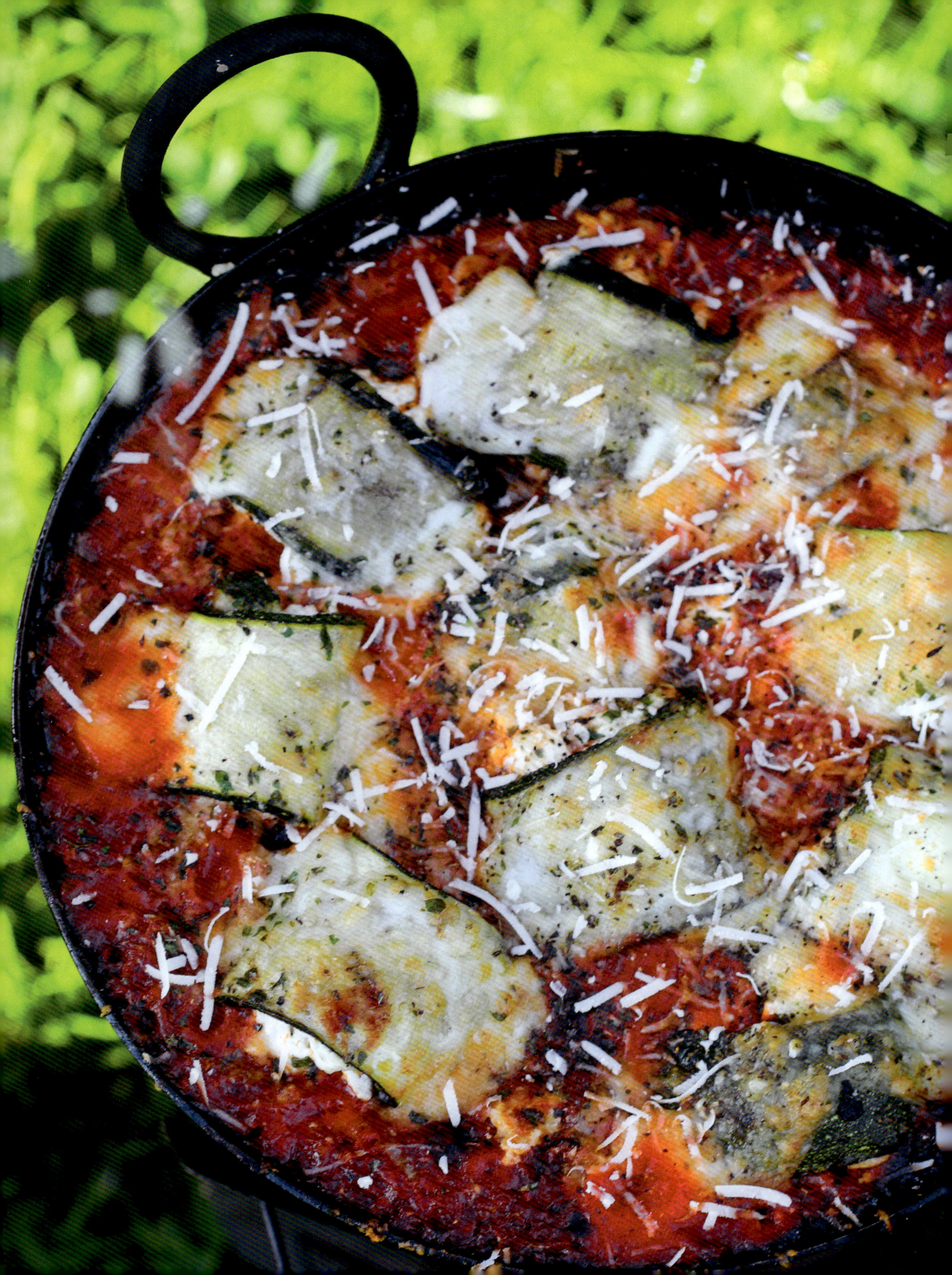

OVEN ROLLATINI *with* COURGETTE & RICOTTA

A scrumptious alternative to a meat lasagne, this rollatini is made with courgette slices that offer a juicy and tender texture. Rolled around a delectable cheesy filling and smothered in our rich marinara sauce, this dish is well-balanced and bursting with flavour.

Prep time: 15 minutes
Cooking time: 20 minutes
Recommended Heat: High

2 large courgettes, sliced lengthways into wide ribbons using a potato peeler
Drizzle of olive oil

For the filling:
250g ricotta cheese
1 large egg
150g parmesan, finely grated
½ tsp salt
500g Marinara sauce (see pg. 193)
100g mozzarella, thinly sliced
Salt and freshly ground black pepper to taste

Serves 2

Brush the courgette slices on both sides with a little oil, place them side by side on the Grill Tray, and slide them into the Wood Fired Oven (see pg. 37) to soften for 3 to 5 minutes.

Put the ricotta cheese, egg, parmesan and salt into a medium-sized bowl and mix well.

Pour the Marinara sauce into the base of the medium Skillet.

Lay one slice of courgette onto a flat surface, spoon 1 tablespoon of the cheese mixture to one end and roll up to form a little parcel. Place the roll seam-side down on top of the Marinara sauce. Repeat until all the courgette slices and cheese mixture have been used and there is no more space left in the Skillet.

Place a slice of mozzarella on top of each roll, season with salt and pepper, and slide the Skillet into the Wood Fired Oven. Cook for approximately 20 minutes or until the mozzarella is melted. Serve with crispy bread or salad.

Equipment:
Set of 3 Grill Trays, Wood Fired Oven, Set of 3 Skillets

JACKFRUIT TACOS *with* SMASHED AVOCADO & SLAW

A deliciously flavoursome and clever alternative to pulled pork, these jackfruit tacos are perfect for both meat eaters and vegetarians. Cooked in our classic barbecue sauce, this shredded jackfruit is wrapped in a crispy taco shell with a tangy cabbage slaw and cooling avocado.

Prep time: 15 minutes
Cooking time: 40 minutes
Recommended Heat: Medium

For the tacos:

Drizzle of vegetable oil
1 large red onion, finely chopped
1 tsp cumin seeds
2 tsp smoked paprika
100ml chipotle sauce
100ml Kadai's barbecue sauce (see pg. 54)
200g chopped tomatoes
400g tin jackfruit, drained
150ml water
8 small tortilla wraps

For the Avocado smash:

2 large avocados, halved, stones removed, peeled and roughly chopped
1 lime, juiced
Handful of fresh coriander, finely chopped

For the slaw:

1 red onion, finely sliced
½ small red cabbage, shredded
2 tbsp apple cider vinegar
Salt and freshly ground black pepper to taste

Serves 4

Suspend the Cooking Bowl on the Cooking Tripod over the Grill (see pg. 34) and leave to get hot for about 2 minutes.

Add the oil to the Cooking Bowl and when hot, add in the onion and sauté for about 5 minutes until soft. Add the cumin and paprika and fry for a few more minutes. Pour in the sauces and tomatoes and mix well, then stir in the jackfruit and water.

Cover the Cooking Bowl with the Cookware Lid and cook for about 30 minutes until the jackfruit is tender and the sauce has thickened.

Remove the Cooking Bowl from the heat and rest it on its stand. Use 2 forks to tear the jackfruit into fine shreds then return the Cooking Bowl to the heat.

Place the tortilla wraps over the bars of the Warming Rack, so they are folded in the middle and dangle down either side. Leave them to crisp and brown, ready to use as the taco shells. Smash your avocados in a pestle and mortar adding the lime juice and coriander.

In a small bowl mix the onion, cabbage and apple cider vinegar with a pinch of salt and pepper. Build the tacos starting with the slaw to keep the shell dry, then pulled jackfruit and smashed avocado.

Equipment:

Cooking Bowl, Cooking Tripod, Cookware Lid, Warming Rack

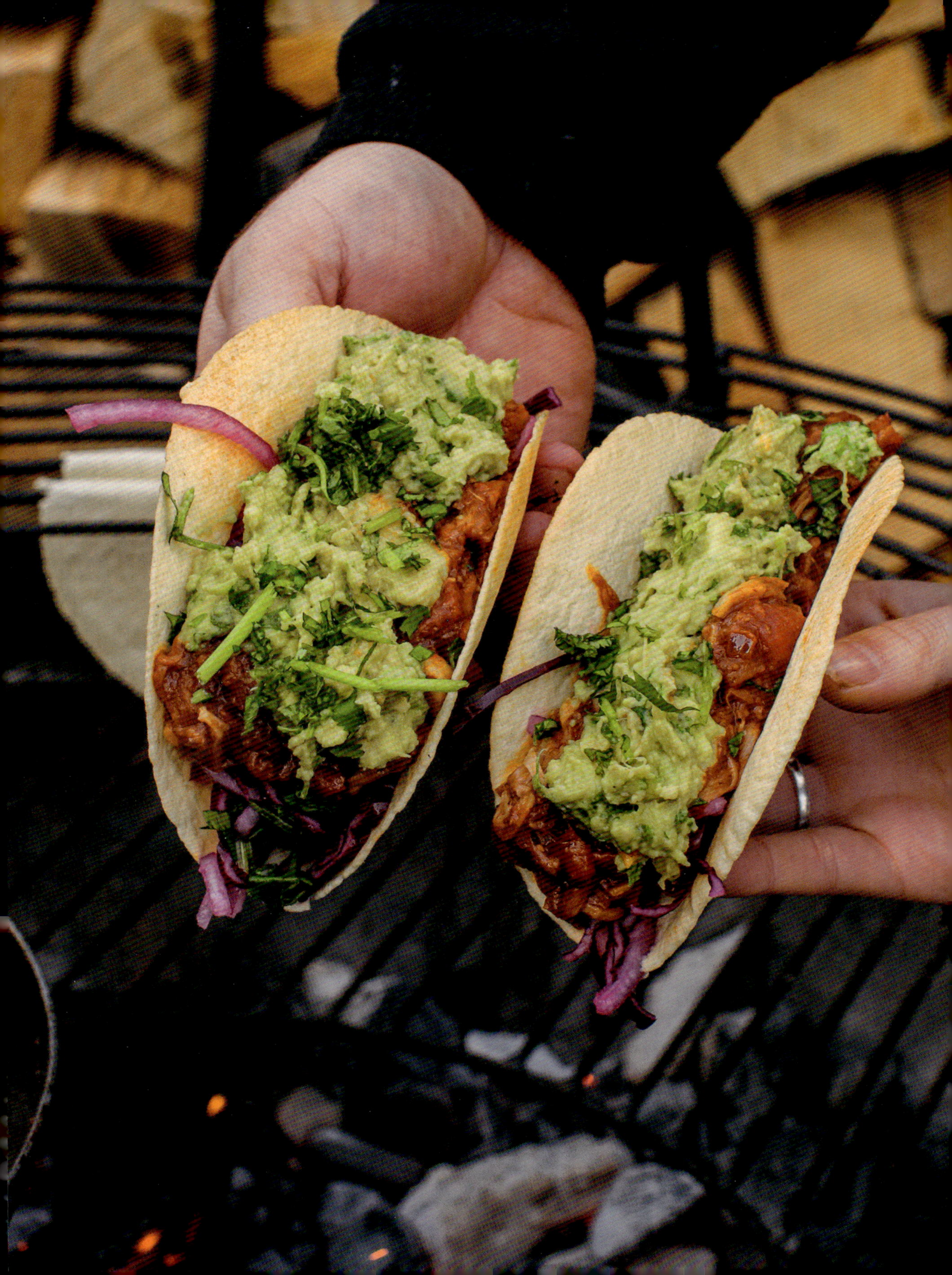

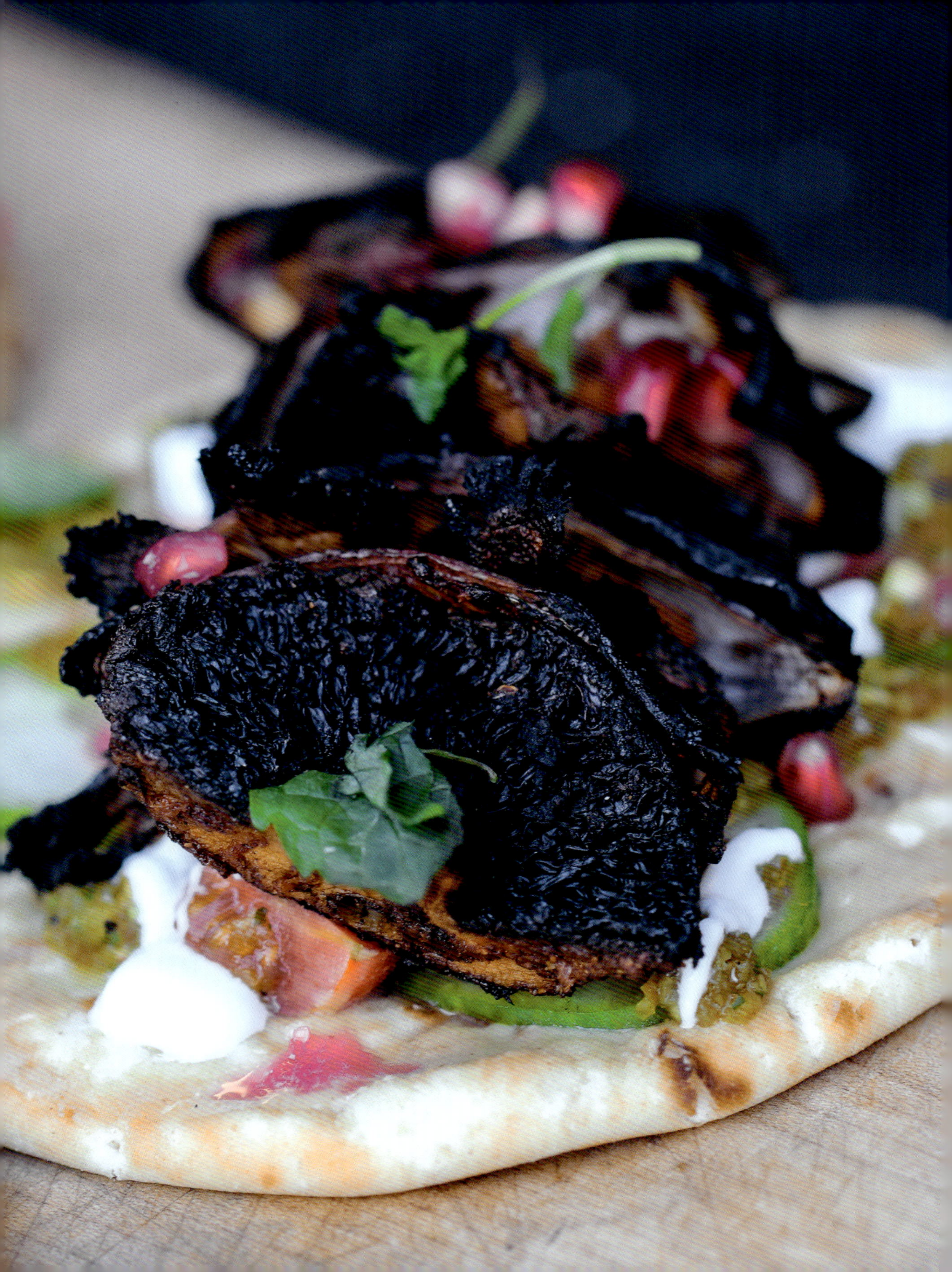

MUSHROOM SHAWARMA *in* TAHINI FLATBREADS

Our variation of shawarma kebabs, a popular street food from the Middle East, is both tasty and special. Portobello and oyster mushrooms are coated in a traditional marinade and slowly grilled on the Skewer Rack. Be sure not to miss out on this delicious combination, served in a tahini flatbread, topped with minted jalapeño salsa and hints of drained yoghurt.

Prep time: 20 minutes
(plus 2 hours marinating time)
Cooking time: 45 minutes
Recommended Heat: Medium/High

For the marinade:

4 garlic cloves, chopped

2 preserved lemons, chopped

1 tsp ground cumin

1 tsp ground allspice

1 tsp smoked paprika

200g natural yoghurt

400g portobello mushrooms, chopped into 4cm pieces

400g oyster mushrooms

1 red onion, chopped into 4cm pieces

200g jar of jalapeños, with the liquid

Handful of fresh mint

2 tbsp pomegranate molasses

4 small Greek style flatbreads

4 tbsp of tahini

10 radishes, sliced

½ cucumber, thinly sliced

100g ripe cherry tomatoes, chopped

Salt and freshly ground black pepper to taste

Serves 4

Line a sieve with kitchen paper and pour in the yoghurt. Give the sieve a gentle squeeze to remove any excess liquid, then leave to drain over a bowl until it is needed. To make the marinade, put the garlic and lemon into a mortar and grind to a paste with the pestle. Stir in the cumin, allspice, paprika and some salt and pepper, mixing thoroughly. Cover the mushrooms and onions with the marinade and leave to marinate for a minimum of 2 hours or overnight.

Alternately thread the mushrooms and onion onto 4 Skewers, then place in the Skewer Rack, leaving a gap between each Skewer. Place the Skewer Rack on the Grill and cook for 20 to 25 minutes turning occasionally. Push the vegetables on each skewer closely together and return to a higher heat, roasting for a further 15 to 20 minutes to get a crispy skin.

Meanwhile, tip the whole jar of jalapeños into a blender with the mint leaves and blitz into a salsa. Just before the Skewers are ready, add a drizzle of pomegranate molasses and leave to caramelise for 3 to 4 minutes.

Lightly toast the flatbreads on the Grill. Once warmed through, transfer to a board and spread each one with a tablespoon of tahini.

Remove the Skewers from the Rack and slide the vegetables onto each flatbread. Top the flatbread with the drained yoghurt, jalapeño salsa, radishes, cucumber and cherry tomatoes, then serve.

Equipment:

Set of Skewers, Skewer Rack

SAMOSA PIE

This pie takes the typically Indian samosa filling of potatoes, onion and cauliflower and wraps it all up in filo pastry. Fried in the traditional spices of India, this Samosa Pie is a great addition to your curry or as a main or side.

Prep time: 20 minutes
Cooking time: 1 hour 15 minutes
Recommended Heat: Medium

2 potatoes, peeled and chopped in 1cm pieces

1 small cauliflower, trimmed and roughly chopped

Drizzle of vegetable oil

1 white onion, finely chopped

2 fresh green chillies, finely chopped (optional)

3 garlic cloves, finely chopped

Thumb size piece of fresh ginger, peeled and finely grated

1 tbsp curry powder

2 tsp turmeric

1 tsp fennel seeds, lightly crushed

175g frozen peas

350ml vegetable stock

Handful of fresh coriander, chopped

6-8 sheets of filo pastry

Sprinkle of nigella seeds

Salt and freshly ground black pepper to taste

Serves 4

Place a large saucepan (suitable for the Kadai) of salted water on the Grill and bring to the boil.

Add the potatoes and boil for 5 minutes. Add the cauliflower and boil for a further 10 minutes, then drain and set aside.

Put the Oven Dish on the Grill over a medium heat and leave to get hot for a minute or two. Add the oil and onion and leave to sauté for 5 minutes. Add the chilli and garlic and fry for a couple of minutes more. Add the ginger, curry powder, turmeric and fennel seed and cook for 2 to 3 minutes until the spices are lightly toasted.

Stir in the potatoes, cauliflower and peas, cover with the vegetable stock and bring to a gentle simmer. Cook for 20 minutes until the stock has reduced and almost disappeared and the mixture has thickened. Stir in the chopped coriander and some salt and pepper to taste.

Take the filo pastry sheets and cut them lengthways, into 2cm-wide strips. Brush each strip with vegetable oil. Roughly crumple the filo pastry strips on top of the pie, creating folds and textures, then sprinkle with nigella seeds.

Set up the Wood Fired Oven (see pg. 37). Slide the Oven Dish into the Wood Fired Oven and leave to cook until the pastry goes crispy, about 25 to 30 minutes.

Equipment:
Oven Dish, Wood Fired Oven

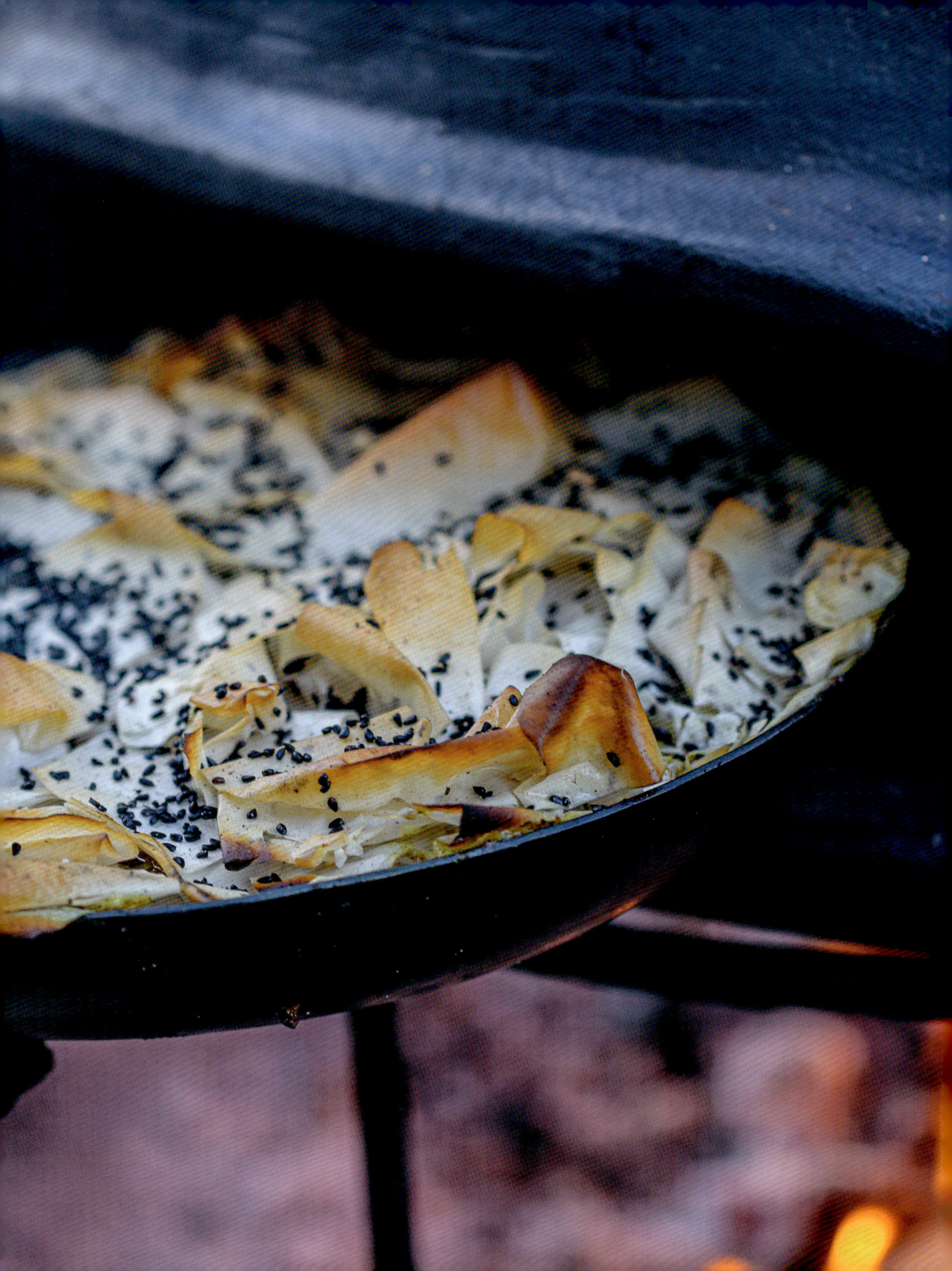

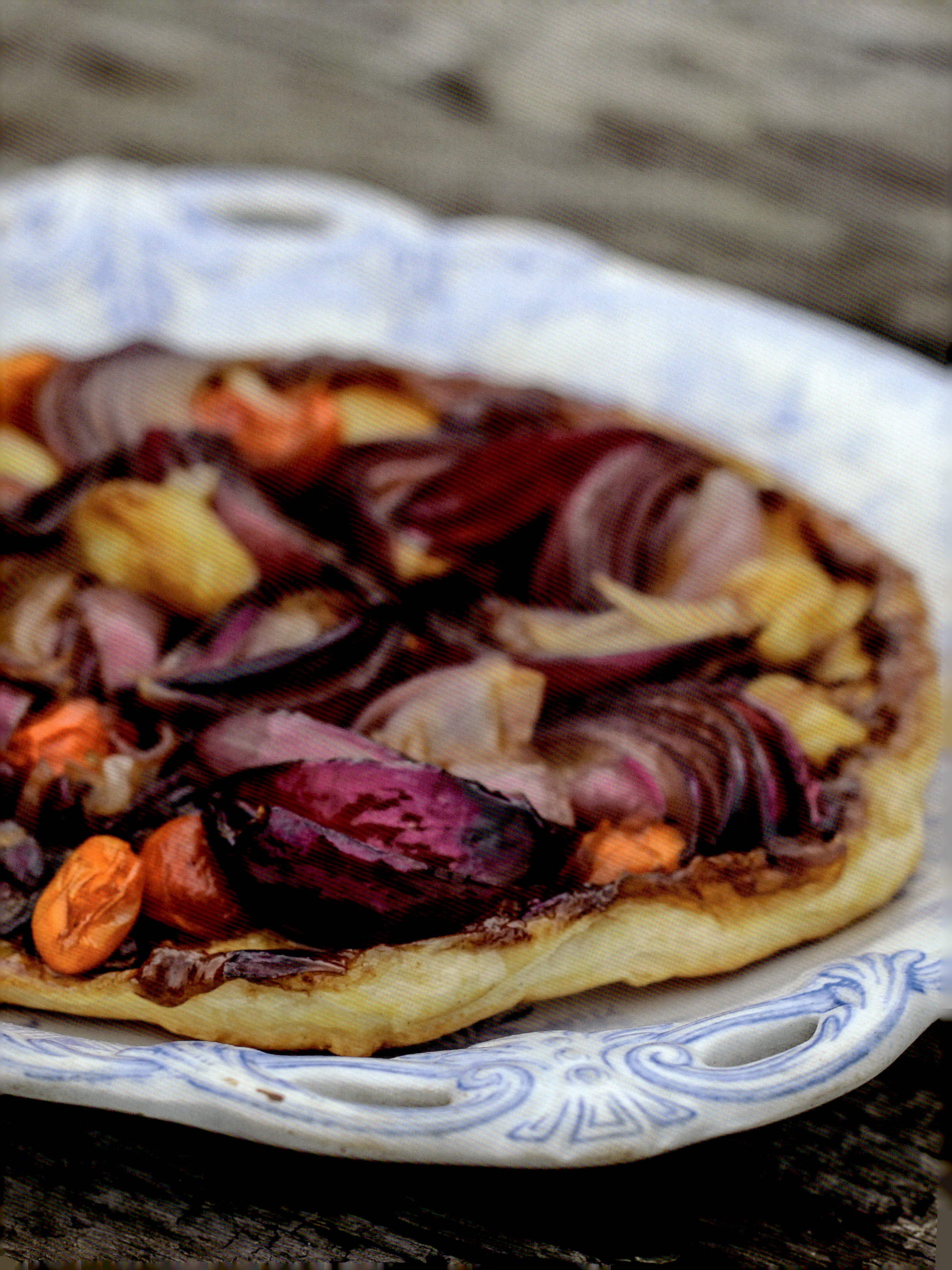

TARTE TATIN

Our interpretation of a savoury Tarte Tatin, this recipe will make everyone curious. Topped with some fresh and seasoned Mediterranean vegetables, this dish makes for a great lunch or light bite to tempt the taste buds when in the garden.

Prep time: 15 minutes
Cooking time: 25 minutes
Recommended Heat: High

3 whole red onions
Drizzle of olive oil
100g unsalted butter
3 red onions, sliced
5 tbsp demerara sugar
6 tbsp balsamic vinegar
100g cherry tomatoes
375g ready-rolled puff pastry
Salt and freshly ground black pepper to taste

Serves 4

Prepare the base by peeling the whole red onions and cutting them in half. Keep the root base intact (so the segments do not fall apart) and cut each half into 6 to 8 wedges.

Put 1 tbsp of oil and half of the butter into a medium Skillet. Add the onion wedges and cook over direct heat on the Grill for about 5 minutes, turning them over halfway through. Remove the segments to a plate.
Add the rest of the butter and oil to the Skillet and heat until sizzling before adding the sliced onions. Cook over direct heat stirring frequently, for 3 minutes. Add 4 tbsp sugar and the balsamic vinegar, season with salt and pepper and cook, stirring constantly, for 5 minutes. Scoop into a bowl and set to one side.

Remove the Grill and prepare the Wood Fired Oven (see pg. 37).

Arrange the red onion wedges and cherry tomatoes in a pattern in the base of the medium Skillet, then spoon over the sliced onion mixture. Unroll the sheet of puff pastry and lay it over the onions, trimming off the excess and tucking the sides down inside the Skillet.
Pierce a few holes in the top of the pastry and cook in the Wood Fired Oven for 15 to 20 minutes until the pastry is puffed up and golden brown.

To serve, invert the tart onto a large serving platter and cut into wedges.

Equipment:
Set of 3 Skillets, Wood Fired Oven

KADAI'S SWISS RACLETTE
with BABY POTATOES & PICKLES

This Swiss-inspired dish uses Wrekin White Cheese, grilled to gooey savoury bliss, served over pickled gherkins and buttered baby potatoes. Feel as though you are in the Alps with this platter - perfect for cheese lovers and sharers.

Prep time: 10 minutes
Cooking time: Approx. 8 minutes
Recommended Heat: Medium

750g baby new potatoes
500g gherkins
½ wheel raclette style cheese (approx. 6kg) (We used Moyden's Wrekin White)
Slices of sourdough bread

Serves approx. 6

Cook the potatoes in lightly salted water for 15 minutes until half-cooked, then drain, slice in half, and place in the large Skillet with the gherkins.

Place the Skillet onto the Grill over a medium heat and cook, turning everything occasionally, until the potatoes are fully tender. After a further 5 minutes remove the Skillet from the Grill and set to one side.

Attach the block of cheese to the Asado Cross (see pg. 34) with the cut-side facing down (with the cheese rind left in place) and position so that it is about 50cm above the bars of the Grill. The time taken for the cheese to begin to melt is dependent on the cheese. Ours took about 8 minutes.

As the cheese starts to melt, slide the Skillet underneath it and scrape the cheese onto it using a knife. Make sure to keep the fire directly below the cheese and move the Skillet underneath only when you are ready to start scraping the cheese. Serve immediately with slices of sourdough.

Equipment:
Set of 3 Skillets, Asado Cross

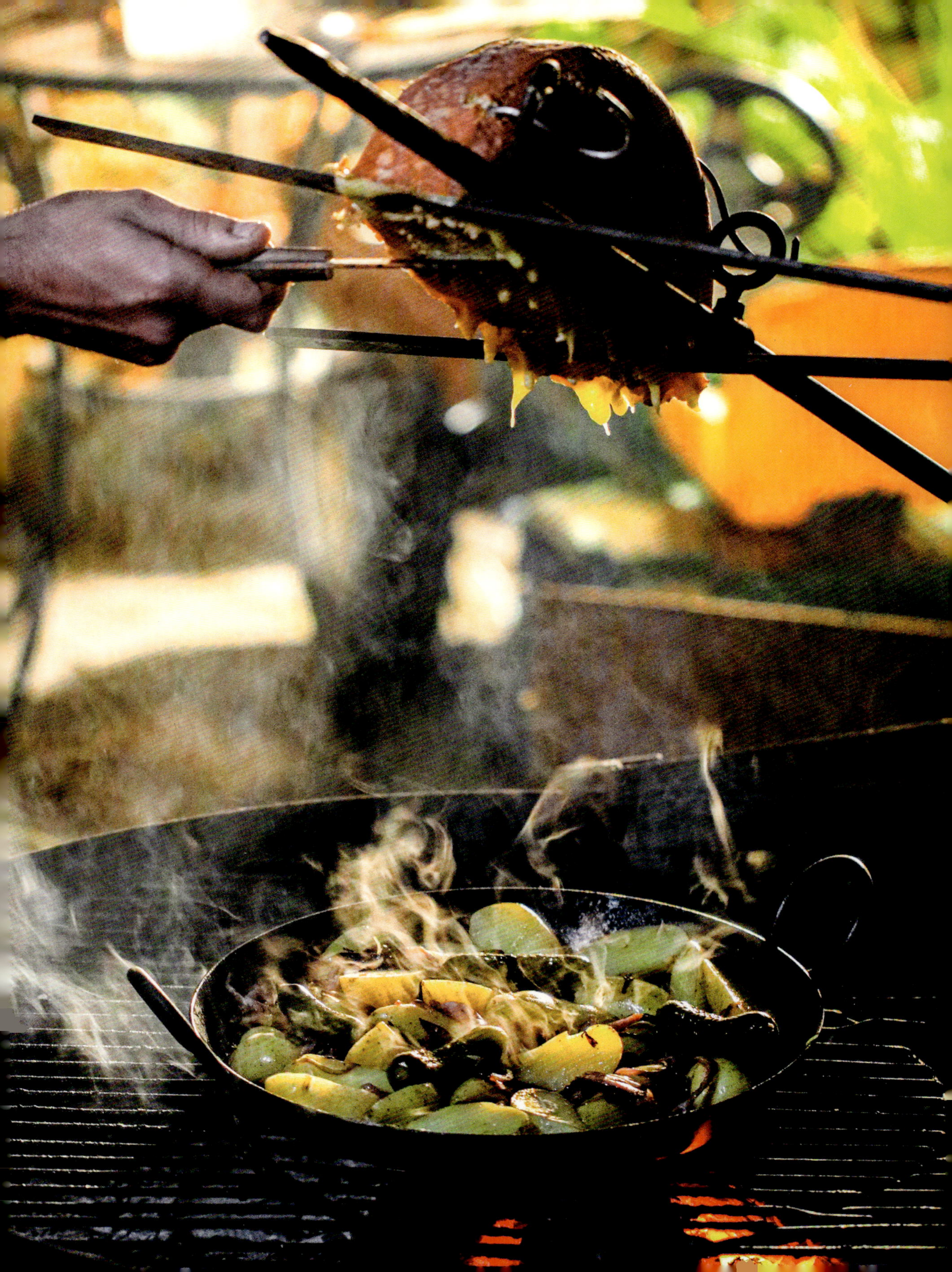

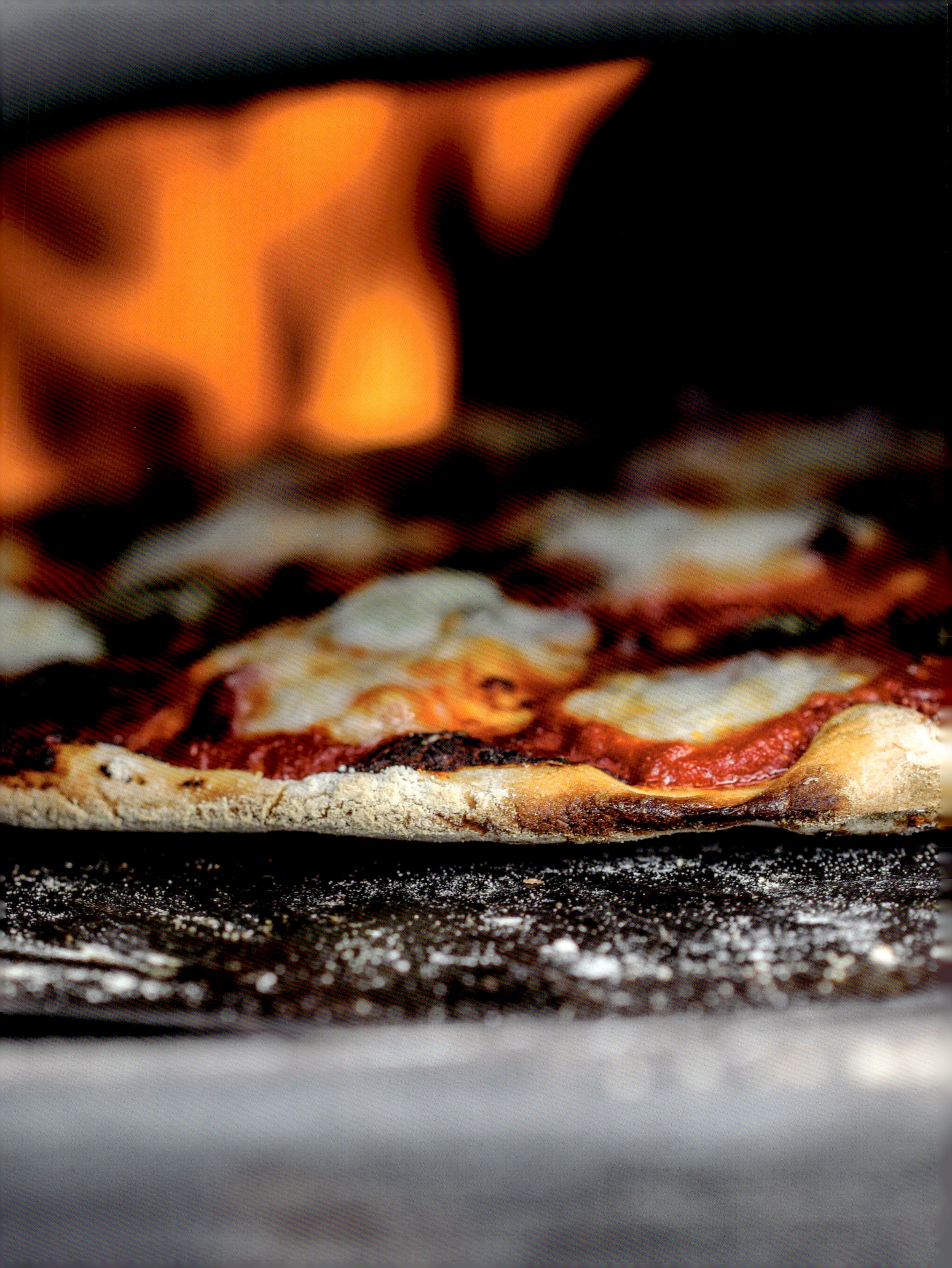

Pizza night

We all love pizza night, and it takes only minutes to make authentic Italian-style pizzas in the comfort of your own garden. Best cooked in the traditional way using the Wood Fired Oven, nothing beats the flavours and crispy perfection a wood fire provides. In this chapter, discover and learn everything you need to know about creating the ultimate pizza and bring this classic meal to a whole new level.

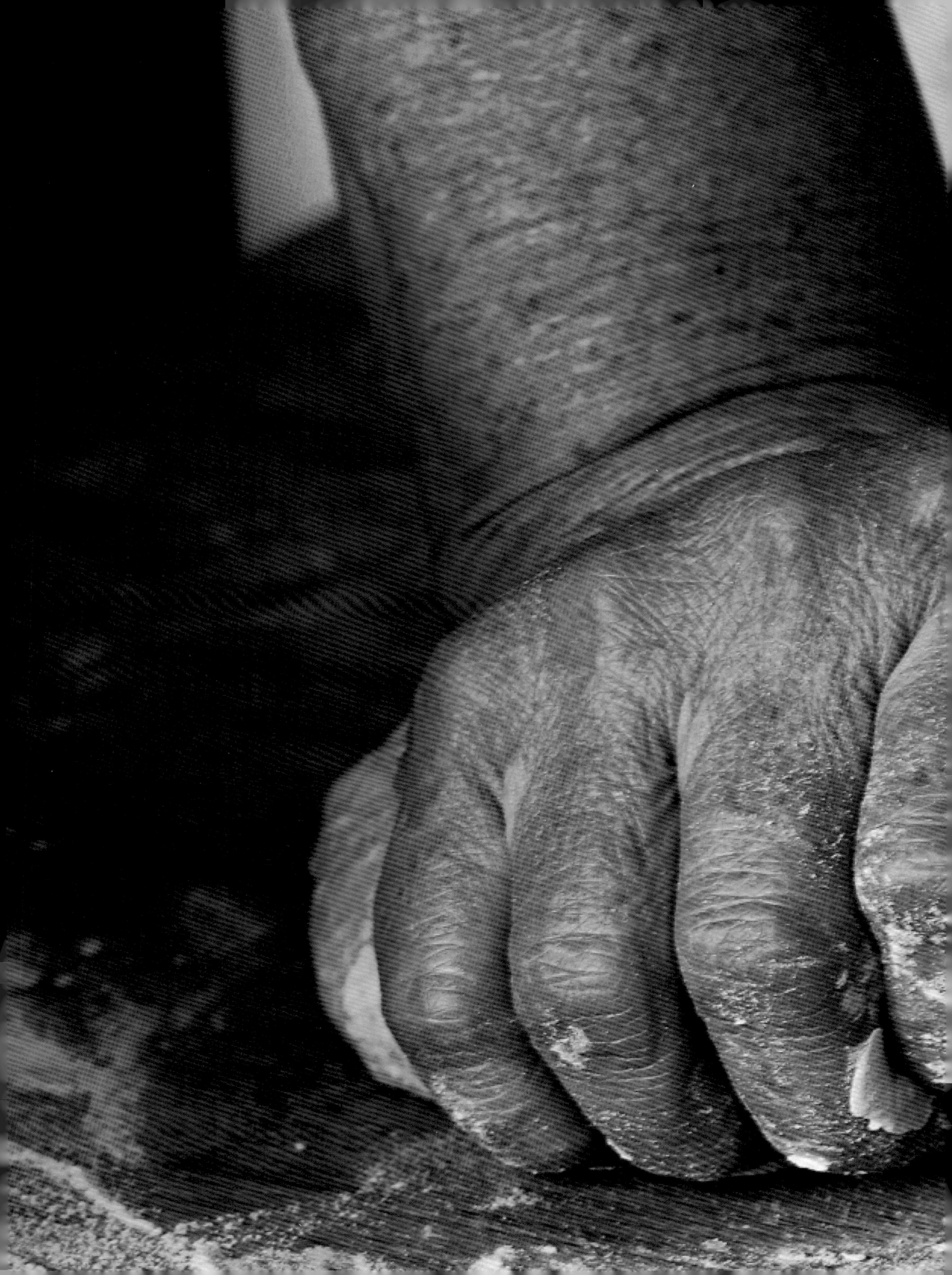

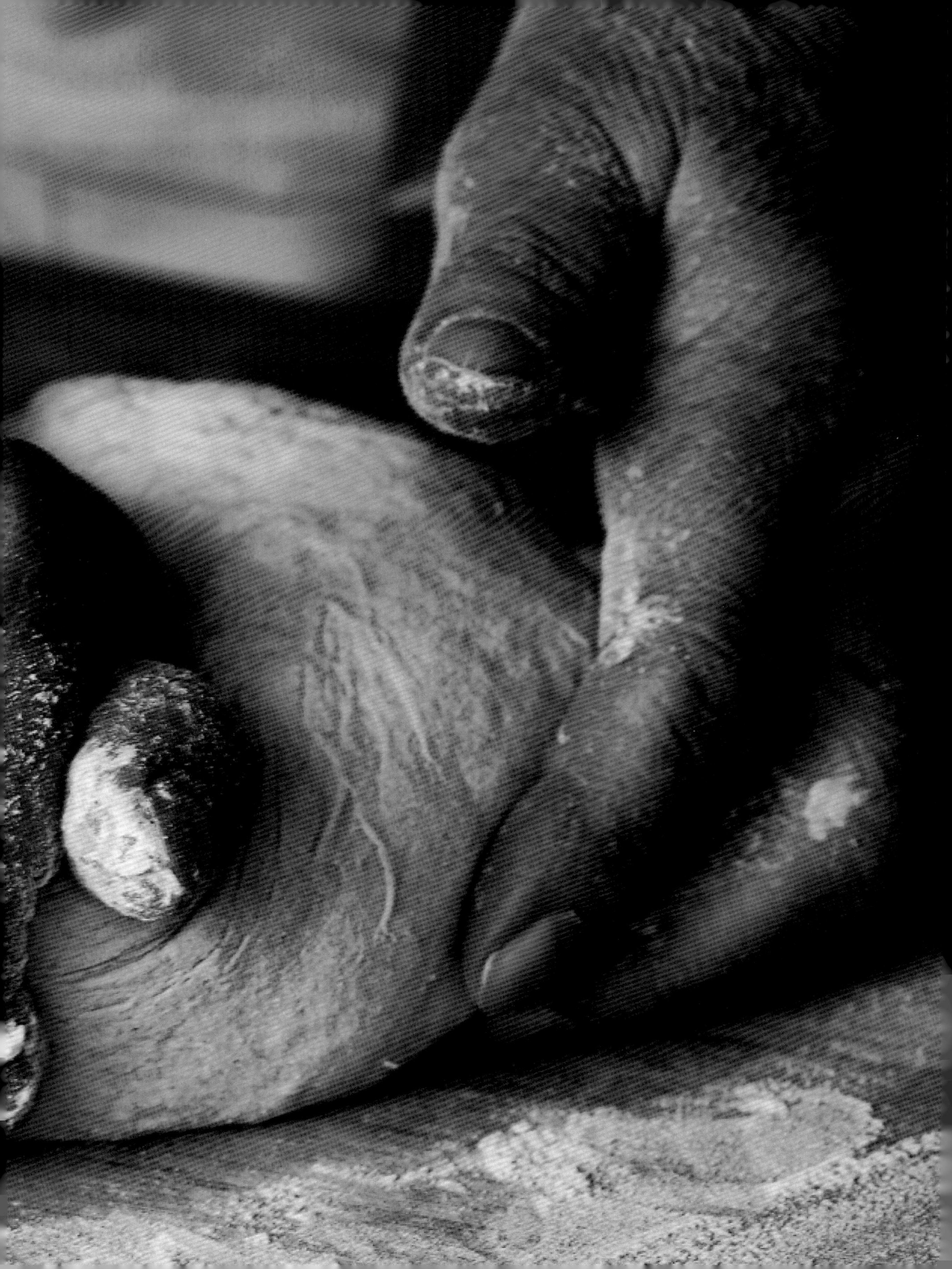

How to make pizza dough

Prep time: Approx. 90 minutes (including proving)

7g dried yeast
2 tsp caster sugar
2 tbsp extra virgin olive oil
325ml lukewarm water
500g strong white bread flour, plus extra for dusting
½ tsp fine salt

Makes 4 (1 medium pizza per person)

Our dough recipe makes the most delicious pizza bases. To save time, it is best prepared in advance. It can also be made the day before and stored in the fridge overnight. You can use any strong bread flour, but, for the best results, we highly recommend using Tipo '00' flour.

....

Whisk the yeast, sugar and oil in a jug with 325ml of lukewarm water. Leave the mixture for a few minutes to activate the yeast and become frothy.

Sieve the flour and salt into a large bowl and make a well in the middle. Pour the yeast mixture into the centre of the well and bring the flour in from the sides with a fork or floured hands.

Scrape the dough out onto a clean, floured work-surface and knead with your hands until the dough is smooth and springy. Form the dough into a ball.

Dust the bowl with flour, drop in the ball of dough, and dust the top with flour. Cover with a damp cloth and leave to prove in a warm room or near to a lit Kadai, for 60 minutes.

The dough will double in size.

Tip the dough out onto a clean, floured work-surface and knead gently with your knuckles to knock some of the air out of it.

Lightly oil 4 pieces of tin foil (slightly larger than the pizza bases) and dust them with flour. Divide the dough into 4 even pieces and roll out into a rough 30cm disc, ½ cm thick and place on the foil. Leave for 15 to 20 minutes to prove before adding the toppings.

TIP: If you are preparing the dough in advance, stack the pizza bases on a plate, cover with cling film and refrigerate until use.

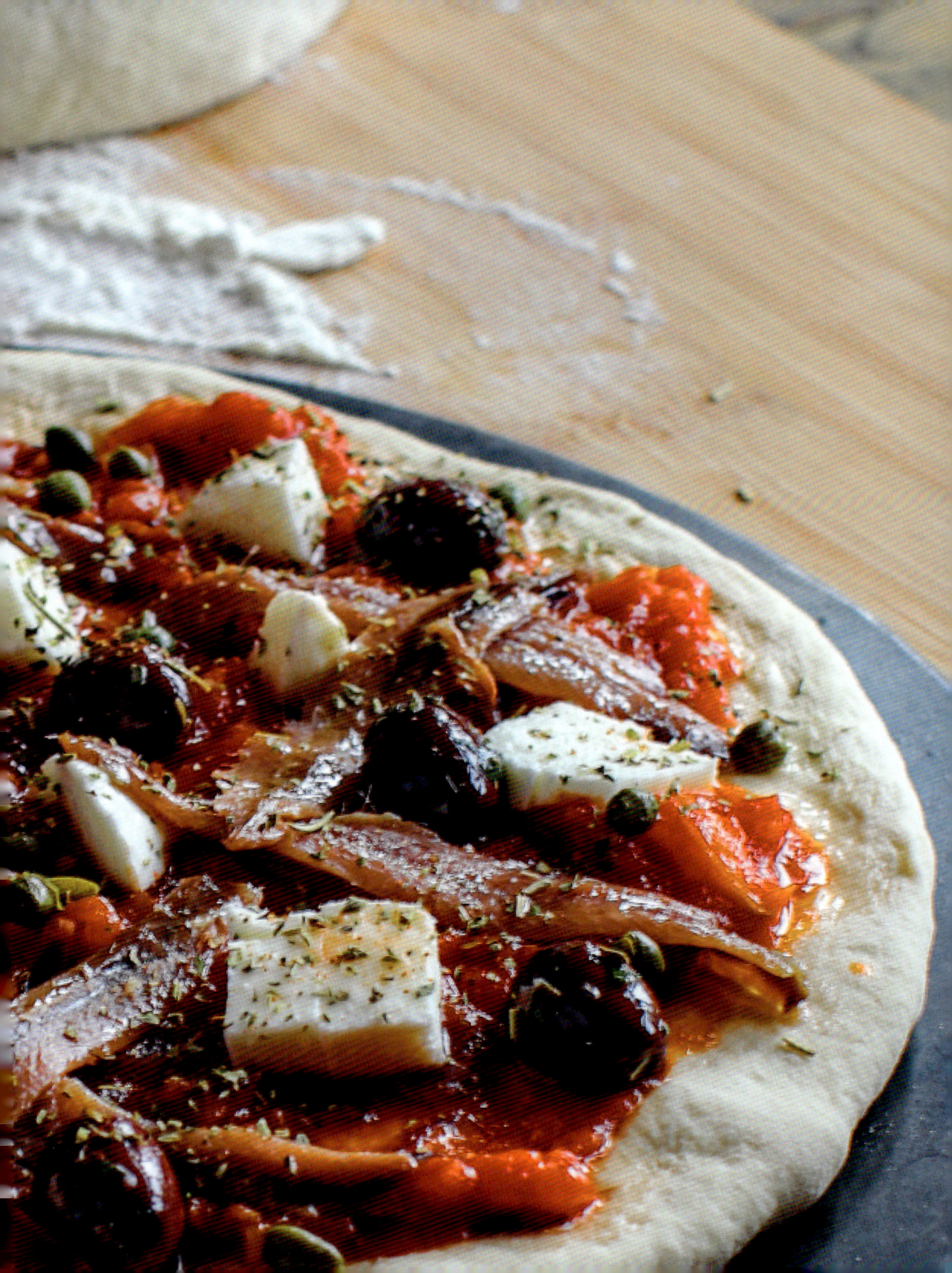

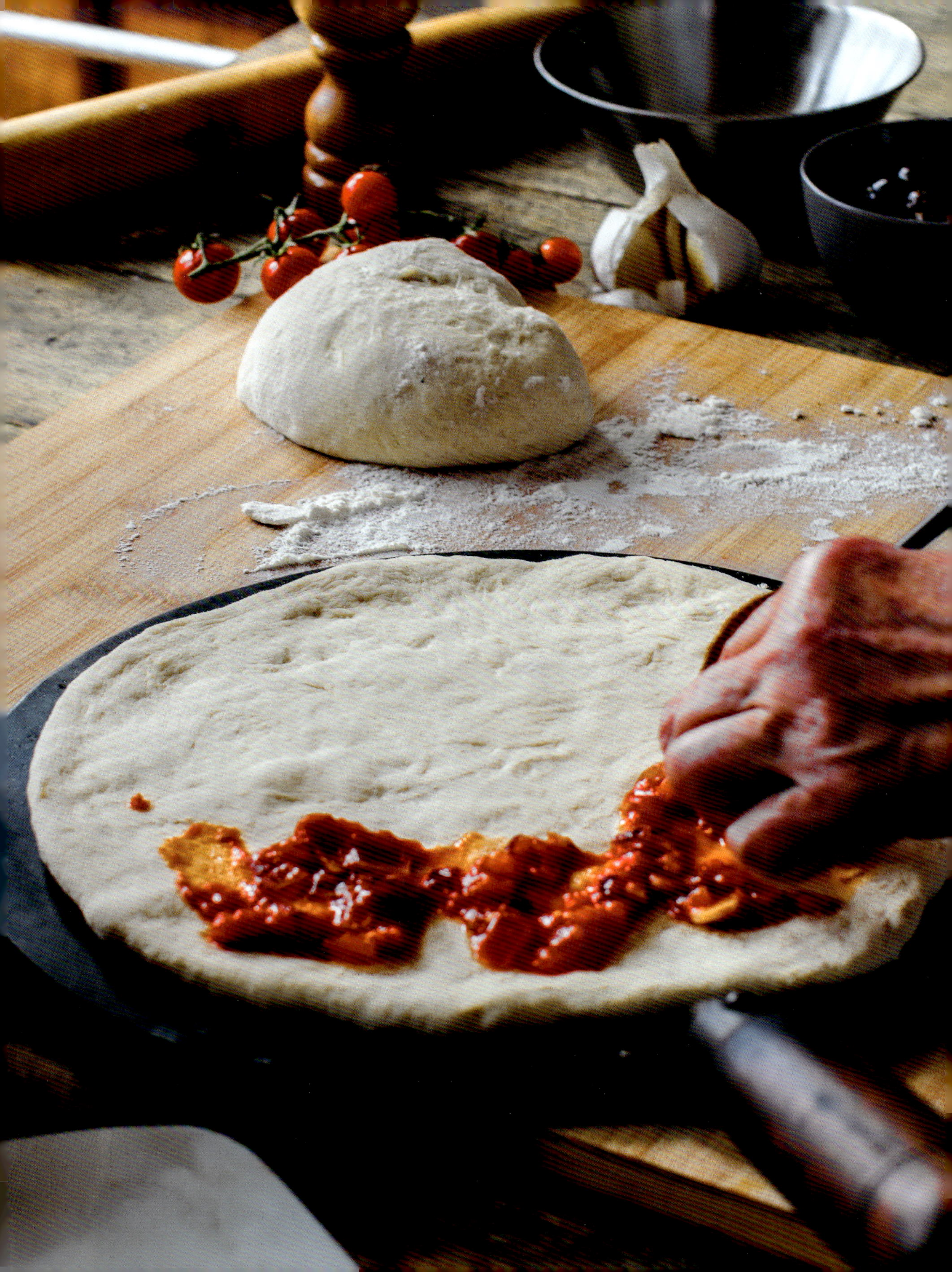

MARINARA SAUCE

Straight from Italy, we bring you the richest and most flavoursome Marinara sauce, which is our go-to ingredient for pizzas and pastas alike. Once you have tried this traditional recipe, no other tomato sauce will do.

Prep time: 15 minutes
Cooking time: 10 minutes
Recommended Heat: High

4 tbsp olive oil
1 medium white onion, finely chopped
2 garlic cloves, finely chopped
800g tinned plum tomatoes
2 tsp dried oregano
½ tsp salt
½ tsp freshly ground black pepper

Enough for 4 pizzas

Suspend the Cooking Bowl from the Cooking Tripod (see pg. 34) over the coals.

Once hot, add the oil and onion and cook gently for 3 to 4 minutes until it becomes translucent and soft.

Add the garlic and tomatoes, squashing them with the back of a long wooden spoon.

Season well with the oregano, salt and pepper and leave to simmer for 10 minutes, stirring occasionally.

Equipment:
Cooking Tripod, Cooking Bowl

PIZZA ALLA MARINARA

Pizza alla Marinara is one of the most traditional Neapolitan pizzas, and perhaps the easiest dish to start with when cooking home-made pizzas in the Wood Fired Oven. Master our dough and sauce recipes, then begin testing out your own combinations and toppings.

Prep time: 5 minutes
Cooking time: 15-20 minutes
Recommended Heat: High

1 quantity of pizza dough (see pg. 190)
1 quantity of Marinara sauce (see pg. 193)
Drizzle of olive oil
Salt and freshly ground black pepper to taste

Serves 4 (1 pizza per person)

Place the first pizza base onto the metal Pizza Peel and spread 3 to 4 tablespoons of the marinara sauce over the centre.

Season with salt and pepper, drizzle with a little oil and slide into the Wood Fired Oven (see pg. 37).

Build up the fire at the back of the Wood Fired Oven with small pieces of kindling, so the flames come up the vent at the back and over the top of the pizza.

Using the Pizza Peel, turn the pizza around a couple of times during cooking to get an even crispy bake.

Cook for 10 to 15 minutes until the base has risen a little and the edges have started to crisp.

Once ready, remove from the oven opening and serve immediately. Repeat for the remaining bases.

Equipment:
Wood Fired Oven

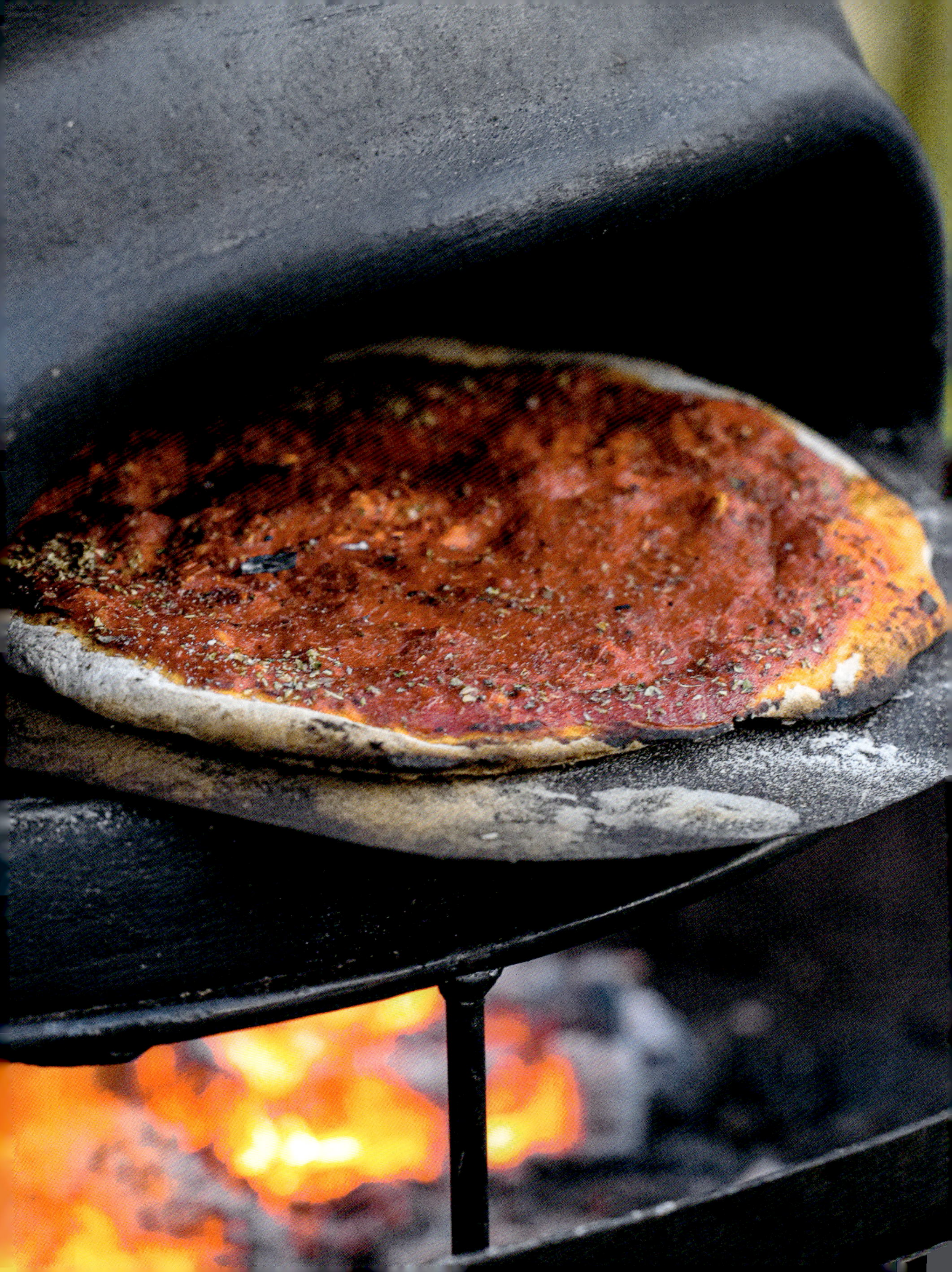

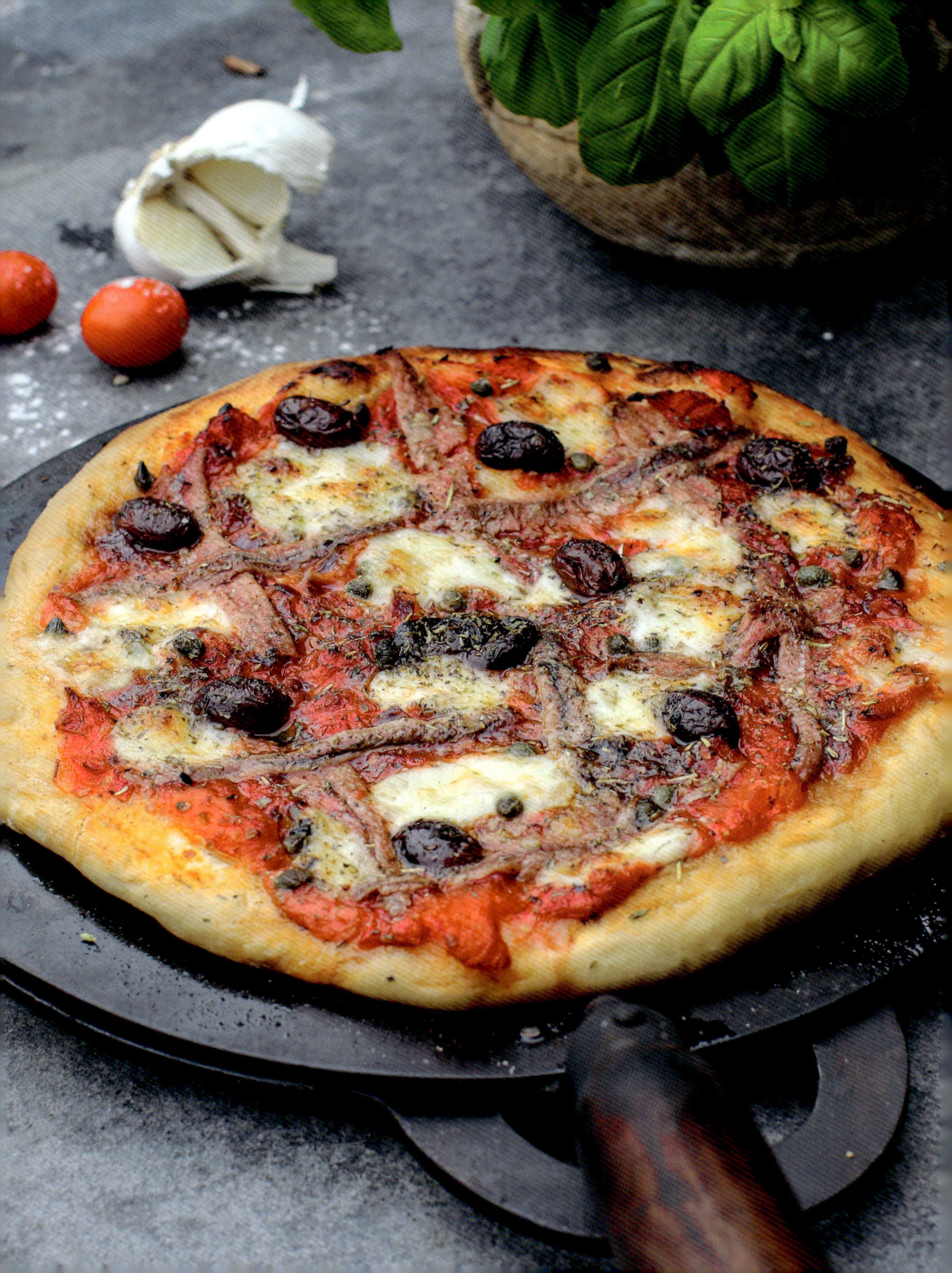

PIZZA NAPOLI

The fish lover's pizza, this Napoli classic with anchovies is a traditional favourite across Italy. On a bed of Marinara sauce, scattered with olives and capers and finished with slices of mozzarella, this pizza delivers an exciting range of flavours.

Prep time: 5 minutes
Cooking time: 15-20 minutes
Recommended Heat: High

1 quantity of pizza dough (see pg. 190)
1 quantity of Marinara sauce (see pg. 193)
10 anchovy fillets, in olive oil and drained
1 tbsp baby capers
8 black olives, halved
125g mozzarella, sliced
Handful of fresh basil leaves
Salt and freshly ground black pepper to taste
Drizzle of olive oil

Serves 4 (1 pizza per person)

Place the first pizza base onto the metal Pizza Peel and spread 3 to 4 tablespoons of the marinara sauce over the centre.

Arrange a few of the anchovies in a diamond pattern on top, scatter some of the capers, olives and mozzarella evenly over the top, season with salt and pepper and drizzle with a little oil. Slide the pizza into the Wood Fired Oven (see pg. 37).

Build up the fire at the back of the Wood Fired Oven with small pieces of kindling, so the flames come up the vent at the back and over the top of the pizza.

Using the Pizza Peel, turn the pizza around a couple of times during cooking to get an even crispy bake.

Cook for 10 to 15 minutes until the base has risen a little and the edges have started to crisp.

Scatter with some of the fresh basil and serve. Repeat for the remaining bases.

Equipment:
Wood Fired Oven

KADAI'S SIGNATURE PIZZA

We invite you to try our signature pizza with Shropshire Salumi and jalapeño peppers for a fiery touch. Our favourite pizza recipe, we cannot get enough of this spicy, rich and refreshing combination, that flawlessly complements the Wood Fired Oven flavour.

Prep time: 5 minutes
Cooking time: 15-20 minutes
Recommended Heat: High

1 quantity of pizza dough (see pg. 190)
1 quantity of Marinara sauce (see pg. 193)
1 red onion, chopped
1 link of Shropshire Salumi (230g), skinned and thinly sliced
1 Jalapeño pepper, thinly sliced
125g mozzarella, sliced
Salt and freshly ground black pepper to taste
Handful of fresh basil leaves
Drizzle of olive oil

Serves 4 (1 pizza per person)

Place the first pizza base onto the metal Pizza Peel and spread 3 to 4 tablespoons of the marinara sauce over the centre.

Sprinkle some of the chopped onion, sliced salumi, jalapeño slices and mozzarella slices evenly over the top, season with salt and pepper and drizzle with a little oil. Build up the fire at the back of the Wood Fired Oven with small pieces of kindling, so the flames come up the vent at the back and over the top of the pizza (see pg. 37).

Using the Pizza Peel, slide the pizza into the oven. Turn a couple of times whilst cooking to get an even bake.

Cook for 10 to 15 minutes until the base has risen a little and the edges have started to crisp.

Once cooked remove from the Oven. Scatter with some of the fresh basil and serve immediately. Repeat for the remaining bases.

Equipment:

Wood Fired Oven

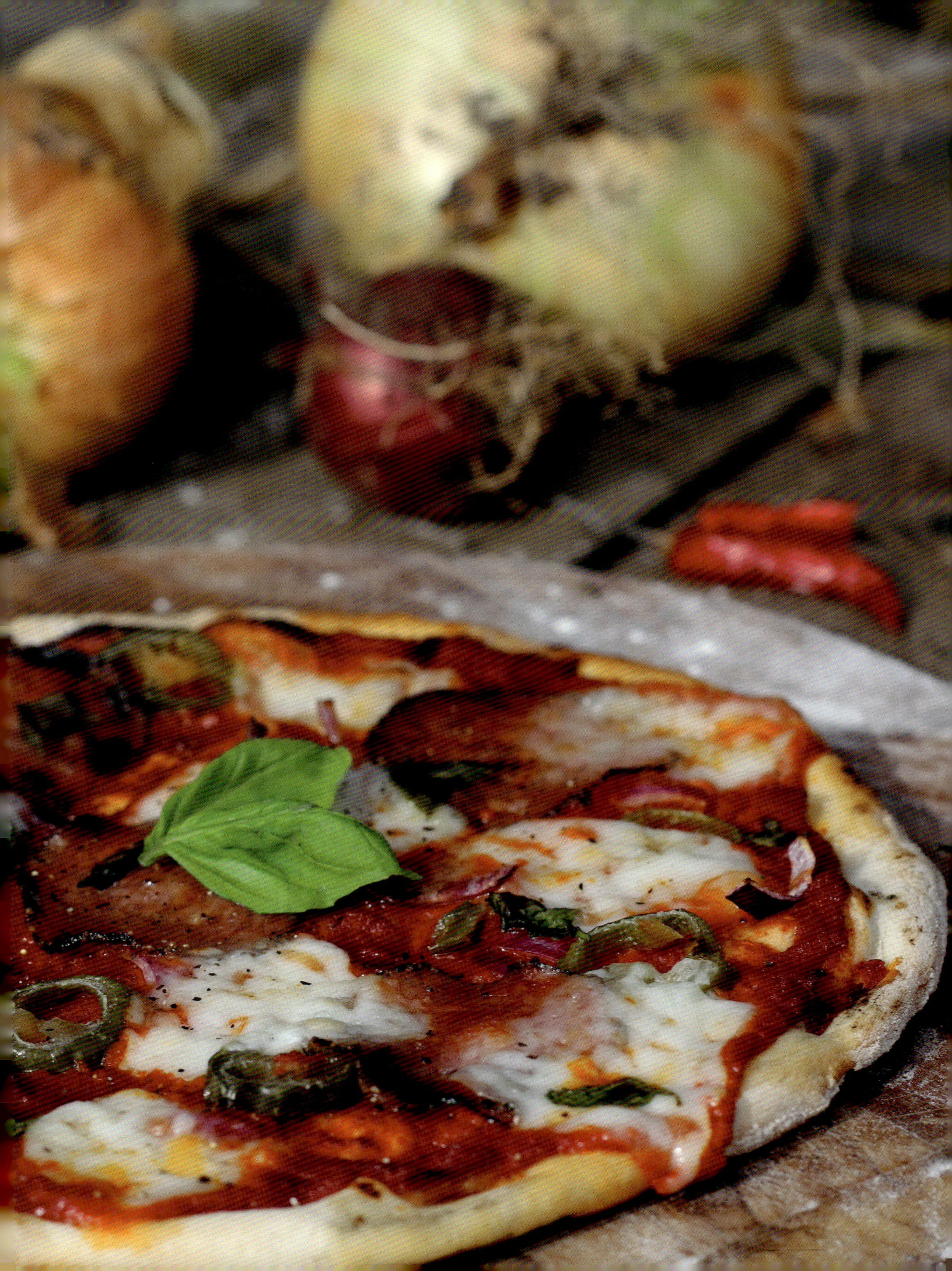

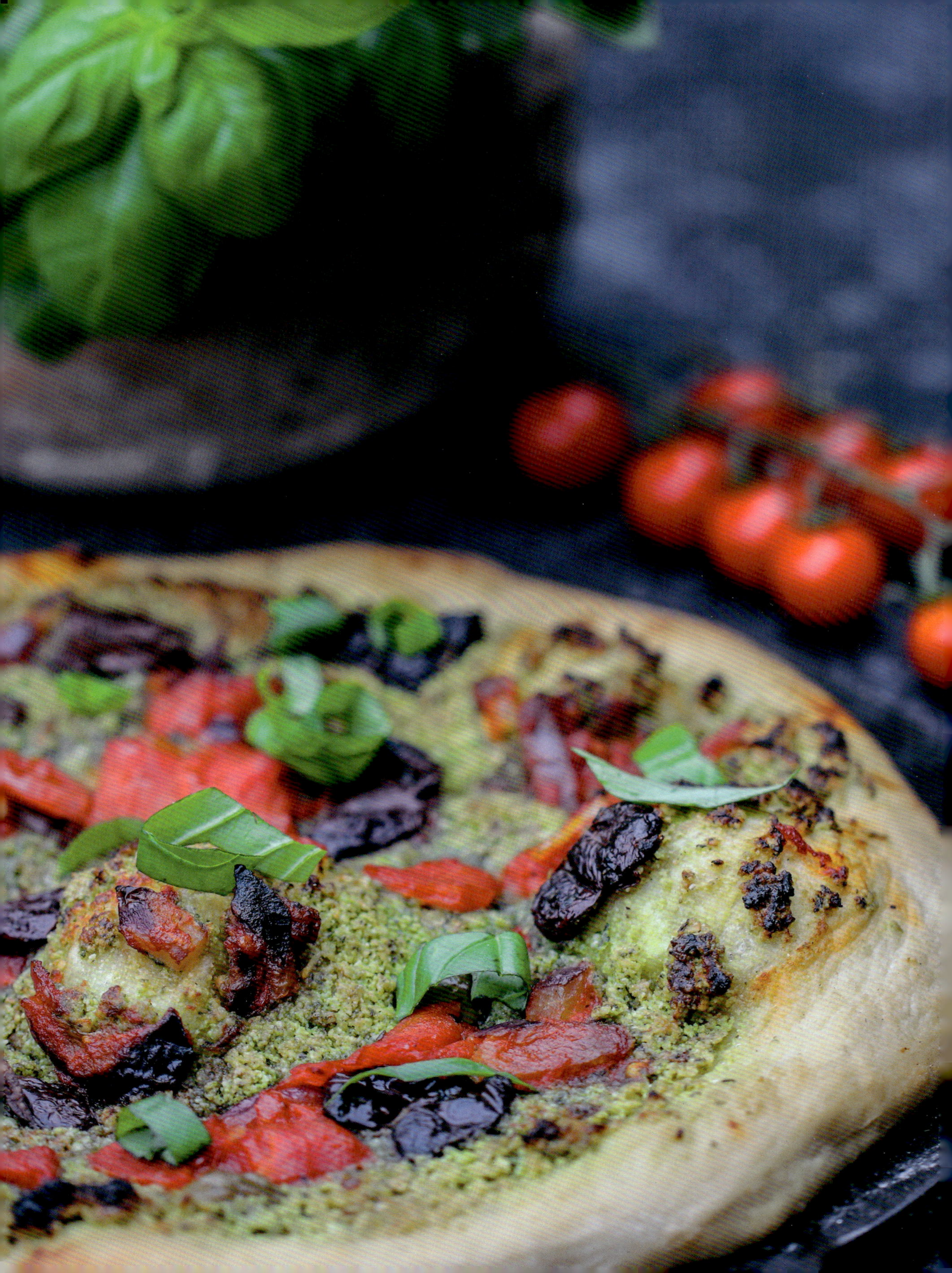

SUN-DRIED TOMATO & PESTO PIZZA

A delicious vegetarian or even vegan alternative to our pizza recipes, this pesto-based pizza is simply fantastic. Harnessing the fresh and herby flavour of our homemade pesto, this pizza is balanced with some rustic sun-dried tomatoes, salty black olives and sweet basil leaves.

Prep time: 5 minutes
Cooking time: 15-20 minutes
Recommended Heat: High

1 quantity of pizza dough (see pg. 190)
1 quantity of pesto sauce (see pg. 55)
6 sun-dried tomatoes in olive oil, drained and thinly sliced
4 tbsp black olives, halved
Salt and freshly ground black pepper to taste
Handful of fresh basil leaves
Drizzle of olive oil

Serves 4 (1 pizza per person)

Place the first pizza base onto the metal Pizza Peel and spread a quarter of the pesto over the centre to within 3cm of the edge.

Sprinkle some of the sun-dried tomatoes and olives evenly over the top, season with salt and pepper and drizzle with a little oil.

Build up the fire at the back of the Wood Fired Oven with small pieces of kindling, so the flames come up the vent at the back and over the top of the pizza (see pg. 37).

Using the Pizza Peel, slide the pizza into the oven. Turn a couple of times whilst cooking to get an even bake.

Cook for 10 to 15 minutes until the base has risen a little and the edges have started to crisp.

Once cooked, remove from the oven. Scatter with some of the fresh basil and serve immediately. Repeat for the remaining bases.

Equipment:
Wood Fired Oven

DIRTY BEETROOT, GOAT'S CHEESE & ROCKET PIZZA

A deliciously light lunch that is both quick and easy; our favourite dirty-cooked beetroots are back but this time on a pizza. Baked with some creamy and tangy goat's cheese, these dirty beetroots add a rustic, charred flavour that works splendidly with sesame seeds and rocket.

Prep time: 5 minutes
Cooking time: 15-20 minutes (plus 45 minutes for the dirty beetroots)
Recommended Heat: High

1 quantity of pizza dough (see pg. 190)
4 large dirty-roasted beetroots, (see pg. 33), peeled and sliced
1 large red onion, sliced
225g soft goat's cheese, chopped
2 tsp sesame seeds
Salt and freshly ground black pepper to taste
Large handful of fresh rocket leaves
Drizzle of olive oil

Serves 4 (*1 pizza per person*)

Place the first pizza base onto the metal Pizza Peel, sprinkle some of the sliced dirty beetroot, onion, goat's cheese, and sesame seeds evenly over the top, season with salt and pepper and drizzle with a little oil.

Build up the fire at the back of the Wood Fired Oven with small pieces of kindling, so the flames come up the vent at the back and over the top of the pizza (see pg. 37).

Slide into the Wood Fired Oven and cook for 10 to 15 minutes, turning the pizza around a couple of times during cooking, until the base has risen a little and has started to crisp at the edges.

Scatter with some of the rocket leaves and serve immediately. Repeat for the remaining bases.

Equipment:
Wood Fired Oven

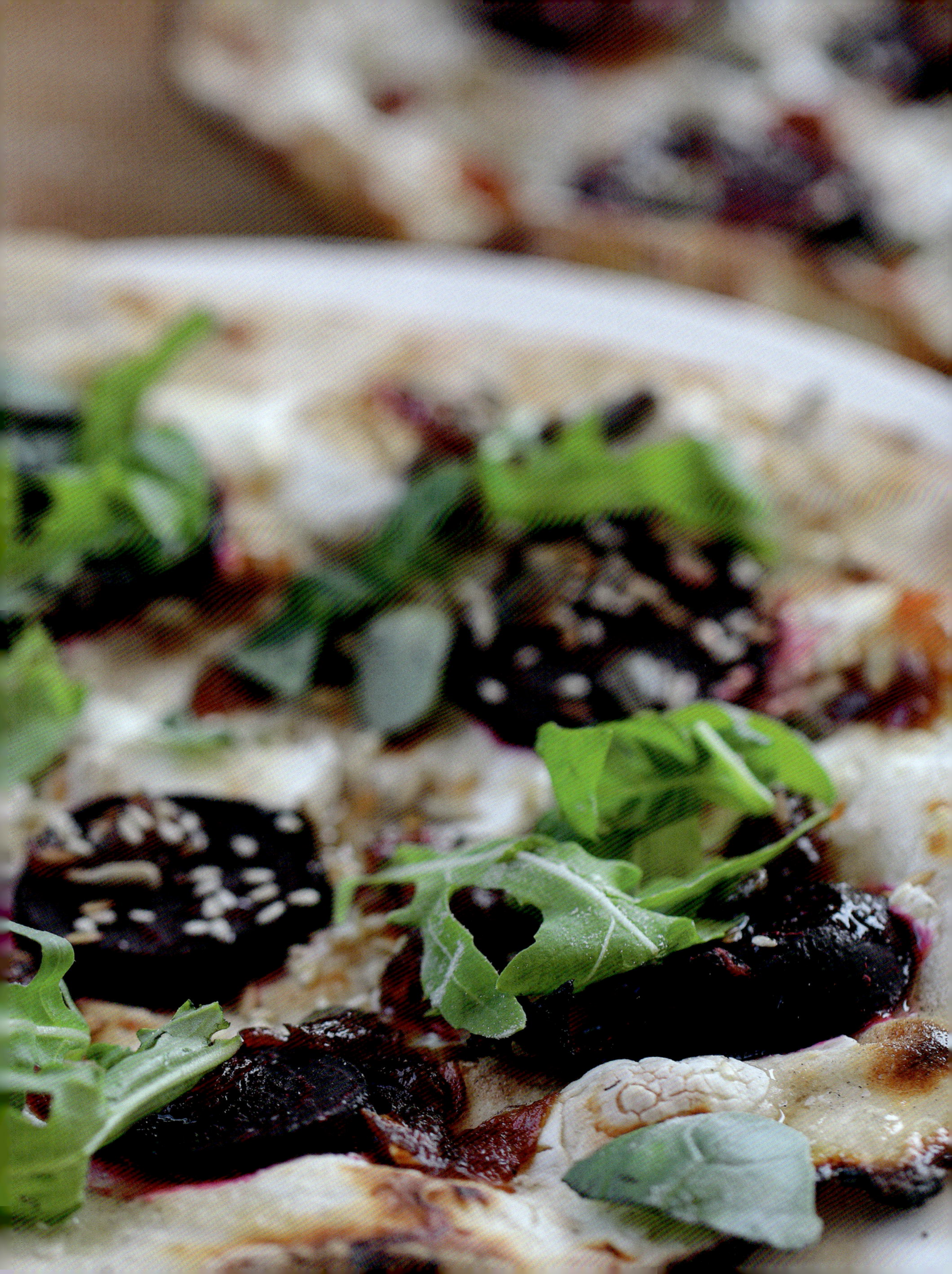

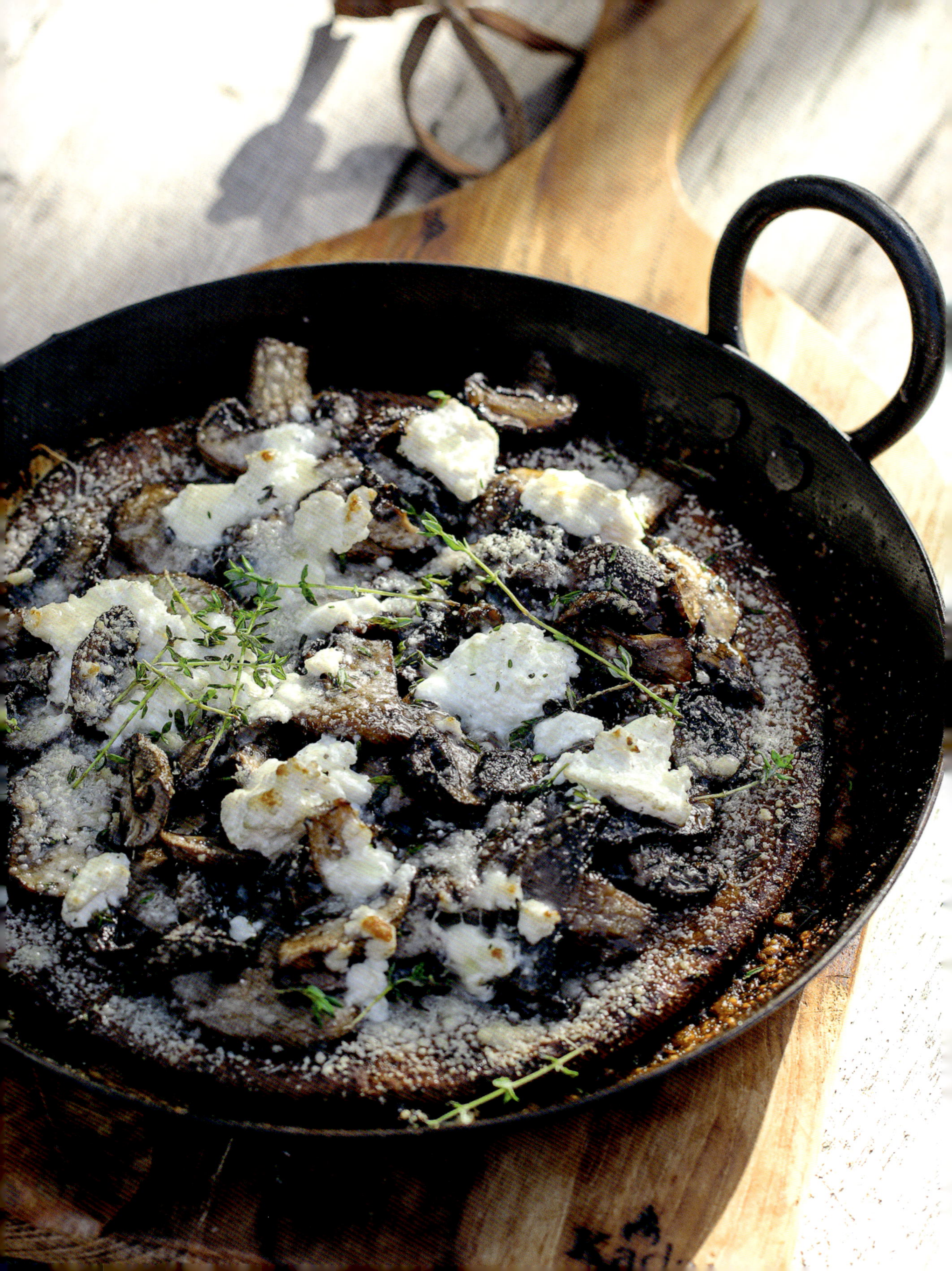

TRUFFLED MUSHROOM & THYME NAAN PIZZA

A fluffy and fragrant naan topped with truffled mushrooms, thyme and ricotta cheese. Prepare with the whole family as a quick snack or as an impressive sharing plate.

Prep time: 25 minutes (plus 1 hour proving)
Cooking time: 15 minutes plus 20 minutes per pizza
Recommended Heat: High

For the naan:

130ml warm water

7g dried yeast

2 tsp golden caster sugar

320g strong wholemeal bread flour

½ tbsp baking powder

½ tsp salt

30g unsalted butter

170ml natural yoghurt

2 tbsp nigella seeds

For the topping:

Drizzle of olive oil

200g mixed mushrooms, chopped

Small handful of fresh thyme, finely chopped

3 tbsp ricotta cheese

25g parmesan, grated

Drizzle of truffle oil

Equipment:
Set of 3 Skillets, Wood Fired Oven

TIP: Add a sprinkle of dried tarragon to your sautéed mushrooms for extra flavour

Serves 4 (1 pizza per person)

To make the naan bread dough, put the water, yeast and 1 tsp of sugar in a bowl. Leave it to stand for 10 to 15 minutes for the yeast to start working (when the mixture has started to bubble).

In another bowl, add the remaining sugar, flour, salt and baking powder; mix together and make a well in the centre. Add the butter, yoghurt, yeast mixture and nigella seeds to the well.

Combine and bring the mixture together into a soft dough ball. If it is too wet, add another spoonful of flour or, if it is too dry add a touch of water to soften. Knead the dough for 5 minutes until you get a good elasticity, and the dough bounces back. Place it into a lightly oiled bowl, cover with a damp towel and leave to prove for 1 hour. Once the dough has doubled in size, cut it into 4 even size balls and roll them into the desired shape.

In the large Skillet add a drizzle of olive oil, mushrooms and thyme. Sauté in the Wood Fired Oven (see pg. 37) for approximately 15 minutes, stirring occasionally. Drizzle olive oil into the medium Skillet and place 1 of the dough balls into the pan. Press down on the dough to flatten it, until it evenly covers the bottom of the Skillet. Drizzle the top with a little olive oil. Slide the Skillet into the Wood Fired Oven and bake for 10 to 15 minutes until the top starts to go golden brown.

Spread ¼ of the ricotta cheese across the top of the naan and sprinkle over ¼ of the sautéed mushrooms. Add a light dusting of parmesan and put back into the Wood Fired Oven until the ricotta cheese starts to melt.

Remove the pizza from the Wood Fired Oven, drizzle with truffle oil, cut in half and serve immediately. Repeat for the remaining bases.

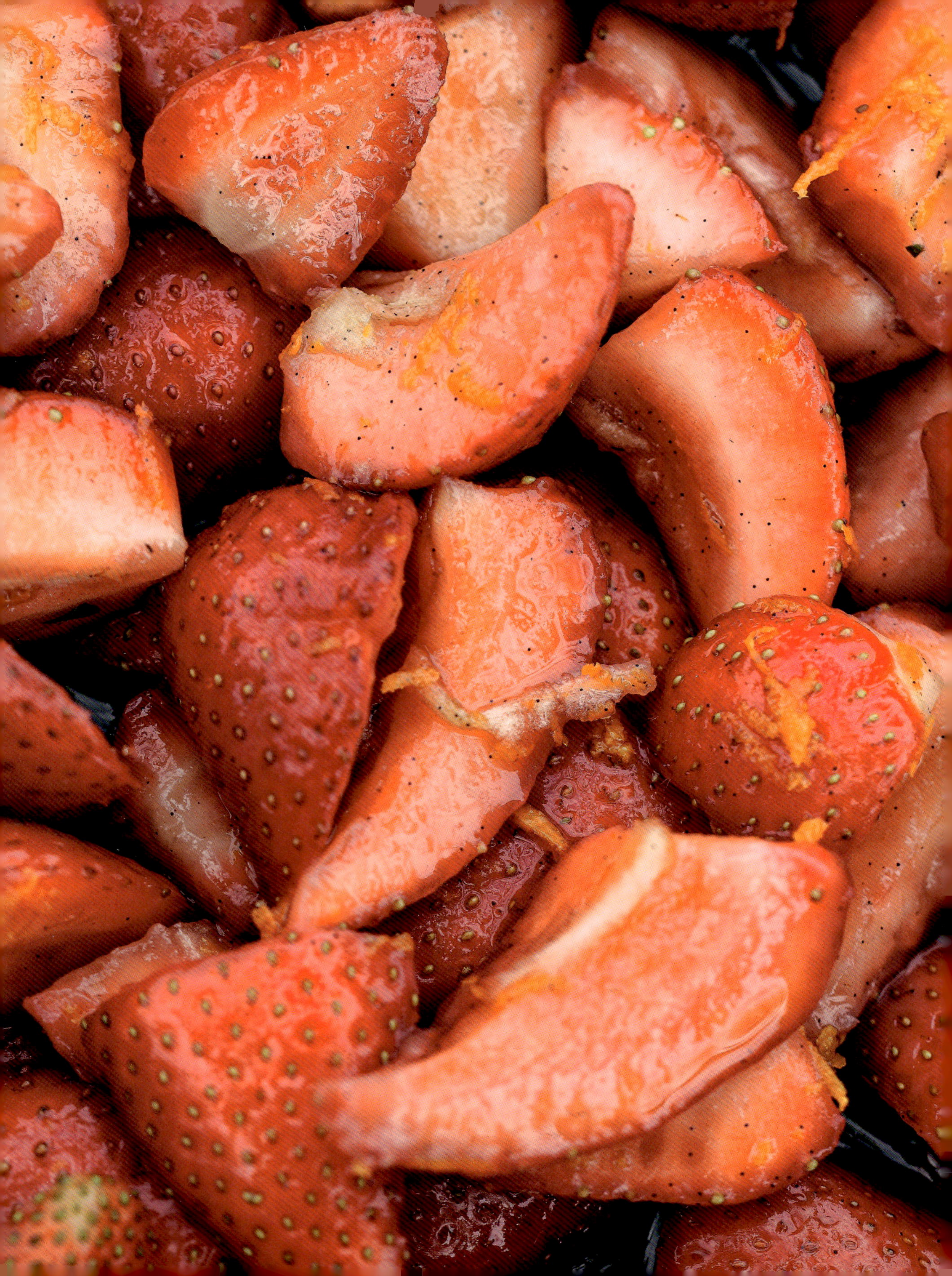

Something sweet

Having a sweet end to a barbecue feast is a great idea. Barbecuing desserts opens a world of new flavours. Try baking apples so they are sweet and soft; poach pears so they are succulent; or slowly bake a fruity pie. Here you will find "sweet" inspiration for treats using those smoky aromas.

PIMM'S & STRAWBERRY SUMMER CRUMBLE

Nothing says summer quite like Pimm's and strawberries. Marrying the two together makes a delicious pudding for a balmy evening in the garden.

Prep time: 15 minutes
Cooking time: 30 minutes
Recommended Heat: High

700g fresh strawberries, hulled and halved
80ml Pimm's
1 orange, zest grated
150g brown sugar
150g plain flour
100g salted butter, cubed
Handful flaked almonds
Dollops of whipped or clotted cream or ice cream

Serves 4

Put the strawberries, Pimm's, orange zest and 1 tablespoon of the sugar into the medium Skillet and mix well.

Put the flour and cold butter into a mixing bowl. Rub the butter and flour between your fingertips until the mixture resembles breadcrumbs.

Add the remaining sugar and mix thoroughly before sprinkling over the fruit mixture. Sprinkle with flaked almonds.

Bake in the Wood Fired Oven for approximately 30 minutes, or until the top is golden brown and the strawberries are tender.

Leave to cool slightly for 5 minutes or so before serving with cream or ice cream

Equipment:
Set of 3 Skillets, Wood Fired Oven

TIP: This is delicious with a glass of Pimm's, served in one of our Chai glasses.

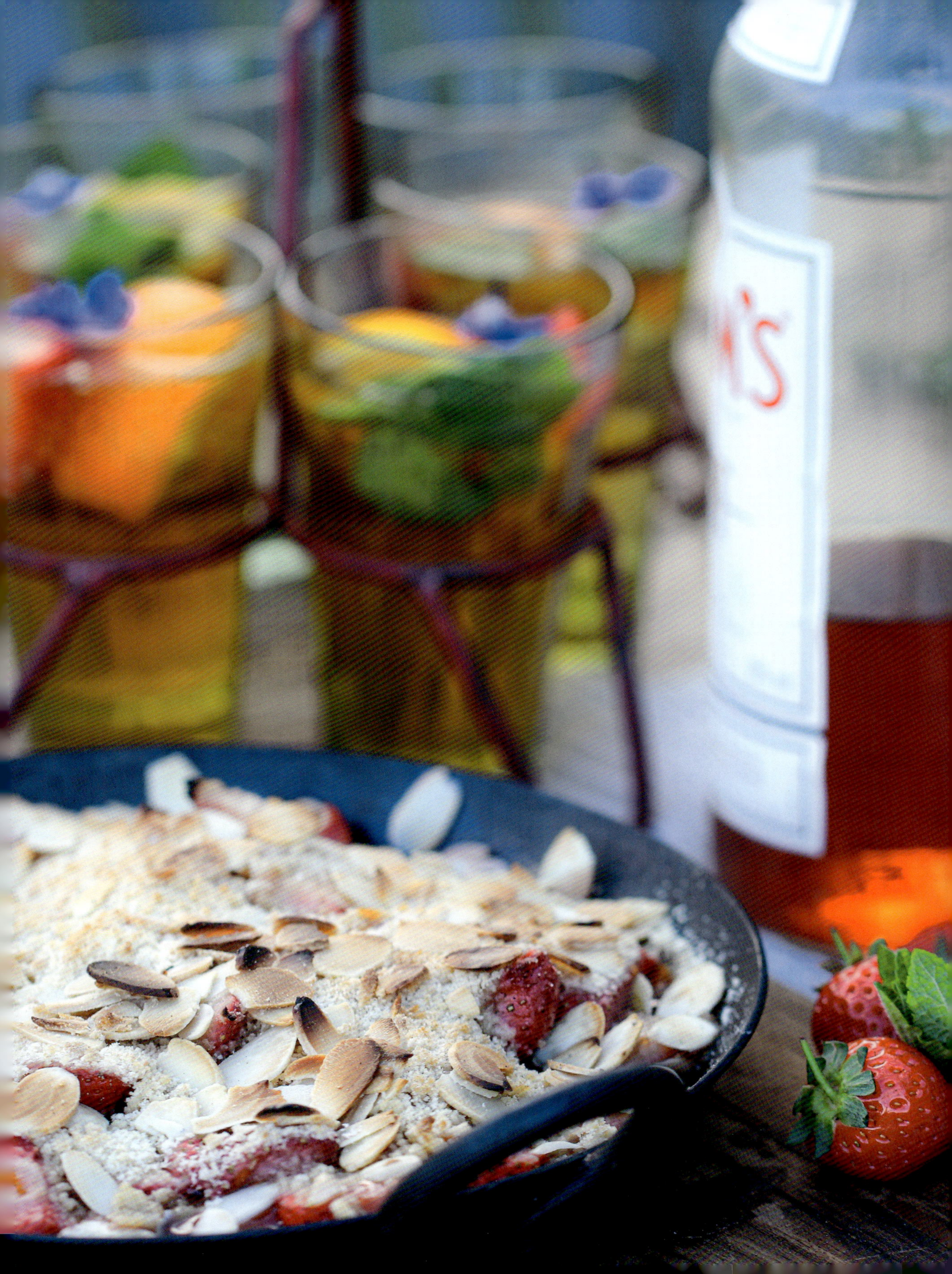

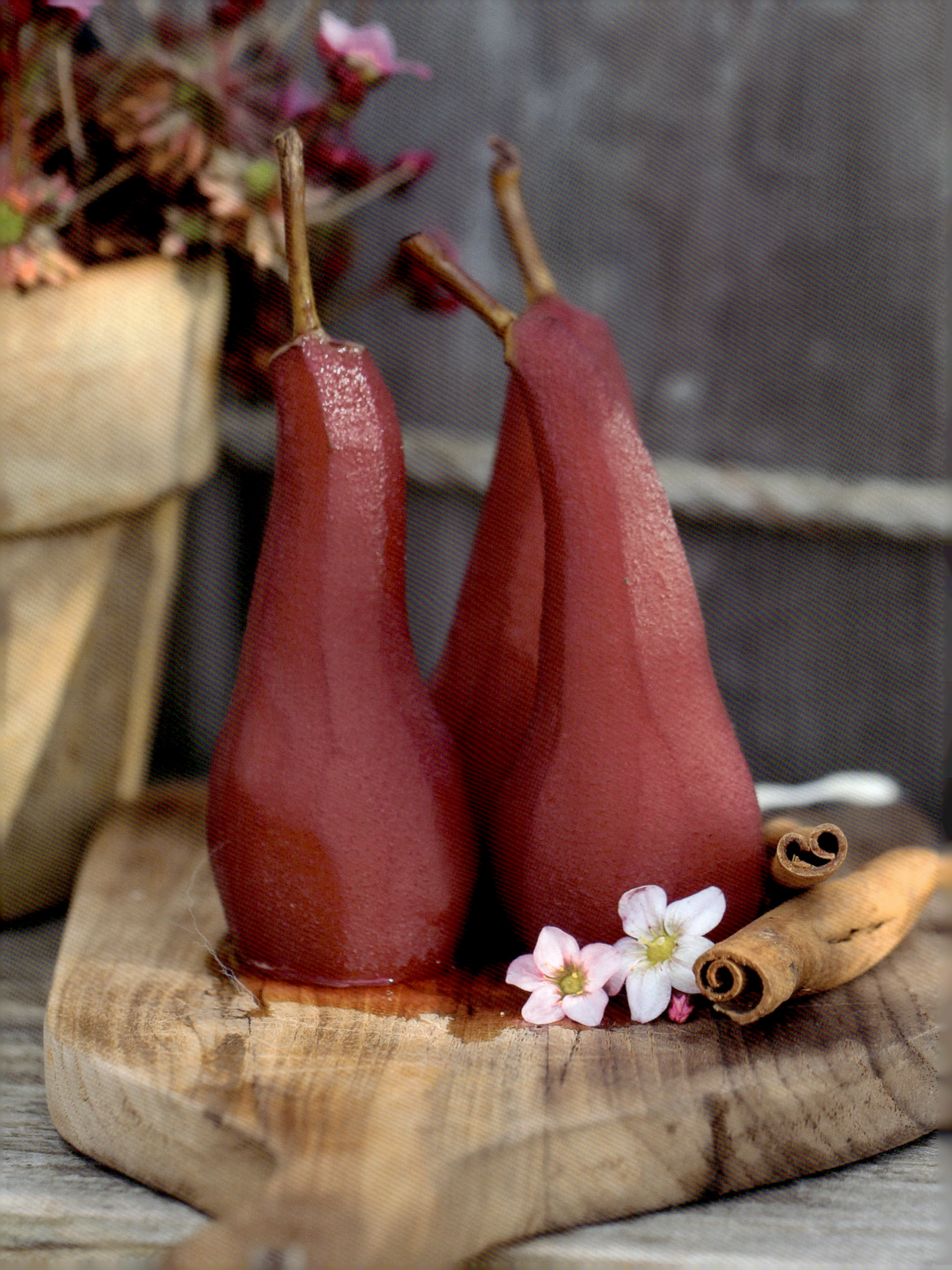

SMOKED & POACHED RED WINE PEARS

This red wine poached pear dessert is simple yet elegant. The hint of spices and delicious red wine enhances the pears' natural sweetness and is contrasted by the deep smoky flavour of the barbecue.

Prep time: 5 minutes
Cooking time: Approx. 30 minutes
Recommended Heat: Medium/High

750ml red wine
100g white sugar
50ml orange liqueur
90ml orange juice (or water)
2 tsp vanilla extract
2 cinnamon sticks
4 medium-sized pears
Whipped mascarpone cheese or cream to serve (optional)

Serves 4

Add the wine, liqueur, orange juice and vanilla extract to the Cooking Bowl suspended from the Cooking Tripod (see pg. 34). Allow enough room in the poaching liquid for the pears to be totally submerged. Bring the wine to a simmer and stir in the sugar. Once simmering, add the cinnamon.

As soon as the poaching liquid is ready, peel the pears (early peeling will cause them to discolour) and lower them into the poaching liquid. Poach the pears in the liquid on medium to low heat, simmering for 20 to 25 minutes, rotating every five minutes to ensure even poaching.

Remove the Cooking Bowl from the heat and place on its separate stand. Keep the pears upright in the poaching liquid and allow to cool down. Remove the pears from the Cooking Bowl and keep them upright.

Return the Cooking Bowl to the Cooking Tripod and bring to a gentle simmer. The liquid should thicken into a syrup after a few minutes. The cooking time will vary depending on how much liquid remains. If the syrup is too thick, add a little water.

Place the pears on serving plates, drizzle with syrup and top with whipped cream or mascarpone cheese and enjoy.

Equipment:
Cooking Bowl, Cooking Tripod

BAKED APPLES

Baked in the Kadai, these apples are juicy and soft, bursting out of their skins. With cinnamon, sultanas and brown sugar, our baked apple recipe is just the thing for a cosy autumn afternoon in the garden.

Prep time: 10 minutes
Cooking time: 20-30 minutes
Recommended Heat: Medium

2 large eating apples
40g sultanas
3 tsp soft light brown sugar
1 tsp ground mixed spice
3 tbsp unsweetened apple juice, orange juice or water
vanilla ice cream (to serve)

Serves 2

Make sure the Kadai is at a medium heat.

Place each apple on the worktop and insert the apple corer to remove the centre.

In a small bowl, combine the sultanas, 2 teaspoons of sugar and the mixed spice. Fill the centre of the apples evenly with the sultana mixture, using your fingers to push in the mixture.

Place the apples side by side in the Roasting Oven.

Add the remaining sugar to the apple/orange juice and stir to dissolve. Drizzle the juice over the stuffed apples.

Place the Roasting Oven on the embers and bake for 20 to 30 minutes (this will depend on the size and type of apples), until they are cooked through.

Serve with ice cream and enjoy.

Equipment:
Roasting Oven

TIP: Try using ground cinnamon instead of mixed spice. Or swap the sultanas for chopped ready-to-eat dried apricots or figs.

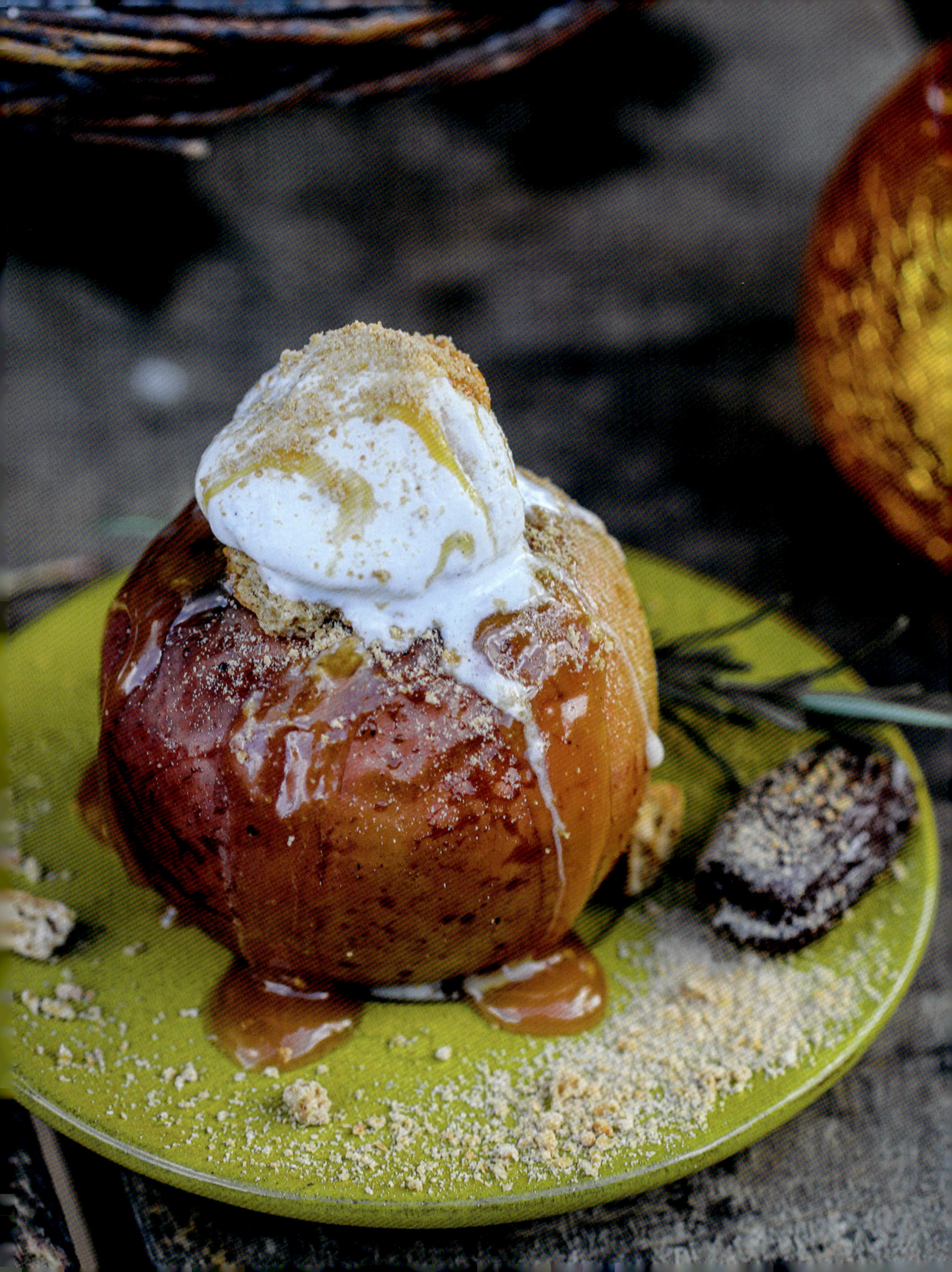

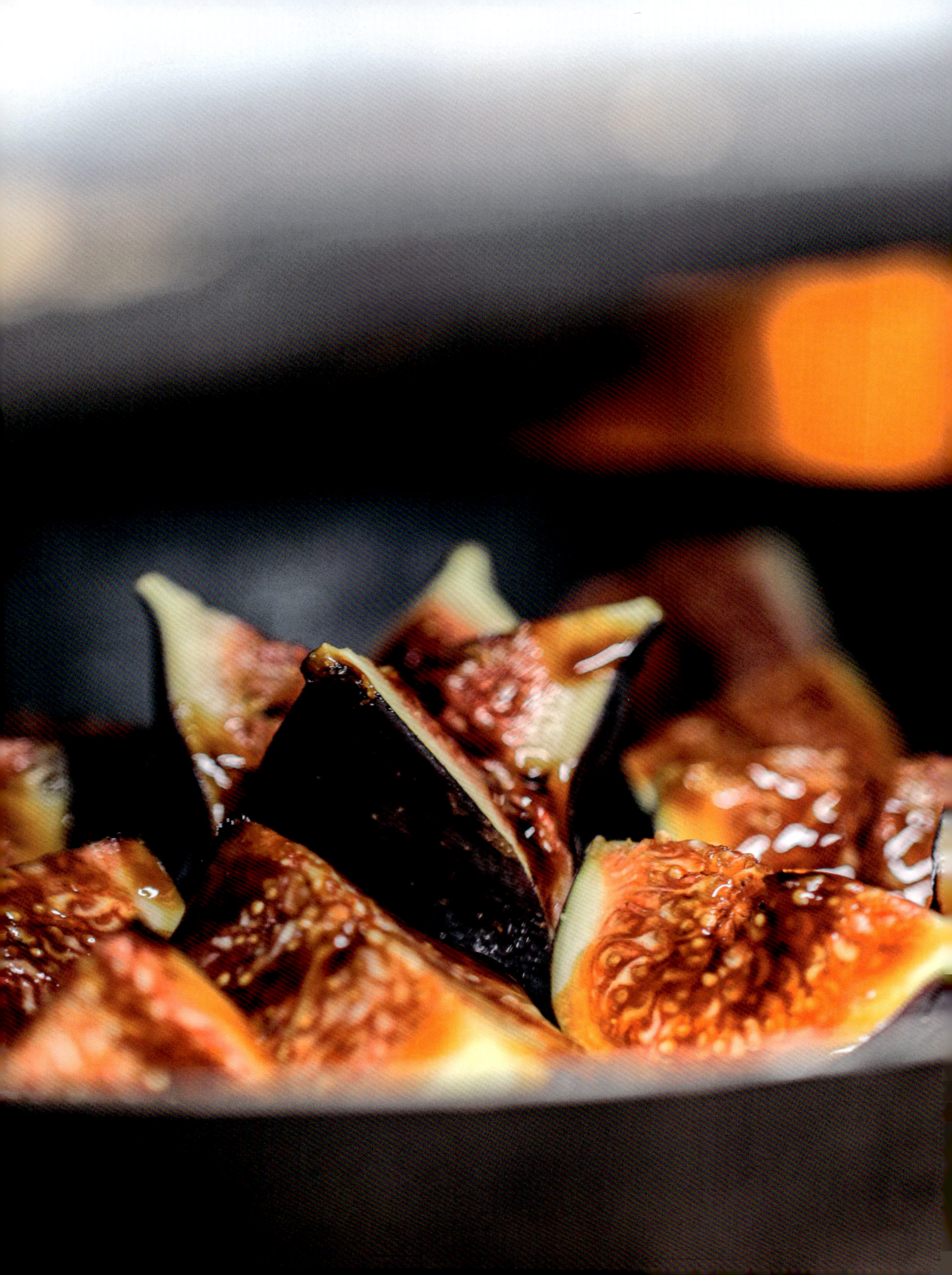

FIGS *with a* CARAMELISED GLAZE

A decadent dessert cooked over fire. A beautifully rich treat that combines the luxurious flavours of figs, balsamic glaze and fresh mint for a real fine-dining experience.

Prep time: 10 minutes
Cooking time: 20 minutes
Recommended Heat: High

4 fresh, soft figs
2 tsp brown caster sugar
Drizzle of balsamic vinegar glaze
1 scoop vanilla ice cream or Chantilly cream
2 sprigs of fresh mint

Serves 2

Stand the figs upright and cut each one in half down through the stalk. Place the figs, flat side down, into a Skillet. Sprinkle the figs with the sugar and a good drizzle of balsamic vinegar glaze.

Place the Skillet into the Wood Fired Oven (see pg. 37) and allow the figs to simmer until the balsamic glaze reduces and starts to thicken.

Remove from the Wood Fired Oven, after about 20 minutes and serve with a large scoop of ice cream or a generous drizzle of Chantilly cream, and a sprig of fresh mint.

Equipment:
Set of 3 Skillets, Wood Fired Oven

PUMPKIN PIE

A quick bake in the Wood Fired Oven and this scrumptious treat uses up all those leftover Halloween pumpkins. Enjoy the beautiful autumn days with this sweet and filling pie.

Prep time: 10 minutes
Cooking time: 40-45 minutes
Recommended Heat: High

400g prepared pumpkin, cut into small cubes
375g ready-rolled shortcrust pastry
3 free-range eggs
100g brown sugar
50g granulated sugar
175ml single cream
1 tbsp ground cinnamon
1 tbsp ground ginger
1½ tsp nutmeg, grated
½ tsp salt
Salted caramel sauce, to serve (optional)
Whipped cream, to serve

Serves 4

Place the pumpkin into a colander and rest it over a pan of simmering water. Cover and steam for 15 minutes or until soft. Purée in a blender until smooth and leave to cool slightly.

Unroll the sheet of pastry, reserving the paper it is rolled up in. Use this paper to line the base and sides of a medium Skillet, then line the pan with the pastry. Crimp the edges with a fork.

Whisk the eggs and both types of sugar together in a bowl until light and fluffy. Add the pumpkin purée, single cream, spices and salt and mix until smooth.

Pour the filling into the pastry base and bake inside the Wood Fired Oven (see pg. 37) for 20 to 25 minutes until the pie is firm in the middle. Leave to cool before removing from the Skillet.

Slice and serve with whipped cream and caramel sauce.

Equipment:
Set of 3 Skillets, Wood Fired Oven

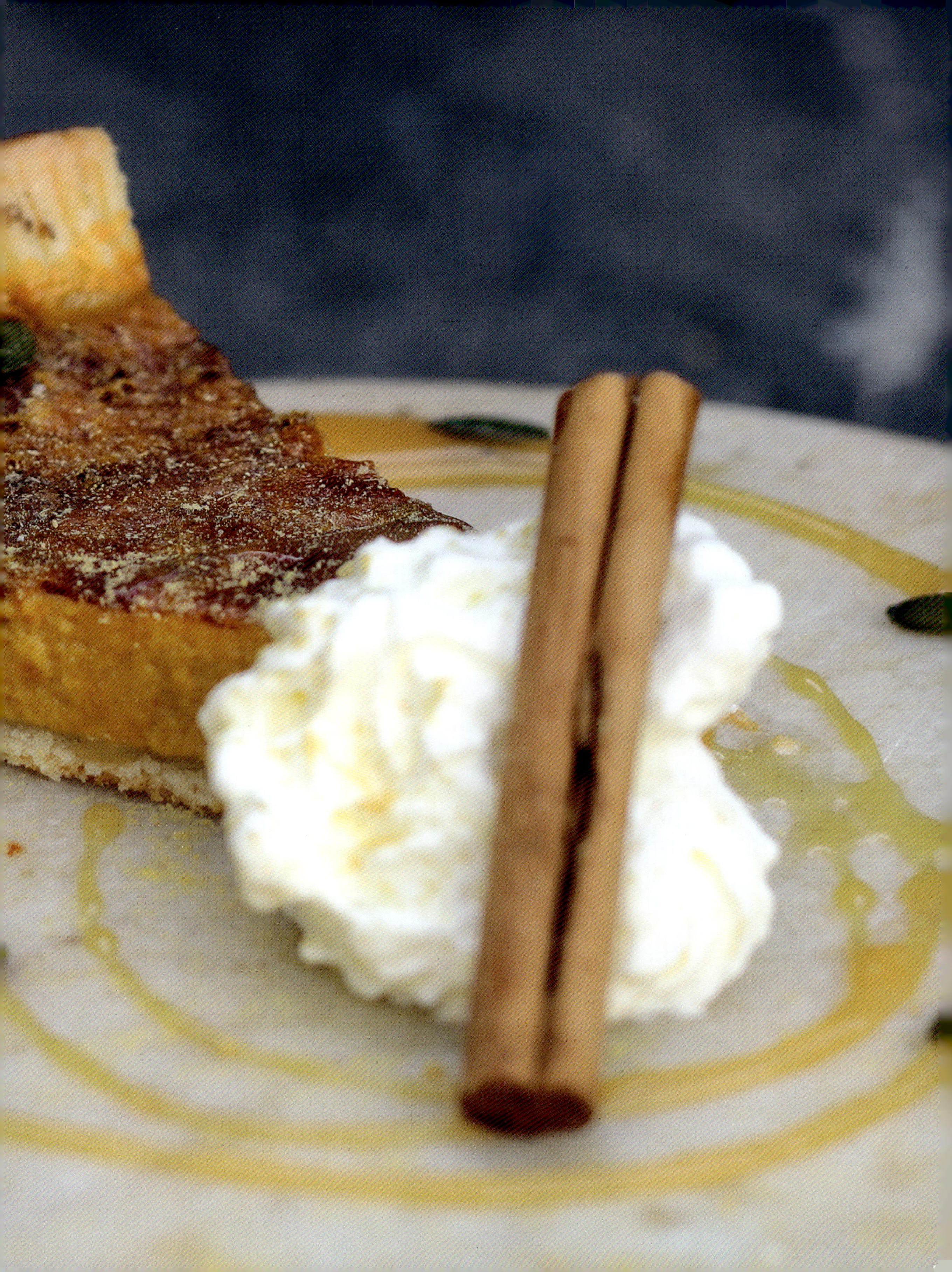

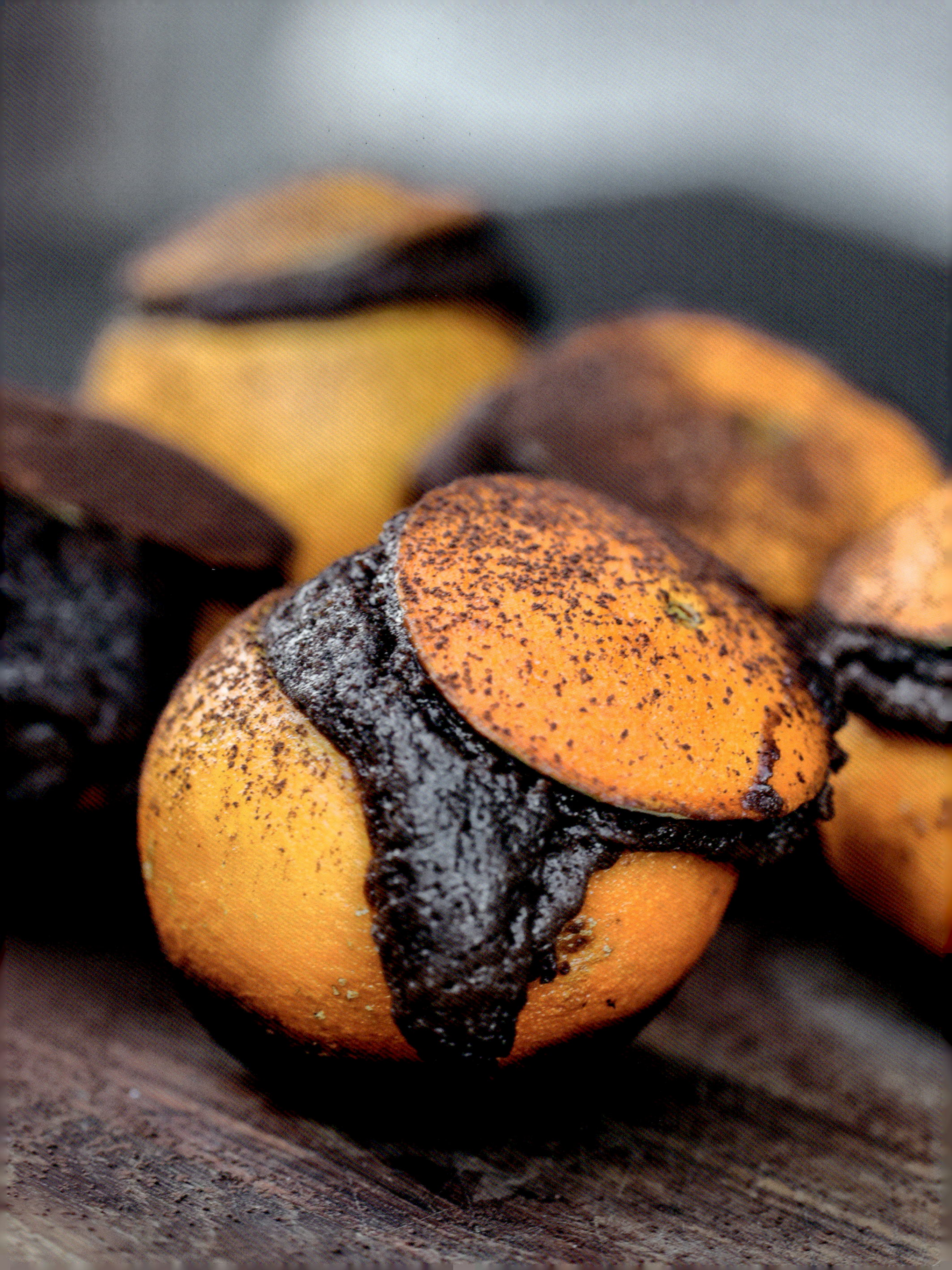

ORANGE BROWNIES

There is a beautiful balance between orange and chocolate. The sweetness and acidity of the orange complement the rich, slightly bitter flavour of the chocolate. Combining these two flavours into a fun presentation makes these orange brownies a tasty treat.

Prep time: 15 minutes
Cooking time: 35-40 minutes
Recommended Heat: Low/Medium

220g dark chocolate
170g unsalted butter
220g granulated sugar
115g dark brown sugar
4 medium free-range eggs (at room temperature)
2 tsp vanilla extract
215g all-purpose flour
2 tbsp cocoa powder
1 tsp salt
6-8 medium oranges

Serves 4

Place the chocolate and butter into a pan over a low heat and stir constantly until the mixture is smooth. Remove from the heat and allow to cool.

Add the sugar to the melted chocolate and mix until completely combined. Whisk in the eggs and vanilla extract.

Sift the flour, cocoa powder and salt over the mixture and fold it in to make a batter.

Using a serrated knife, cut the top off each orange and carefully take out most of the flesh to make room to add some batter. Leaving some flesh will add to the flavour of the brownies.

Pour the batter into the oranges until they are three quarters full, leaving space for the mixture to rise whilst it is cooking.

Place the oranges directly on the Grill over a medium heat and cover with the Kadai Lid.

Cook for 35 to 40 minutes until the brownies are done, remove from the heat and enjoy.

Equipment:
Kadai Lid

TIP: If you don't have a Kadai Lid, these can also be cooked in the Wood Fired Oven

AMARETTI S'MORES

Finish off your barbecue with these deliciously gooey, melted, amaretti s'mores. Each sweet biscuit sandwich is filled with oozy, chocolate spread and melted marshmallows.

Prep time: 5 minutes
Cooking time: Approx. 4 minutes
Recommended Heat: Medium

8 amaretti biscuits
8 tsp milk chocolate spread
4 marshmallows

Serves 2

Paste the chocolate spread evenly onto the 8 biscuits.

Using a Marshmallow Fork, warm the marshmallows through for approximately 1 minute on each side, over an open fire, careful not to lose any marshmallows to the flames.

Remove the toasted marshmallows from the Marshmallow Fork and place each one on top of a biscuit.

Place another biscuit on top of each marshmallow and the s'more is now ready to serve.

Equipment:
Marshmallow Fork

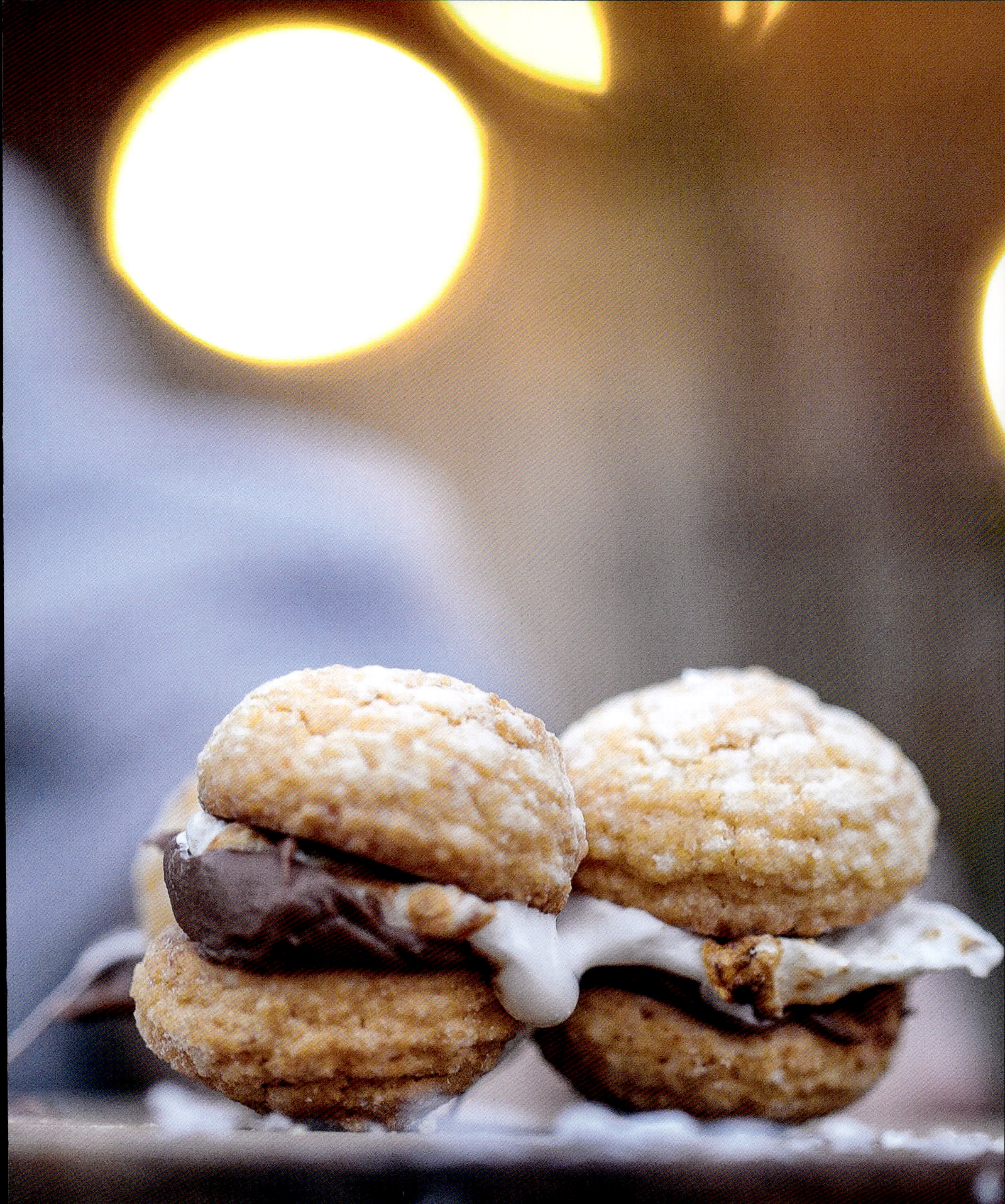

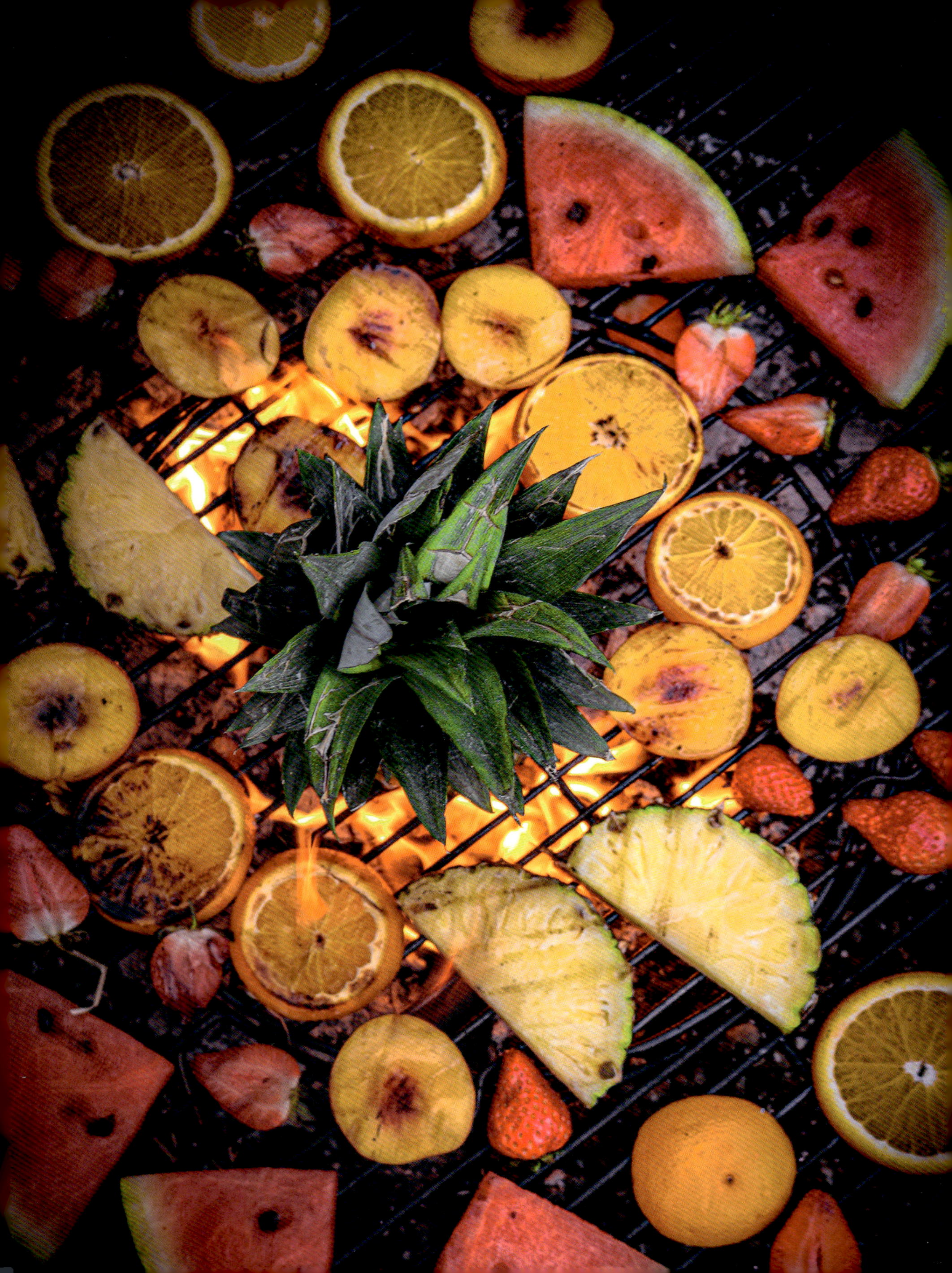

Drinks from the grill

Your barbecue can be even more creative by adding some unusual cocktails to the mix, and welcoming guests with an aperitif with a difference. Grilling fruit adds a delicious, charred flavour to balance out the sweetness of other ingredients. Or why not try toasting marshmallows for an indulgent, chocolatey cocktail to end the perfect evening?

BURNT ORANGE GIN

An elegant cocktail that pairs gin and citrus, perfect to serve as an appetiser before your Kadai feast.

Prep time: 10 minutes
Cooking time: 5 minutes
Recommended Heat: Low

4 small slices of orange
200ml orange-flavoured gin
Tonic water (we used Mediterranean)
Few drops of ginger bitters
Ice cubes
Small bunch of dried thyme sprigs

Serves 4

Place the slices of orange on the bars of a heated Grill.

Once they are nicely marked with the bars of the Grill, remove them from the heat to a Chopping Board and leave them to cool for a couple of minutes.

Mix the gin and tonic in glasses, with a tiny splash of ginger bitters and some ice.

Add a slice of charred orange and a sprig of dried thyme to each glass and serve.

Equipment:
Chopping Board

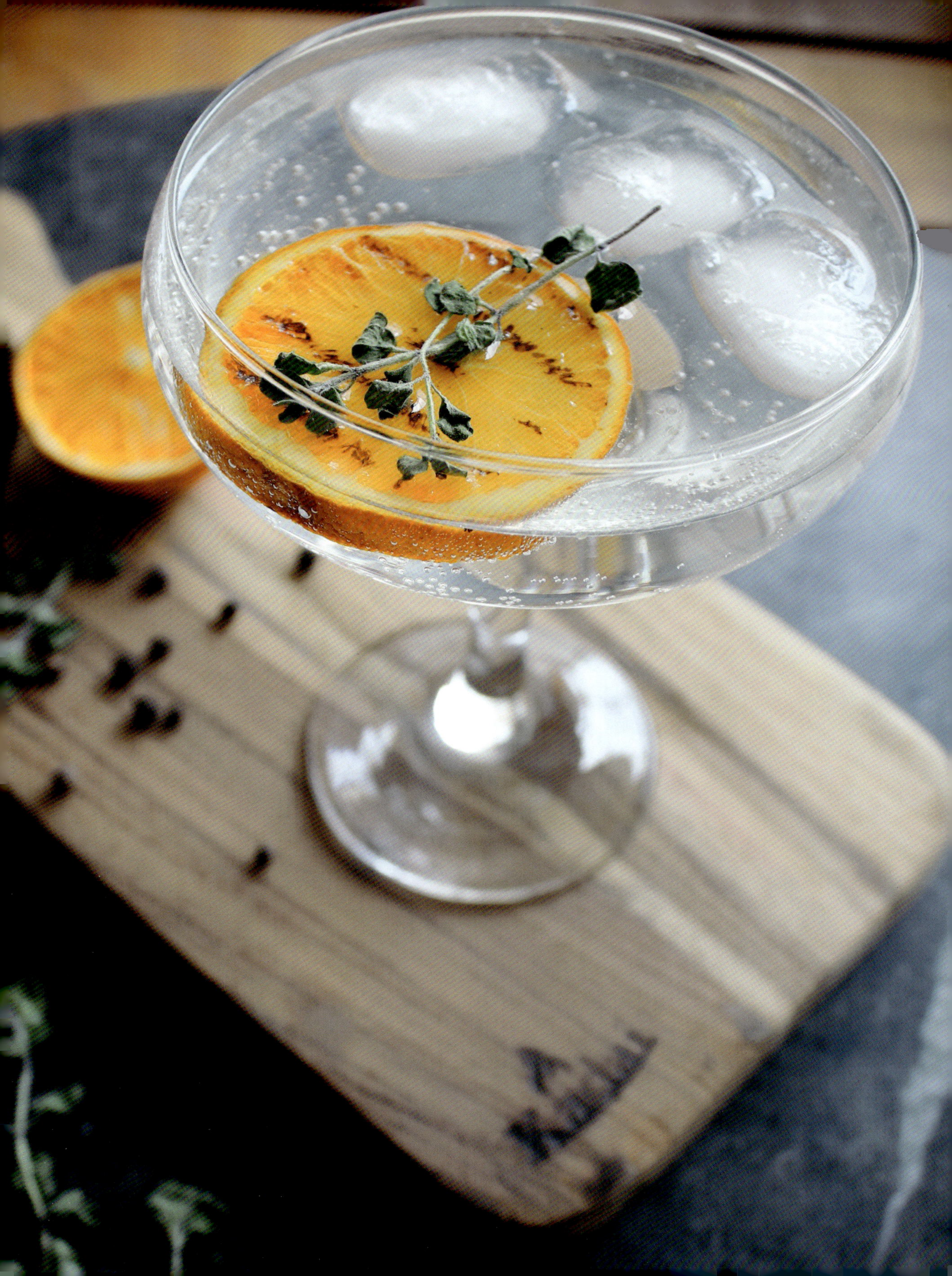

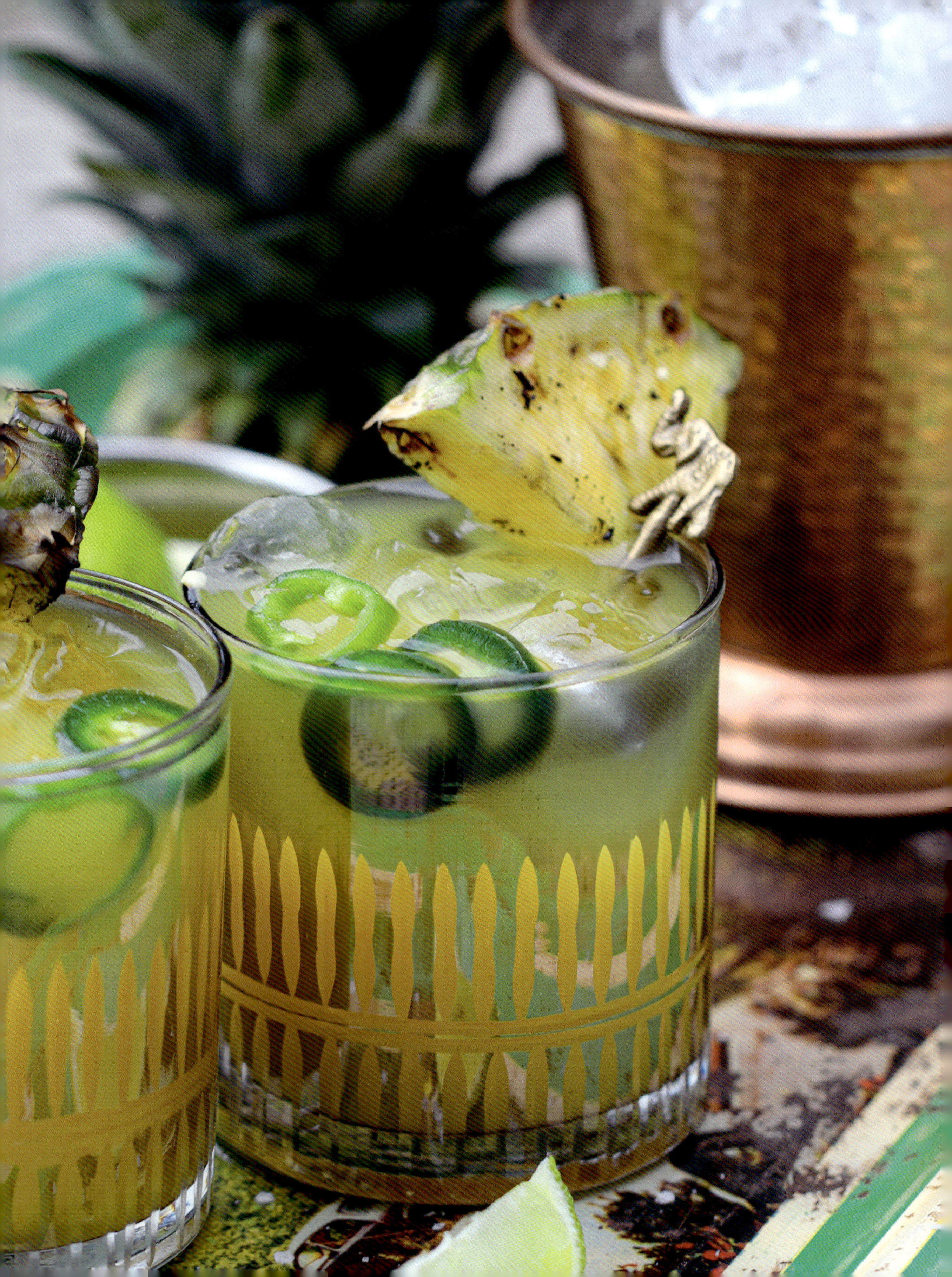

GRILLED PINEAPPLE
with JALAPEÑO MARGARITA

This sweet and sour cocktail is bursting with tropical summer flavours you can enjoy in your garden.

Prep time: 5 minutes
Cooking time: 5 minutes
Recommended Heat: Medium

1 slice fresh unpeeled pineapple, cut into 4 small wedges
Ice cubes
4 tbsp lime juice
240ml Tequila
300ml pineapple juice
120ml Cointreau
1 jalapeño chilli, sliced across

Serves 4

Place the wedges of pineapple directly onto the heated Grill.

Once they are nicely marked with the bars of the Grill, remove them from the heat to a Chopping Board and leave them to cool for a couple of minutes.

Half fill a cocktail shaker with ice and add the lime juice, Tequila, pineapple juice and Cointreau.

Shake vigorously and pour into 4 glasses.

Garnish with a wedge of the charred pineapple and the jalapeño slices.

Equipment:
Chopping Board

CHARRED SANGRIA

Feel the Spanish sun on your face as you fall in love with this charred sangria – a Kadai twist to a summertime classic.

Prep time: 10 minutes
Cooking time: 5 minutes
Recommended Heat: Medium

2 oranges, quartered
1 lemon, quartered
Small bowl of brown sugar
750ml red wine
500ml lemonade
50ml of brandy
1 ripe peach, sliced
200g berries, sliced (we used strawberries and cherries)
Ice cubes
Sliced lemon and orange to garnish

Serves 4 (with enough for top ups)

Lightly dip the orange and lemon quarters into the sugar.

Place the orange and lemon quarters skin-side down in a small Skillet and slide onto the Grill.

Leave for about 3 minutes until they start to char, then take off the Grill and leave to cool.

Squeeze the juice from each quarter through a small sieve into a large serving jug.

Add the red wine, lemonade and brandy to the jug, add the peach, strawberry and cherry slices and serve in a large wine glass, poured over ice.

Equipment:
Set of 3 Skillets

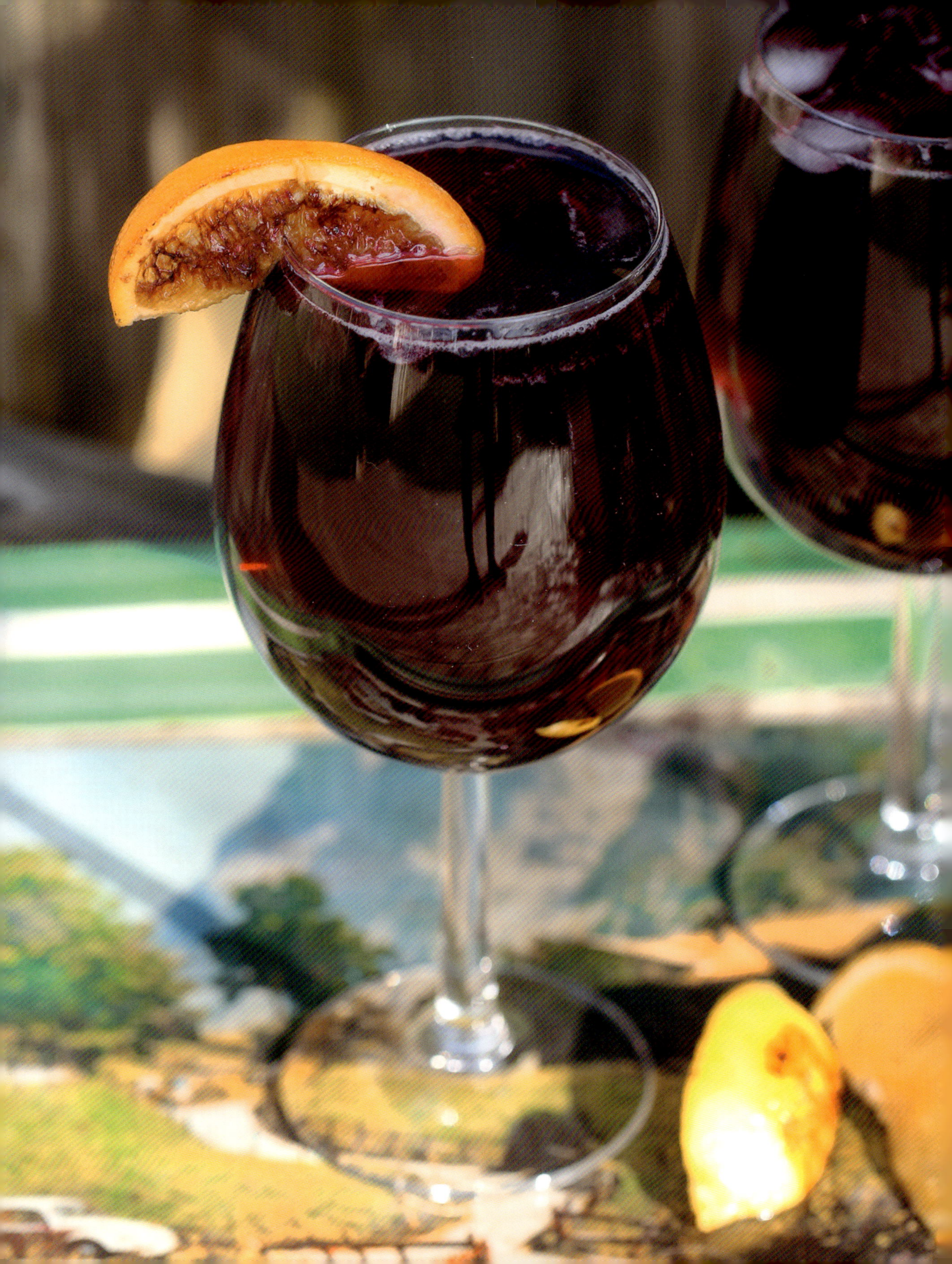

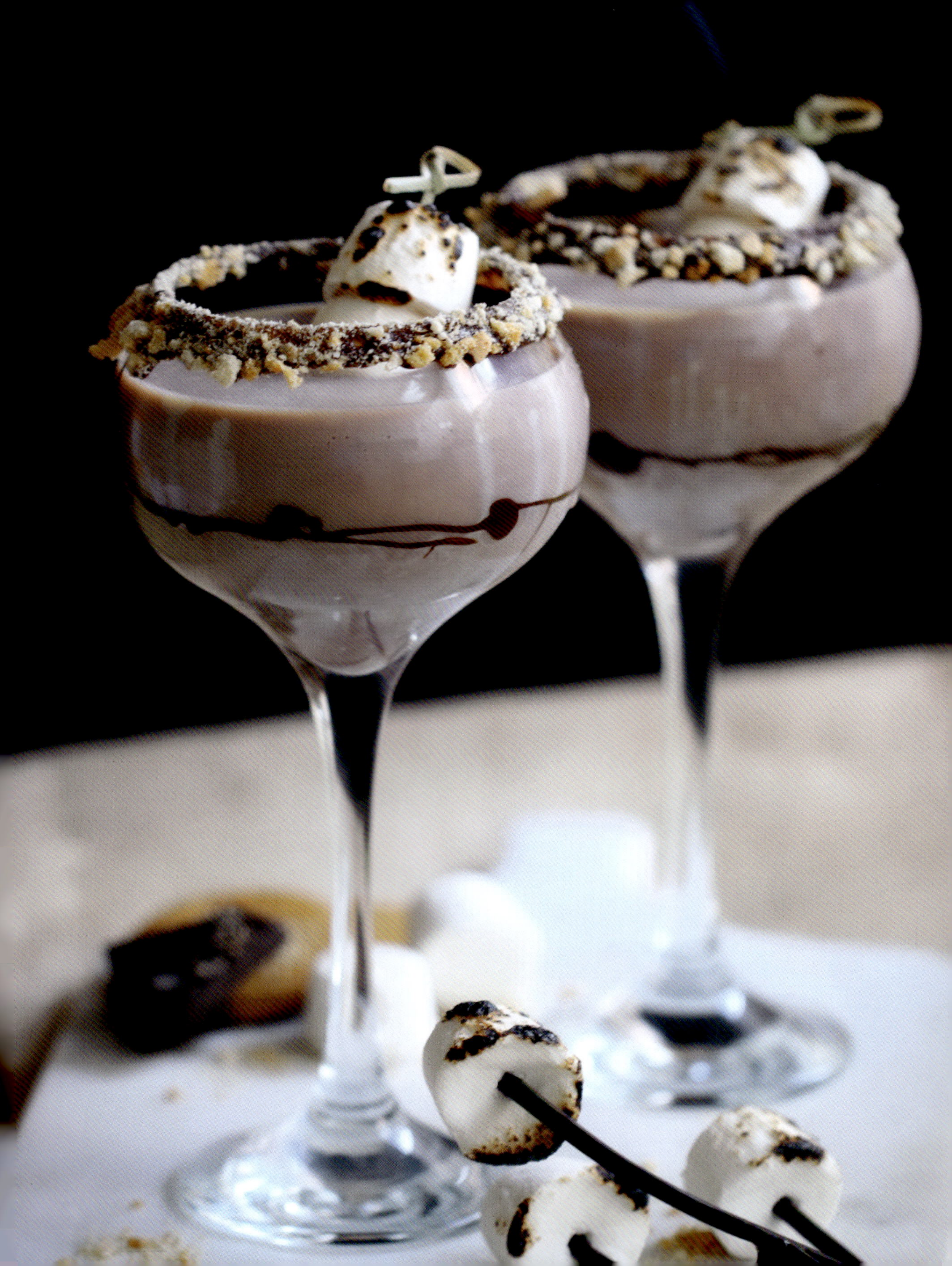

TOASTED MARSHMALLOW KADAI COCKTAIL

A rich and utterly indulgent treat, this boozy hot chocolate must be enjoyed around a warming fire.

Prep time: 10 minutes
Cooking time: 5 minutes
Recommended Heat: Medium

50g chocolate chips
1 tsp butter
3-4 ginger biscuits, crushed
340ml Baileys chocolate luxe liqueur
Ice cubes
8 marshmallows
8 wooden cocktail sticks

Serves 4

Put the chocolate chips into a small Skillet with the butter and place over a low heat. Stir constantly until the chocolate has melted, then remove the Skillet from the heat.

To decorate the glasses, dip the rim of each glass into the melted chocolate and then carefully into the crushed ginger biscuits.

Turn the glasses right-side up again and using a spoon, swirl the chocolate around the inside of each glass. Place in the fridge to cool.

Once the sauce has hardened in the glass, pour approximately 85ml of Baileys into each glass (dependent on the glass you are using) and top with ice.

Using a Toasting Fork or Marshmallow Fork, quickly toast the marshmallows over the Kadai flames and thread onto wooden cocktail sticks.

Rest them on the top of each glass, serve and enjoy.

Equipment:
Set of 3 Skillets, Toasting Fork or Marshmallow Fork

A

alcohol, *see drinks*; red wine
apples: baked apples 212
asado cross 34
aubergine: baba ghanoush 88
avocado:
    smashed with bacon bagels 62
    smashed with jackfruit tacos 176

B

bacon: maple bagels with avocado 62
baking 30
beans: smoky with beef ribs & 'slaw' 131
beef 45
    brisket with barbecue sauce 128
    pulled brisket 132
    ribs, smoky beans & 'slaw' 131
    rub 46
    Sunday roast 152
    temperature 24
    see also burgers; steak
beetroot:
    and feta salad with spiced oil 84
    goat's cheese & rocket pizza 202
biscuits: amaretti s'mores 220
bread:
    ciabatta with creamy mushrooms 96
    maple bacon bagels 62
    naan pizza with mushrooms & thyme 205
    tahini flatbreads 179
burgers:
    patty stack with burger sauce 109
    surf & turf with crispy shallots 113
    wild boar with apple sauce 155

C

cakes: orange brownies 219
calamari 76
carrots: braised 136
charcoal 12–13, 15, 20
cheese:
    blue cheese dip 168
    cheddar & hazelnut topping 164
    ember-baked camembert 87
    goat's cheese, beetroot & rocket pizza 202
    halloumi salad 83
    ricotta & courgette rollatini 175
    Swiss raclette with baby potatoes & pickles 184
    see also feta cheese
chicken:
    marinade 53
    rub 48
    whole roasted in garlic & lemon marinade 143
    and wild garlic pie with cheddar & hazelnut topping 164
    wings with blue cheese dip 168
chimichurri 55
    onion & wild garlic risotto 148
chocolate:
    amaretti s'mores 220
    orange brownies 219
chorizo: stew 160
cleaning cookware 41
coconut: and prawn Penang curry 172
cooking methods 26–33
cooking tripods 34
cookware 34–38, 40
courgettes:
    frittata with feta & mint 70
    rollatini with ricotta 175
cream:
    charcoal sauce 136
    moules marinière 118
    mushrooms on ciabatta 96
crème fraîche: pancakes & berries 73
curries:
    goat 156
    prawn & coconut 172
    Sri Lankan 167

D

desserts:
    baked apples 212
    figs with a caramelised glaze 215
    Pimm's & strawberry summer crumble 208
    pumpkin pie 216
    smoked & poached red wine pears 211
dips: blue cheese 168
direct cooking 26

dirty cooking 33
drinks:
   burnt orange gin 224
   jalapeño margaritas 227
   marshmallow cocktail 231
   sangria 228
duck: Peking pancakes with Hoisin sauce 171

E

eggs:
   courgette frittata with feta & mint 70
   shakshuka 69

F

fennel: with wild boar steaks 136
feta cheese:
   beetroot salad with spiced oil 84
   courgette frittata 70
figs: with a caramelised glaze 215
fire building 13, 18, 20
fish 45
   fire-smoked kippers with lemon & parsley 66
   grilled sardines with samphire 79
   herb-roasted rainbow trout 122
   marinade 53
   plank-smoked salmon with lemon, dill & parsley 147
   rub 49
   sea bass, vine tomatoes & salsa verde 117
   temperature 24
   see also seafood
fruit:
   figs with a caramelised glaze 215
   jackfruit tacos with avocado & 'slaw' 176
   sangria 228
   smoked & poached red wine pears 211
   strawberry & Pimm's summer crumble 208
   fresh berries & pancakes 73
   see also apples; lemon; oranges; pineapple

G

garlic:
   creamy mushrooms 96
   moules marinière 118
   see also wild garlic
goat: curry 156
grilling 27

H

halloumi: salad 83
herbs 44–5, 58–9
   roasted rainbow trout 122
   thyme & mushroom naan pizza 205
   see also mint; parsley; pesto
honey:
   glaze with charred vegetables 91
   and mint lamb rack with pistachio crust 114

I

indirect cooking 26

J

jackfruit: tacos with smashed avocado 176

K

Kadai kits 10–11, 40–1
kippers: fire-smoked with lemon & parsley 66

L

lamb 45
   honey & mint rack with pistachio crust 114
   marinade 50
   Mediterranean fire-roasted leg 135
   and mint pie 163
   rub 48
   souvlaki 159
   temperature 24
lemon:
   fire-smoked kippers & parsley 66
   plank-smoked salmon 147
   roast chicken & garlic marinade 143
lids 38
lobster: grilled 121

low & slow cooking 28
lumpwood charcoal 15

M

maintenance of equipment 40–1
marinades 50–3
marinara sauce 193
marshmallows: Kadai cocktail 231
mint:
    courgette frittata with feta 70
    honey lamb rack with pistachio crust 114
    and lamb pie 163
mojo rojo 57
muntjac 144
mushrooms:
    on ciabatta 96
    shawarma in tahini flatbreads 179
    and thyme naan pizza 205
mussels: moules marinère 118

N

noodles: pad thai 125
nuts:
    hazelnut & cheddar topping 164
    pistachio crust with lamb rack 114

O

oak plank cooking 30
oils:
    basil 95
    spiced 84
onions: and wild garlic risotto 148
oranges:
    brownies 219
    burnt gin 224
oysters: dirty 80

P

pan-frying 27
pancakes:
    crème fraîche & berries 73
    Peking duck with Hoisin sauce 171
parsley:
    fire-smoked kippers with lemon 66
    moules marinière 118

plank-smoked salmon 147
pears: smoked & poached red wine 211
pesto 55
    roasted peppers 92
    steak salad & rocket 106
    and sun-dried tomato pizza 201
pies:
    chicken & wild garlic 164
    lamb & mint 163
    pumpkin 216
    samosa 180
pineapple:
    grilled with jalapeño margaritas 227
    Hawaiian sauce 110
pistachios: crust with lamb rack 114
pizzas:
    alla marinara 194
    beetroot, goat's cheese & rocket 202
    dough 190
    Kadai's signature 198
    Napoli 197
    sun-dried tomato & pesto 201
    truffled mushroom & thyme naan 205
pork 45
    belly ends 139
    marinade 50
    rub 50
    sticky ribs 140
    temperature 24
see also bacon; salami
potatoes:
    roast 99
    Swiss raclette with pickles 184
poultry 45
    temperature 24
see also chicken; duck
prawns: coconut Penang curry 172
pumpkin: pie 216

R

rainbow trout: herb-roasted 122
red peppers: roasted with pesto 92
red wine:
    sangria 228
    smoked & poached pears 211
resting meat 25
rice: dirty onion & wild garlic risotto 148

rocket:
   beetroot & goat's cheese pizza 202
   seared steak salad & pesto 106
rubs 46–7

S

salads:
   beetroot & feta 84
   halloumi 83
seared steak with rocket & pesto 106
salami: skewers coated with
   Hawaiian pineapple sauce 110
salmon: plank-smoked with lemon,
   dill & parsley 147
salsa verde 57
sea bass & vine tomatoes 117
samosa: pie 180
samphire: with grilled sardines 79
sardines: grilled with samphire 79
sauces 54–57
   apple 155
   barbecue 54, 128
   burger 109
   charcoal cream 136
   Hawaiian pineapple 110
   marinara 193
sea bass: pan-fried, vine tomatoes &
   salsa verde 117
seafood:
   calamari 76
   dirty oysters 80
   grilled lobster 121
   moules marinière 118
   prawn & coconut Penang
     curry 172
   surf & turf 113
shakshuka 69
shallots: crispy 113
slaw:
   beef ribs & smoky beans 131
   with jackfruit tacos 176
slow beef brisket 128
smoking 29
spices 44–5
steak:
   caveman tomahawk 102
   seared salad with rocket & pesto 106
   and vegetable stir-fry sizzler 105

stews: chorizo 160
strawberries: Pimm's summer
   crumble 208
sun-dried tomatoes: and pesto pizza 201

T

temperature 23–4
thyme: mushroom naan pizza 205
tomatoes:
   grilled with basil oil drizzle 95
   sea bass & salsa verde 117
   see also sun-dried tomatoes

V

vegetables:
   baba ghanoush 88
   braised carrots 136
   charred with honey glaze 91
   crispy shallots 113
   onions & wild garlic risotto 148
   pad thai 125
   pumpkin pie 216
   roasted peppers with pesto 92
   rub 49
   samosa pie 180
   'slaw' 128, 131
   stir-fry sizzler 105
   tarte tatin 183
   see also beetroot; courgettes;
   mushrooms; potatoes; 'slaw'
venison:
   temperature 24
   wild muntjac 144

W

wild boar:
   burgers with dirty apple sauce 155
   steaks with braised carrots, fennel
     & charcoal cream sauce 136
wild garlic:
   and chicken pie 164
   and onion risotto 148
   roast chicken & lemon marinade 143
wood 12, 17–8, 20, 29, 30
wood fired ovens 37

Acknowledgements

This book has been compiled and photographed mostly in-house at Kadai HQ, located in the beautiful Shropshire Hills, drawing upon knowledge gained over the past 20 years of trial and error. In addition, we have benefitted greatly from the assistance of local chefs and suppliers, who, along with our loyal customer base, have inspired us to create this cookbook to be enjoyed by all.

To the Kadai team who have supported us on this long journey, we are so thankful for the time and enthusiasm they have contributed towards this project, and most importantly their willingness to taste test the recipes.

Particular thanks to:

The Shropshire Lad (Adam Purnell), who we have had the great pleasure of working with for many years - sharing experiences of cooking over live fire and creating wonderful food. Specifically, Adam generously supplied the following recipes for this book:

Pork Belly Ends (see pg. 139)
Wild Muntjac (see pg. 144)
Dirty Onion & Wild Garlic Risotto with Chimichurri (see pg. 148)
Boar-some Burgers with Dirty Apple Sauce (see pg. 155)

Jess Waller, from Batchcott & Waller, who has kindly contributed some recipes packed with flavour which are utterly scrumptious, exactly suited for Kadai cooking. With special thanks for the following recipes:

Blackened Beetroot & Whipped Feta Salad with a Spiced Oil (see pg. 84)
Chicken & Wild Garlic Pie with a Cheddar & Hazelnut Crumble Topping (see pg. 164)
Sri Lankan Curry (see pg. 167)

Adam Markham, our in-house Kadai chef, whose expertise in live-fire cooking has added new, delicious twists to barbecue food. The following are a sample of his adventurous recipes that really get the tastebuds tingling:

Goat Curry (see pg. 156)
Lamb & Mint Pie (see pg. 163)
Mushroom Shawarma in Tahini Flatbreads (see pg. 179)
Samosa Pie (see pg. 180)
Orange Brownies (see pg. 219)

Additional thanks to...

Yolanda Pearson, who provided Italian inspiration and guidance for our pizza section.

Samuel Legge, who took the stunning photographs on pg. 2 and pg. 21.

Mr Matthew, who back in the very early days helped Christo gain a better understanding of India and its unusual way of conducting business.

....

We believe in always supporting local businesses, and Shropshire is a county full of enterprising people. Our thanks go to all who have helped with the creation of this book, including those below who have generously offered their wonderful products, so that we could create these stunning recipes.

Caradoc Charcoal, our neighbours, who make and supply us with good quality lumpwood charcoal and firewood.

Hough & Sons, a family-run butcher in Church Stretton, whose meat is reared on their own farm.

Moyden's, an artisan, cheesemaking business that uses local, Shropshire milk to make their cheeses, all named after well-known Shropshire towns and landmarks. We used their cheese in our Swiss Raclette recipe (see pg. 184).

Shropshire Salumi, supplier of handmade, richly textured salamis and cured meats, full of flavour from locally reared pigs. We used their salami in our Salami Skewers recipe (see pg. 110).

Sytch Farm Studio, our local potters, whose beautiful hand-thrown plates and bowls have been used in many of the photos.

And, of course, none of this incredible journey would have even started if it were not for the highly skilled craftspeople of India, who, with simple mechanical machines and traditional ironworking methods, hand-make the majority of elements for Kadai. Without them, none of this would have been possible, and a Kadai would still just be a very large cooking bowl in Rajasthan. Firebowls, therefore, may not have evolved into such versatile barbecues with a multitude of accessories.

Thank you to all

Kadai

Cooking with Kadai

The information in this book was correct at the time of publication, but the Authors do not assume any liability for loss or damage caused by errors or omissions.

First Edition Copyright ©2023 Christo McKinnon-Wood

All rights reserved. No part of this publication may be reproduced, stored in a retrieval system, or transmitted, in any form or by any means, electronic, mechanical, photocopying, recording or otherwise. For permission to publish, distribute or otherwise reproduce this work, please contact support@kadai.com.

ISBN: 978-1-80352-157-2

Written by:	Christo McKinnon-Wood and the Kadai Team
Lead Photographer:	Lucy Hatton
Designer:	Lucy Hatton
Editorial Director:	Tasha Hunt
Co-editors:	Debbie Major, Victoria Wilson
Creative Assistant:	Tula McKinnon-Wood
Fire Master:	Will Madeley

Printed in the UK by Swallowtail Print

Published by Kadai Ltd
www.kadai.com

All trademarks and brands are the property of their respective owners, and no claim is made to them and no endorsement by them to this book or recipes is implied or claimed.

FSC — MIX — Paper from responsible sources — FSC® C113523